ISLAND of CHILDHOOD
Education in the Special World of Nursery School

EARLY CHILDHOOD EDUCATION SERIES
Millie Almy, Editor

Elinor Fitch Griffin, *Island of Childhood: Education in the Special World of Nursery School*

Sandra R. Curtis, *The Joy of Movement in Early Childhood*

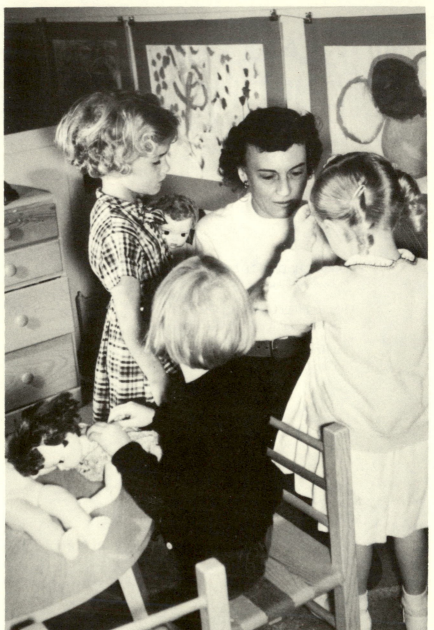

ISLAND of CHILDHOOD

Education in the Special World of Nursery School

ELINOR FITCH GRIFFIN, Ph.D.

Director, Griffin Nursery School and
Former Head of the Child Development Department,
Washington State College

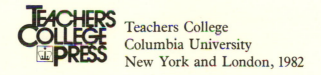

Teachers College
Columbia University
New York and London, 1982

Published by Teachers College Press, 1234 Amsterdam Avenue,
New York, N.Y. 10027

Library of Congress Cataloging in Publication Data

Griffin, Elinor Fitch.
  Island of childhood.

  Bibliography: p.
  Includes index.
  1. Nursery schools. 2. Education, Preschool.
I. Title.
LB1140.2.G73   372'.216   81-9256
                                  AACR2

ISBN 0-8077-2659-1 (cloth)
ISBN 0-8077-2690-7 (paper)

Manufactured in the United States of America

87 86 85 84 83 82   1 2 3 4 5 6

In memory of
Myron M. Griffin
and
Clara Lynn Fitch

At two hours after midnight . . . they arrived at an island of the Bahamas that was called in the Indians' tongue Guanahaní.

The Admiral says that he never beheld so fair a thing: trees all along the river, beautiful and green, and different from ours, with flowers and fruits each according to their kind, many birds and little birds which sing very sweetly.

— Christopher Columbus
Journal of the First Voyage, Oct. 1492

Contents

PART II.   SELF-AFFIRMATION

Preface

The education of three- and four-year-old children has become an important part of our culture and, since the latter part of the 1960s, has been proliferating rapidly in many directions. There are private, fee-supported schools, laboratory schools attached to colleges and universities, both community-sponsored and commercial day-care centers, licensed homes for group child care, as well as adult education programs and high school courses that include assisting in nursery schools or play groups. The Head Start program has brought many children into a school situation earlier than heretofore, concentrating on disadvantaged groups that might be expected to do less well academically in public schools than more privileged groups.

The traditional nursery school in the 1940s was soundly based on child development research and could provide a rich environment for exploration and independent learning. Though the daily schedule included teacher-directed periods, there was also an effort to respond to interests and needs as they arose. In their open classrooms and variety of activities, the nursery schools continued to become more and more oriented toward the development of the whole child. As time went on, they moved further away from many customs inherited from conventional schools, such as expecting all the children to sit still and listen to stories, to join in teacher-directed activities at a specified time each day, and to eat, dress, rest, and use the bathroom as a group, rather than according to individual need. Attention was also given, more and more, to underlying feelings, rather than to behavior alone.

At the time of this writing, there is a popular "back to basics" movement in education. It stresses teaching the three R's, which is thought to prepare children for a competitive society and, in the case of the youngest, to prepare them for school. But there is also a strong countermovement, expressing the belief that every child has a right to live in the present and experience it fully. Many exciting ideas are coming from this forefront of the field, and books by some of its leaders are listed at the end of this one for those who would like to know more about it. I see today's nursery schools as a part of that movement. In the end, I believe this kind of teaching will overcome many of the problems our heterogeneous class-rooms now face. Respecting each learner as he is—a unique individual with something special to offer—opening up possibilities, and facilitating and supporting his choice of interests will help him to develop confidence in himself and in his future. He will see the world as a fascinating place to explore and also as one to which, as in school, he will be able to make a contribution of value. Because of their wider scope for the expression of mind, body, and emotions, schools like these are more related to home and community life than those whose orientation is only academic. But for children of any age, even for college students, an intensification of the kind of schooling that has in the past led to failures, dropouts, apathy, or outright rebellion can only repeat old mistakes.

The basic goals of young children, described in this book as the achieve-ment of relationships and self-affirmation, are shared by older children as well as by everyone else. But the three- and four-year-olds with whom this book deals are different from older children in important ways, too. What is needed for them is education that reflects the previous and current research that has explored those differences and is also sensitively respon-sive to their special qualities. Their education must take into account what they are ready to learn, what they want to learn, and their own ways of learning. It especially needs to recognize their creative force and their individual differences. And vitally important will be an emotional climate in which they can grow. More dependent on this than older children, they are correspondingly more vulnerable to the lack of it. When the sense of self is beginning to take shape, the warmth, support, and steady accept-ance of children by their teachers is crucial. It is increasingly evident from the emotional and behavioral disturbances all around us that we must have more concern about mental health. The teaching of much else can cer-tainly wait, but there is no postponing the making of sound relationships and the forming of a healthy self-concept. With all these very young children now coming more and more under society's influence in nursery schools and day-care centers, we have an opportunity such as we have never had before.

My own education in preschool teaching, supported by the comments of teachers now in training, suggested the form of this book. Though we found a good deal written about the science of teaching, there was much less about the art of it. Where these two came together for us in our reading was in the all too rare case study, record, or description of what a child did, what a teacher did, and what happened next. All of us, I think, were looking for experience, or as close a substitute for it as we could find. Extended apprenticeships in nursery schools are seldom possible, so, to fill this gap, I have used examples drawn from records and notes kept for twenty years at a nursery school, representing some two hundred children interacting with teachers and with each other and using materials. My hope is that to some degree the quantity and variety of these examples may approximate the richness of the experience that would be found in an actual nursery school apprenticeship and that both information and empathy may be acquired easily and naturally, much as they would be, day after day, in a real-life setting. The examples will also help, I hope, to illustrate responsive teaching and its results.

Just as might happen in an apprenticeship, a reader will perhaps not agree with what a teacher says or does at one time or another or with the interpretation of an incident. This might be because the child involved was unlike the one the reader had in mind, because the reader is a different person from the teacher and cannot imagine doing or saying the same thing, because the reader's orientation and goals are different, or because the teacher in the example missed something. But because the continuous impact of examples resembles what would be experienced in an extended apprenticeship, some of the same growth can occur. At first an apprentice teacher focuses on details of the master teacher's approach and tends to imitate these. Later, as examples multiply and are analyzed and interpreted, he or she identifies instead with an overall attitude. In the end, some aspects of the teaching are absorbed, some are conditionally accepted with modifications, and some are dropped off. Then the apprentice, realizing that, just as no two children are alike, no teacher is like any other, becomes himself or herself, ready to go on alone.

The examples used in this book were selected from records made during a twenty-year period at Griffin Nursery School in Berkeley, California, a fee-supported center serving prekindergarten children from age three. There are eighteen children to a group, attending sessions two and a half or three hours a day, from two to five days a week. The teachers, two for each group, are college trained and experienced, and the director, who teaches part of the time, has a Ph.D. in Child Development and Nursery Education and is a consulting psychologist. Six poems in Chapter Nine were recorded by the author at the University of Michigan Nursery School.

Because it is a fee school, many of the children come from middle-class families. Through the years, however, children from poverty-level families have also attended, with the help of scholarships offered by the school or with the aid of county and state welfare funds. Berkeley has large Hispanic, black, and Asian groups, and this, too, has influenced the composition of classes. Also, because of the school's proximity to the University of California at Berkeley, students and faculty have provided children from India, Kenya, Japan, West Germany, Holland, Italy, France, the Philippines, and other parts of the world.

Over the twenty years, similarities among the children always seemed more impressive than cultural differences. All the children were just preschoolers, with the same kinds of developmental characteristics and needs. Though some poverty-level children had disrupted families, many middle-class ones did, too; marriages break up anywhere. Some children could not play outside near their homes because of violence on their streets, but the "hill homes," where the higher-income families live, were more apt to be burglarized, and a few children of very wealthy or well-known families had to be watched for fear of kidnapping. Language differences, too, were soon submerged. While a child who spoke no English at all was not admitted until he had learned a little, because of the possibility of language shock, soon, aided by his preschooler's quick ear and speech readiness, he would not be distinguishable from the baby-talkers.

For these reasons, and because I am, in any case, not comfortable with the idea of different kinds of teaching for different races and economic levels, feeling that a good school meets the needs of individuals of all varieties, the emphasis in the book has been upon children as people, and not as members of any class or special group. Sex differences were not emphasized either; teachers in the school looked at boys and girls simply as people, too, avoiding stereotyping them as much as possible. One's sex is a part of one's identity, and young children, in search of a sense of self, observe sex-linked behavior closely and tend to adopt it. But unless there is reinforcement, this phase will pass, and children will gradually have less need to assert to themselves and others that they are boys or girls (or are four years old, or four and a half, or four and three-quarters). Sometimes, too, a child may be what is considered feminine or masculine in our culture because of personality makeup, no matter what his or her actual sex is. Whatever the case, the aim is to accept the child, leaving both present and future options open.

Records were kept in the form of tape recordings of nursery school sessions, written observations by visiting teachers and students, and, most frequently, notes taken by the staff. Names and identifying information have been changed, and an occasional child, teacher, or parent described in this book is a composite of several similar examples combined into one.

Because, until fairly recently, there were few qualified male teachers for this age, "she" has been used for the teacher, and, to avoid pronoun confusions, "he" is most often used for the child in generalizations. I am sorry about this language requirement and hope "he or she" will be understood in such cases.

I am grateful to more people than can be listed, but some are: Janet Beal, my sister, who helped and encouraged me all the way.

Helen Czaja, long-time teacher at Griffin Nursery School, and my supporter as both colleague and friend.

Teachers: the late Hazel Roger, Alice Kuznets, Dorothy Baker, the late Josephine Poynter, Miki Austin, Sharon Hammond, Madeline Hendricks, Anne Yeomans, Tory Beale, Moreen Libet, Penny Tees, Deborah Tarrson, Ann Kadyk, Peter Rengel, and Rose Weilerstein.

Signe Allen, whose photographs contribute so much to the book.

Robert Overstreet, who graciously allowed me to use his photograph as frontispiece.

Robert Erickson, composer and professor at the University of California at San Diego and the school's music consultant, who read and commented on the music section.

Others whose interest never failed: my sister Mary Wernham, my cousin Helen Geisness, Ruth Straus, Bernice Fried, Anne Apfelbaum, Fay Libet, Lisa Thompson, Mamie Goodman, Becky Temko, and Thelma Harms.

The children of Griffin Nursery School and their parents, to whom the book really belongs.

Berkeley, California, 1981

1 Toward Purpose and Plan

I can play all day,
I can play all day,
I can see all sun,
And I can cry.
                —Joshua

I

We have a very special institution in our culture—a somewhat strange one. The children served by it, mostly three- and four-year-olds, are like changelings, rather as though they came from a different land from the rest of us. The places where these children first came together under teachers, in England in 1909, were called Nursery Schools, the name reflecting the feeling of the founders that the new institutions were neither homes nor schools, exactly, but something halfway in between. Later such places became known as Pre-schools, an odd name again expressing the idea of something that is not really school but, rather, leads up to it. The terms Day Nursery and Day-Care Center, also used today for such institutions, convey the idea of a substitute for home rather than a school, yet those who work there are called teachers and think of their function as at least partly educational. Similarly, dedicated teachers are found in Child Development Centers, although this name, too, is confusing, signifying only an interest in study and research concerning young children's growth and development.

All these names reflect the problem of setting up an educational institution for a group of human beings who are as different from others as these children are. It is not so strange that these places for three- and four-year-old children are somehow neither one thing nor another, but, so far, undefined; so are the children themselves. They are on an island of childhood set apart from what came before and from what will come later. This time in their lives is neither baby-hood nor childhood as we adults remember it. Thus, providing nurs-ery care only for them is as inappropriate as providing an extension downward of an educational system designed for children from kin-dergarten age on.

Yet education solidly based on an understanding of these children and designed especially for them could bring to our society, as the children mature, a new richness we cannot afford to be without. Very early childhood is the time of life when personalities are basically determined. Attitudes toward the self and toward others are both learned then. Young children have an immense capacity for de-velopment through beneficent influences, as well as an extreme vul-nerability to destructive ones. The effect of environment during the first five years far outweighs the effect of an equivalent period of time in later life. It follows that since these experiences in early years play such an important part in helping or hindering the grown man or woman to fulfill his or her potential, our society could prosper in ways now inconceivable to us if we gave dedicated attention to the problem of early childhood education.

It is time to think about offering education for three- and four-year-olds that is addressed to their uniqueness as a group and also expresses a deep regard for the extraordinary individuality and variety they show among themselves. But the task is not easy. The under-standing needed requires not only study and observation of their developmental characteristics, but, even more, an accepting attitude and an open mind toward what one sees. Teaching them in a new, more aware way means seeing below the surface of their behavior. And both the planning and the carrying out of their education require a delicate interweaving of what, in our culture, we feel most valuable to pass on, and what, at their time of life, they themselves value.

A baby first experiences a relationship in a passive, receptive way. As he makes more and more efforts toward reaching goals of his own choice, if his mother or whoever cares for him responds with interest and pleasure, sharing the goals and trying to help him reach them, the baby can turn toward her more actively, thinking something like "She is for me; she is on my side. Her interests are my interests." They are then, at this early stage, symbiotically identified, one with the other, and the baby begins gradually to identify with her goals, too. Because of this deep assumption of common goals, he begins to be sad when she is sad, angry or frightened when she is, and disappointed in himself when she is disappointed in him. And he feels joy and pleasure when she does, too, responding to her smiles with his own. If all goes well with them, he will go on from this point and reach a stage at which he can accept the idea that his mother has goals of her own, and separate feelings, too.

It seems possible that progress toward future altruism comes about through an extension of the process of identification. If a baby's early identification with his mother has been well learned and fully experienced, he then has the ability to use it with each person with whom he later comes in contact. What this means is that the child he grows into, and the adult he becomes, can not only empathize with others but also care about their welfare. Because he identifies with them, it makes him happy to see them happy, and he can also share their sorrows. When he helps another person toward a goal, the achievement is partly his, and there is mutual reinforcement. Similarly, when he sees another's pleasure in doing something for him, his own pleasure is increased by theirs; thus he can accept easily, as well as give.

The ability to identify with others grows something like this. A child's early identification with his mother is followed by identification with his father and other members of his family. Next come relatives and family friends. In nursery school he moves from playing with one child to two, then three or more, but when he has become identified with his group, he is still not yet able to identify with outsiders; he often calls, "Go away!" to a strange child peering through the gate. Gradually, step by step, as he grows older he talks of "my neighborhood," then "my hometown." Next it will be "my state" and "my country," with the latter especially emphasized in wartime. Those who continue to grow will be able to identify more and more with the needs of people not in their immediate environment, including people different from themselves. This can come to mean the economically or culturally deprived, people of other races, religions, or politics, or the delinquent and mentally ill. Through identification and empathy, the divisions between people begin to melt away. Those who have grown to the point of feeling identified with all mankind are made profoundly uneasy if expected to look upon another nation as an enemy; the idea of warfare is incompatible with their state of development. They must refuse to believe that there is no middle ground between war and isolationism; they want to work with, not against people, and are optimistic about the peaceful resolution of difficulties.

Schools for very young children can play an important role by providing a climate in which the first social relationships can develop in the ways described, and in which a child can also find ways to affirm his growing sense of himself as a valuable and unique individual. These two goals are actually inseparable; each supports the other. When one feels good about oneself, one feels good about others; and, in the same way, when one likes others, one likes oneself. It works in both directions. At any age there may be unfinished business left over from baby days; perhaps love was not offered in recognizable form at the right time. Then growth cannot proceed naturally and normally until the block is removed. People who are blocked are limited in their ability to have both healthy relationships and positive attitudes toward themselves, and, unless release comes, behavior, work, and relations with others faithfully reflect the problem. Because the nursery school deals with children at the time of the first step away from home, it has a special opportunity to help a child through any frozen stages in his development, so that he can continue to grow and learn.

II

Is help in learning these things more important than teaching anything else at this age, and is the nursery school the place to give it? The answer to the first question comes easily. To love oneself means to have the attitude a good parent would have toward oneself: warm, encouraging, tolerant, friendly, interested, indulgent when possible but steadfast and strong when necessary, and accepting in the way that a good companion is. With this attitude toward the self comes the ability to love others in the same way. Such a person has within him the ingredients of a good life. As to the world's needing this kind of person, it is painfully obvious. We have only to look at our world, with its mental illnesses, delinquency and crime, race prejudice, and exploitation of the poor and uneducated to see that it does. Negative attitudes toward other people are everywhere expressed in our social institutions and customs, above all in war, where killing, maiming, and destruction are taken for granted. We have difficulty maintaining in ourselves, and inspiring in others, even a minimum amount of the trust needed to work out solutions with our enemies even though we know that if such solutions are not found, we are all in danger of extinction.

The second question, whether the nursery school is the place to help children with this kind of learning, needs careful consideration. To stress these goals over all others means to go against a number of traditional ideas about schools. One is that personality development is the province of the home, not the school—even the nursery school—and that if there are problems in this area, psychologists and psychiatrists, rather than teachers, should be concerned with them. But evidence is everywhere that the job is too much for parents alone. And what nursery schools would be undertaking is not psychotherapy, which involves an exclusive relationship that a teacher cannot have with a child in a classroom. Nevertheless, in these schools there can be a kind of natural group therapy, with some individuals receiving special attention. It would be accurate to call the milieu of such a nursery school a prophylactic one as far as emotional health is concerned. One could perhaps think of this as preventive psychiatry. But essentially a nursery school with the goals described would be doing what any school purports to do. It would be educating for better living. The difference would be that, because of the age of its pupils, it could take a more direct route.

These goals for nursery schools also sometimes meet head-on with another accepted view about schools, the idea that their foremost purpose is to foster intellectual achievement. However, young children are, by and large, tied to a developmental clock. A few children have been painstakingly taught to recite classical Greek, to play chess, to read at two, to skate in ice shows, and so on; usually the motivation was the adult's, rather than the child's, and the feats apparently had little or no immediate value to the learner. Teaching that proceeds from adult goals fosters dependent, rather than independent learning. Projects designed for the teaching of science, mathematics, biology, reading and writing, and many other academic subjects have been developed, but children can learn any of these more easily when they are older. Though they will learn a good deal in these areas through enriched play activities and exploration of the environment, anything that cannot be independently learned by direct experience is best postponed. However, children can be much more easily helped with their relationships and their feelings about themselves before the age of five—in fact, often later is too late. To postpone the achievement of academic goals is in no way a deterrent to their later achievement, but, in fact, the contrary. If children are helped toward independence and confidence in themselves, they will be open to new experiences of all kinds, including academic learning, and later, when their minds are more mature, they can become not merely good students but true scholars (if such is their bent), able not only to acquire knowledge but to evaluate what they learn and apply it in both personally satisfying and socially useful ways.

But the real answer to whether the nursery school is the place for the kind of learning that is more social and emotional than academic lies in the fact that children at the age of three or four are particularly adapted for such learning. Their own drives, needs, and special gifts at this age make them ripe for it. At no later time in his life will a child be so well suited for learning about relationships and feelings. He is so ready, in fact, to learn to be his own friend and the friend of others that he cannot help trying continually to move in that direction, with or without our aid. He is not beginning his course in love; he is well into it, because it began in his earliest infancy. It is only necessary to tie into this powerful momentum. What does a little child care about most? Mother: his feelings about her and hers about him. Father: the same. Other children: Will they play with him? How can he express his love, his indignation, his fear, with the limited vocabulary at his command? There is everything here to work with. It is the time, too, for the child to become acquainted with himself. By making his own choice of activities, he learns who he is, discovering where his interests lie and what gives him the deepest pleasure. Many an adult has never found the answers to these questions.

Those who are convinced that the kind of teaching just described is of great importance may still have doubts about whether it can be successful. Most of their experience may have been with older people, for whom such learning is harder. Can "human nature" be changed? Can such things be taught at all? One answer can be found in the experiences of patients in psychotherapy who have made major changes in attitude toward both themselves and others. And evidence is accumulating that specialists in group dynamics can help totally inharmonious factions in adult groups move toward mutually acceptable compromises. If this is true of adults who have had years of acquiring negative attitudes, imagine how much more can be expected from young children having their first experiences and open to all impressions. Today's trend toward day care and the admission of younger children into our educational system will offer us an opportunity to give people the kind of start that was never before possible.

A teacher who wishes to help children learn about themselves and others must herself believe that what she is doing is valuable. She learns more and more about how to achieve her goals as she goes along, but her eyes must light up when she is asked about them. She needs to believe in her goals with both her mind and her feelings so that they are expressed in her behavior and communicated to children. Once she is at this point, the "how to do it" aspect begins to fall into place. New methods and techniques occur to her as she needs them. She begins to be highly focused and alert, allowing unessentials to drop away. There will be the main job, and the lesser ones. Of the latter she will say, "Well, if it falls out that way, I'll include them in my program, but not if they interfere in any way with my doing the main job." Whatever goes on in her nursery school or day-care center then builds toward her goals. The rest of this book describes how it all works out for teachers and children in actual practice.

This design for the education of young children has a circle —from the self to others, and back again to the self. It has depth as well —a third dimension—being tied to deep layers of feeling. And there is an ongoing rhythm in it—the orderliness of a progression that connects early infancy to adulthood. But the most outstanding feature of this kind of education is its emphasis on wholeness, on developing all parts of the personality in harmony, so that the life force that was in these children from the beginning can continue to flow into all aspects of behavior—physical, mental, social, and emotional— without fragmentation or distortion along the way.

III

What can nursery schools actually do to contribute to the achievement of these goals? Schools vary in many ways, reflecting the special interests of staff and parents, the education, experience, and backgrounds of the teachers, the kind of family or community involvement, the facilities and equipment of the school, the length of the school day, and so on. Whatever is different about them, however, they are alike in their potential to help children achieve satisfying relationships and self-affirmation. And children, too, whatever their cultural differences, are more alike than different at this age, owing to the influence of the developmental stages through which they are all passing, the traits of which they all exhibit. Some generalizations about these young children in school may help, therefore, to answer the question.

With few exceptions, three- and four-year-olds show their feelings very clearly in the prepared school environment, tuning out what has no interest for them and pursuing, with remarkable vigor and great persistence, what does. It becomes plain, when one watches them, that they themselves pursue the two goals that have been discussed. Their play is purposeful. In playing, they seem to want to relate to others and also to experience themselves as feeling, thinking, and acting individuals. Spontaneously, they explore the school, indoors and outdoors, and, in so doing, also explore the potentials of their own bodies, minds, and senses, as they interact with materials of all kinds. They are like self-motivated, independent scientists or artists. In these explorations they learn a good deal about the world, about each other, and about themselves, but all of their activity can be seen as allied to the two basic motivations. The information to which a child is most responsive is the kind that helps him establish a relationship with someone or that makes him feel like a person in his own right, at home in his world and happy to be himself. And he seems to want only those facts for which he can readily see a use in the present. He does not anticipate future needs; he lives entirely in the moment.

Certain of the child's activities seem to contribute with special directness and immediacy to his sense of himself as both a likeable and valuable individual. Among these are music and art experiences, especially if offered in such a way that the child's own ideas and feelings, rather than the teacher's, are expressed through them. Toys and equipment that help a child play out scenes from his life or fantasies also seem to serve this purpose well. Challenges to physical coordination and strength help him to know his body better, and problem-solving materials, if he can use them without need for a teacher's help, allow him to experience satisfaction with what his mind can do. There are also means for wide-ranging enjoyment through his own senses—sand and water play, things to taste, smell, and touch, and space and special materials to enhance kinesthetic experiences in movement play.

Less successful in helping the child achieve those aims are activities in which an adult's attention and help are all-important. It seems that if a child is completely dependent on the teacher and cannot have the experience without her, it is not the kind of give-and-take relationship with an adult that he really prefers. Sometimes one can also see relationships with other children suffer in such situations, since, while a teacher is helping one child, the others, unable to function alone in the project, become competitive and resent not only the teacher who has put them in that position, but also the child she helps. As for the sense of self, a child feels diminished to the extent that he can neither cope with the activity by himself nor evaluate himself; he must depend on someone else to explain what to do and to decide whether it was done well or poorly. And meanwhile the child wonders whether the teacher's expectations are being met, rather than feeling sure that she accepts him no matter what he does. Usually, whenever a teacher is the center of attention, the impact of her personality seems a little overpowering. If this makes a child feel less sure of his own value, he shows a need to attract attention to himself, to escape, to play dumb, or to change the subject. One striking way in which these small children appear different from older ones and from adults is in their sensitivity to feelings of inferiority, perhaps because of their size and relative helplessness.

With these points in mind, teachers who want to emphasize good relationships and self-affirmation try to facilitate independent, rather than dependent, learning. They also focus on making their interactions with any child express acceptance of him just the way he is at the time, helping him to change only in the direction of the goals they both hold. Just as they are unlike the rest of us in many ways, very young children also differ widely from one another, even though they share developmental characteristics and basic motivations. Each is uniquely himself or herself. It follows that teachers learn to see each child as a new and different person and discipline themselves as to their expectations. If a teacher cannot do that—if she expects a child to be like the others, or like some ideal she has in mind—then he will not have the kind of experiences that will enable him to discover, and like, the person he really is. So teachers study the children and try to understand what each one is seeking, feeling, and thinking, in order to understand who everyone really is. Only after such empathizing can teachers respect children as individuals; then a school environment has been provided that will greatly contribute to a child's positive feelings about himself and enable him to move on ahead in a process of self-affirmation that includes self-expression, learning, and achievements of many kinds.

RELATIONSHIPS

2 Transition

The first day I stayed at school alone,
I thought a big, terrible cough was coming,
And you held me on your lap,
And you talked about "lonesome,"
And a little bit of crying came,
And I played.
Remember?

—Russel

I

Starting school is deeply meaningful for children. It symbolizes for them the crossing of a bridge from babyhood over into childhood. Most children who have had a good relationship with their mothers have confidence in her plans for them and, when she leaves them for the first time at nursery school, rely on her returning as arranged. Feeling this basic security, they can accept the teacher as a substitute protector and soon feel safe. But even those who have already taken a few steps away from home may well feel some hesitation on approaching the new situation and need first to establish a relationship with the teacher, who can then help by introducing them to another child or two or interesting them in play.

Most nursery schools invite new children to make a visit before actually starting school, if possible. This provides a chance to evaluate the child's readiness and also helps the mother (or father) to learn how the school operates, how the teacher works with the children, what the atmosphere is like, and how the child responds. For the child, it is always a special experience. As a guest, he has a chance to size things up with no commitments or requirements. He can be relaxed, and enter or not enter into play as he wishes; he can admit the teacher to his world or reject her and relate only to his mother, and he can approach children, watch them, or turn his back on them altogether. The mother usually remains seated near the toys; for a while her child will need to know where she is, so that he can orient himself around her.

After the first greeting, which does not focus too much on the child, the teacher goes on about her work in the room, observing him as inconspicuously as possible. It is advisable not to press him with questions or invitations to play. If he makes no move toward the toys on his own, after a time the teacher will bring an interesting one close to his mother's chair, with just a quiet "You might like to play with this," moving on without waiting for an answer. Perhaps she will arrange the furniture and people in the dollhouse nearby, talking casually about them. The idea is to indicate, in one way or another, "You can play if you want to," and also "It's all right to do nothing, too." This makes it clear to the child that nothing is required of him, and that whatever he does will be of his own choosing. A timid child might climb on his mother's lap, and the teacher would then respond to that choice, saying "You'd like to sit on your mother's lap"; this assures him that nobody will try to separate him from his mother, and often wins a first smile.

Mothers, too, have various ways of reacting to the situation. Usually the teacher has made some preliminary suggestions, but sometimes she helps a mother understand her role during the observation of the child by saying "Could you be as passive as possible?" (Sometimes she might add, sympathetically, "It's hard, isn't it?") Some mothers see for the first time, through this experience, that they tend to point out things rather than letting the child do his own discovering, try to push him into activity, help or direct him too much, or hold him back anxiously. Soon it becomes interesting for such a mother to see what the child does with this chance to react entirely on his own. As the teacher tries to show a child that whatever he does is acceptable, his mother, too, can soon relax. It is also reassuring to her to see that if the child interferes with other children, the teacher will be understanding but, at the same time, will protect them. "This is Lee; he's a visitor. You can tell him, 'I'm using this truck, now.' And we'll find him another one."

When Binky came to visit, his mother was a little worried about sitting in one place as was suggested. "If I stay here, he'll just stay here with me," she said. But soon she could see that he was gradually stretching his tie to her by going back and forth from her to the toys that interested him, and was spending longer and longer periods away from her. She was encouraged to be warm and responsive when he came to show her things and to hold him close a moment when he sought physical contact, but not to say, or suggest by her attitude, "Go away and play," or, on the other hand, keep him with her by playing with him or asking him what he had been doing. The teacher tried to make Binky feel that she was aware of him and looking after him in place of his mother during this period, frequently making eye contact, providing what he needed for his play, and building his sense of a separate self by verbalizing his choices: "You're choosing the tractor this time; you decided to change." And when Binky finally said, "I want to go out there," pointing to the playground, she responded similarly, "You're ready to go out now?" and let him open the door by himself.

Once enrolled, children can find many ways to help themselves adjust to the transition from home to school if adults are prepared to go along with them and support their solutions. For example, some children are bringers, carrying with them their links to home. Donavan brought a lunch box containing his toy monkey and a snack. Paul stuffed his bear in a backpack and carried it everywhere with him at school. Gerald always had a small car in his locker, and Bobby always had one of his dad's large handkerchiefs. Georgia brought flowers or pictures for the teacher. Max wore his big boots, rain or shine; Kathy wore her party dress; and Felicia wore a long overblouse of her mother's, with the sleeves pinned up. Annabel packed a large shopping bag with home mementoes, as though going on a long trip. And of course many a nursery school child finds it helpful to bring the stuffed animal, doll, or blanket he takes to bed.

And children find other ways of coping. Lowell, in his early days at nursery school, attached himself to the big train so no one else could use it at that time. When children protested, the teacher helped them understand how he felt, deciding this was a better learning experience for them than the use of the equipment. "He's a new boy. The train helps him get used to school. Remember when you first came? I don't know quite why, but I can see Lowell feels he really needs that train. We'll watch awhile and see." The children helped protect Lowell and his train, telling each other, "He needs it." After a few days he no longer stayed glued to the train. They were pleased. "Look! He doesn't need the train any more now," they said, proudly, as though they had done it. Sammy led his father in to meet the teacher. Earlier Sammy had asked her, "Do you love me?" She replied, "Mommy and Daddy love you; I like you." "Do you love my Mommy and Daddy?" he went on. These questions had probably meant he was wondering how she fit into his family. After she and his father shook hands warmly, he was satisfied. Barbie invited one child after another to play at her house, and the mothers arranged for these visits. Jodie, for quite a while, refused to have his hair brushed or be washed for school. (He seemed to have decided that if people there accepted him au naturel, he would accept them.) Little Miguel kept his own potty chair at school for a time and brought his own apron for painting. Cecily always made a picture for her mother first of all; perhaps she then felt less disloyal for enjoying herself so much at school. And Helen made something for the baby; then she probably felt less guilty for her resentment of his having her mother's complete attention while Helen was away.

Sometimes children need the teacher's cooperation in their plans for coping. Several wanted to go to school at the same time as their older siblings, and sometimes this could be arranged. Amy, for a time, set up her own home away from home in the waiting room where her mother had formerly been sitting, and kept her belongings in the big chair there instead of her locker. When she felt out of her depth in play, she could retreat to her room, and she was offered a "Do Not Disturb" sign for her door. At first Al sought close physical contact, wanting to sit on his teacher's lap or be carried about. Next he progressed to going everywhere with her, holding her hand, and then to just keeping an eye on her. Augie entered the building by slow stages, and the teacher brought him a basket of small trucks to play with just outside the door until he felt ready to come in. Oliver, though most children like to be greeted, preferred entering invisibly. Theo liked to telephone his mother now and then during the first few days, and kept his phone number, printed on a large card, in his pocket. Sammy asked to have his six-year-old sister stay on the first day his mother left, and she did. And Bill made a circle of the big floor trucks around him on his first day; he stayed inside it and played there all morning. (A year later he still remembered how the teacher had let him do that. "I did that because I was afraid of the kids," he told her then.) And many children may go to a front window to wave good-bye to their mothers. They seem to feel better if they take an active part in the separation by waving their mothers away than if they passively allow themselves to be left.

II

Mothers, too, can have separation problems. Those mothers who say no at once when asked whether they think their children will need them to stay probably can leave. They say good-bye calmly and confidently, and their children usually respond in the same way. But when a mother replies, "I don't know," or "Yes, I'm sure he will want me to stay," it is a good plan for her to remain with her child for a while. The teacher can then observe not only the child—his forays away from his mother, his willingness to accept teacher help, and other signs of readiness for nursery school—but also the mother. Is she reading, or writing letters, thus indicating that she has no doubts about the school and is giving her child time, trusting that he will handle things himself? Is she watching everything interestedly, to see what the school is like as well as how her child is responding? Or are her eyes anxiously fixed on her own child all the time? If the latter is the case, the teacher, too, will need to watch the child carefully that day; his mother may be afraid that there may not be help when he needs it, or perhaps that he will do something "wrong." By helping her child promptly and appropriately, the teacher can reassure her.

When a teacher judges by his independent behavior that the child of an anxious mother is ready to be left, she will need, next, to find out how the mother feels about leaving him, because the child may have become ready for separation first. A mother cannot tell a child comfortably and easily that she is ready to go unless she feels that way, and even if the child wants her to go (some do—Johnny pushed on the back fender of his mother's car, saying, "Go!"), the mother needs to gain enough confidence in the school and the teacher to feel happy about doing it. If she thinks her child is not ready, it is usually best that she stay a little longer. She may be right, and in any case the child would feel her uneasiness when she said good-bye. The period of watching helps mothers come to their own conclusions. Those who are undecided whether to go or stay can move from "I'll do anything you say" toward an independent decision.

The teacher can also operate as an intermediary between the child and the mother. She can report how he is coming along when he is not in his mother's view and point out that he is increasing the space between them. Sometimes the teacher can ask the child how he would feel about staying without his mother. If his mother asks him this question, he might be upset, fearing that it meant she was going immediately, whereas, if the teacher asks, he may be able to tell her what will help him to accept it. "If you sit by me I can," Daphne said. "Tomorrow, but not today," said Sebastian, and he was right. "At story time," said Betty.

Susan, though apparently enjoying school and the children, was unable to stay without her mother for quite a while, although she was four years old. She would be well involved when her mother tried to leave, but in a moment panic would sweep over her, and she would run after her mother, begging her to stay. When the teacher watched Susan's mother trying to leave, she saw how anxious this mother was. "Is it all right? Are you happy now? Are you sure?" she would say to Susan. Her expression was so worried and concerned that Susan was unable to keep her own poise. So it was arranged with them both that the teacher would carry the message to Susan when her mother was ready to go and would then say goodbye to the mother for Susan. The next day, when Susan was in the swing, her favorite place, the teacher told her, "Mother is ready to leave; shall I tell her goodbye for you?" and she nodded in apparent relief.

After several days her mother asked for an interview and confided that she had always been needlessly overconcerned about Susan, and she analyzed some of the causes. She was then able to say good-bye successfully herself. A mother's asking, "Can I go now?" or "Can you stay alone?" may increase a child's anxiety, because he cannot really know the answer. He would like to feel that his parents know what he can or cannot do. However, he can answer a question like "Are you ready for me to go now?" because that has to do with his feelings. But even easier for him is for his mother or father to tell him the plan and then leave the subject open for a moment, in case the child wants to discuss it further: "I think I'll go along now, and pick you up at story time," with a short pause for his response, but without insisting on an answer. Many children feel that this statement requires no answer at all. But those whose readiness has been misjudged can usually be relied upon to protest, and then the parent can say, "Oh, you're not quite ready? I see," and quietly sit down again. At home the parent can reassure the child that it takes a while to get used to going to school but that he surely will in time.

Sometimes a working mother cannot stay with her child during an adjustment period. In that case she may be able to bring him a little early for a while and remain a few minutes to get him started in play and to be his link to the teacher. Sometimes the father, another relative, a family friend, or the baby-sitter can stay awhile as the link from home. Another mother in the school might help, too, by inviting the child to play with her own child, then bringing them to school together and staying if needed. A friend with whom to enter school helps in many a transition problem.

Dicky, at three and a half, never made the transition, because he was brought by a maid who said at the gate each day, "Well, do you want to go in or not?" He had courageously asked to be brought several times, but then he felt shy and was unable to cross the threshold alone. Without an adult's backing, the change from a home child to a school child was impossible for him. A decision as to whether or not he is to go to school is too hard for a child to make by himself. It is more helpful to say, "You'll soon be ready to start nursery school," or later, "Today is a school day," so the child takes it for granted that he is going and proceeds to put his energies into solving the problems this may present him, not upon whether or not he is to go.

III

A more intensive look at problems that individual children had in entering school follows.

● Jodie shows in detail the movement from a secure base into unfamiliar territory by means of using links between them. When first seen, he was being carried in his mother's arms to the school door, screaming and wailing, "No! No! I don't want to go to school!" As he clutched his mother, Jodie was showing where he felt his safety lay. The teacher recognized that feeling by saying, "You don't *want* to go to school. You just want to be very close to your mother. So you could both go into the waiting room here, and she could sit in this big chair and hold you on her lap." Previous planning had prepared the mother, and she held him quietly and comfortably, without in any way pressuring him, with the door closed.

The waiting room contained a basket of small trains and tracks. After sitting on his mother's lap awhile, Jodie slid to the floor and began to put a train together, leaning against her legs. A train seems to symbolize a growing person to children; probably when complete it stands for the father, the power, noise, and the train's ability to carry smaller things all possibly contributing to this idea. The fact that a child can either use just the engine or go on to attach as many cars as he wishes, one at a time, makes a train appropriate for playing out a growth process he can control.

Jodie's train ran in and out around the legs of his mother's chair, and now and then the teacher looked in and commented on what was happening. "Your train is going around your mother's feet. It's going underneath her chair," she said, recognizing in this way his use of the symbol which represented his growing self, desiring to be like his father but also needing to be close to his mother right then. A little later the teacher sat down on the floor, not looking at him but saying, "We have some tracks here. They fit together like this," demonstrating. Judging his readiness by his interested watching, she handed him a piece of track, reaching it out to him at arm's length. After a second's pause he took it, also at arm's length. (If he hadn't, she would have laid it down by him. Children cannot take anything from the hand of a person they don't trust.)

Jodie placed the first section of track in contact with his mother's foot. Then the teacher handed him a second one from the basket, across the arms' length between them, and then a third, and so on, in a kind of simple ritual. He built the track outward from the chair in this way toward the doorway, then slowly through the door into the big playroom. The teacher brought the basket out and put it near him, and protected the track from the other children as he worked on it, saying to any who wanted to help him build it or put other trains on it, "This is Jodie's train track; he's building it by himself, just the way that he wants it." Had anyone broken Jodie's links then, he could only have retreated. While to the hasty glance it might have looked as though he were "playing with the children, now," in reality they were merely trying to play with him. He himself was not ready for social contacts until much later.

The teacher commented, "The track's getting longer," and so on, but she was careful not to push him with comments like "Can you make it longer?" "Let's make it over to the block shelf," or "My, what a fine long track." Growth must come from inside; it cannot be hurried. All of a teacher's comments must stay as close as possible to simple statements about what is going on, when a child is, as at that point, delicately balanced between staying with mother and moving on. But the remarks that she makes are an essential part of the process, helping the child to see that what he is doing is understood and respected.

At last the little train track reached a big floor train which stood in the middle of the room. "The little track has come to the big train," the teacher said then. Perhaps the big train was father, perhaps it was herself, the biggest person in the school. In any case, the little train could now move on a track safely anchored at both ends. And now Jodie, himself, described what was happening. "The train goes away, and it comes back on the track," he said, and this was just what the little train did. "Away from your mother and back again; it goes where it wants to go," the teacher replied.

After a few trips, the little train paused by the big train, and Jodie put the little one on the big one's flatcar; then he dragged the large floor train around the room on his hands and knees, ending up back in the waiting room, by his mother. He parked the engine under her chair and hopped up on her lap again, leaning back against her with a sigh. "That was a long trip," the teacher said, "and now the train wants to rest." But very soon Jodie was down on his knees again, pushing the big train out into the playroom. "It's going for a *really* long trip this time," he told the teacher, crawling almost to the door that led to the playground before retreating. In this stage he only crawled or sat, never stood; in that way he probably expressed his need to be little a while longer, even though using grown-up symbols like trains. He could thus have it both ways.

By now the teacher could see how sound Jodie's approach to his problem was — how he wanted to move ahead within the safety of his links. She therefore picked up his idea of going on a *"really long trip"* and put a rubber train used for sand play just inside the door leading to the playground. Because he might not be ready to stand up and carry the new train down the low flight of steps, she put a board there so he could crawl down. True to prediction, the old train met the new one, and Jodie's hand slid off the one and onto the other. The teacher said, "That's a sand train; it can be used outdoors," and Jodie pushed it through the open doorway and down the board to the foot of the steps. A bucket filled with sand and a small shovel awaited the train there, and Jodie loaded up the cars. When the sand was gone, he crawled with his train to the sand area and refilled his bucket there. This ended his first day.

On his second day, Jodie was again wailing as his mother carried him in. Again they were invited to sit in the big chair with the door closed for a while. After a few minutes, Jodie's teacher opened the door and pushed in the big train's engine, saying, "Well, here we are again"; then, closing the door, she left them alone. When next she opened the door, he was on the floor at the foot of his mother's chair, pushing the engine around her feet as he had done before. The teacher reached a long arm through the door, not crossing over the threshold, holding out the flatcar. "Do you need this, too?" He reached out his arm as elaborately, not leaving the foot of the chair, and they made contact in this way until the train was complete. A few minutes after the teacher returned to the playroom, the door banged open and Jodie emerged, crawling on a fast trip around the room with the train.

Again the big train connected with the little sand train at the door to the playground, and the sand train and Jodie went down the board. But this time Jodie pushed the sand train, filled with sand as before, to the foot of the slide; then he crawled up the slide and slid down, smiling. The teacher felt he was nearing the time when he would stand up, thus identifying himself with a later developmental stage less tied to his mother. For this step she planned to have the right materials ready, but she watched and waited, avoiding showing anything resembling expectations on her part, since they would have come through to him as a lack of acceptance of his wish to remain in the safety of babyhood. However, not offering links would also be to ignore his way of progressing. The right material for the next day seemed to be a pull-toy, such as those that give babies confidence when they first stand up. But to be sure he was really ready, rather than offering it to Jodie she left it (a dog on a leash) where he would pass it on his next indoor train trip. He took it as soon as he saw it, stood up, and pulled it around the room and back to the train. Next he pulled his dog outside. The board had been put away when the teacher saw him stand up, and he walked down the steps, bumping the dog behind him. Pulling the dog to the familiar sand bucket, he gave it some sand food. Next, he walked on his own feet to get a rubber dog and cat nearby. These three animals he carried about and fed for some time. It seemed Jodie was almost there. But he showed a small child's sense of his own needs when another child offered him a cracker by saying, "No." Certainly to return to being an eater (a baby) when engaged in being a feeder of baby animals was inappropriate.

So far, this had been the progression. First Jodie had blended with his mother's body, sitting on her lap. Then he had leaned against her legs and feet and attached his train tracks to her chair. Next he had built himself something like an umbilical cord, using train tracks leading from her to another source of safety, the big train. Then he had linked his hand to the big train, crawling at its level like a crawling infant, yet, by means of it, feeling big and powerful, too. Thus he moved back and forth between the old and the new. Next he had begun to move from identifying with a train to feeding it sand, and here he took the important step of identifying himself with the parent who cares for and feeds an infant, rather than attaching himself to the train for support. Now he could move on and seek a more clear baby symbol, the dog, using the dog's leash as a kind of umbilical cord, but this time with himself as parent. In feeding the dog and other animals, he also fed himself vicariously, and the two parts of himself—the big and the little—came together.

Now Jodie could be himself, somewhere between the two extremes. On his fourth day he moved independently, exploring the room. Finding a ukelele hanging on the wall, he took it down and said, "Big people play guitars like this" (moving all his fingers together), "but this is for boys, so I do like this" (strumming it with his thumb). He also tried to hang it back up, and when he couldn't, he said, "I can only do this part; you do the hook." Thus he showed his realistic acceptance of himself as a child, who is able to do some things alone and needs help with others. By the following week, Jodie was moving about freely and relating to the children. The time was right for his mother to leave. Jodie made only a token protest to this, and later in the day he was heard explaining to another child, "Mothers don't stay; they have their own things to do. *Children* go to school."

The best transition from home to school is a gradual one in which the child has a real part and is not a helpless creature to whom things are done regardless of his feelings. One can see the use that children make of the challenge, then—how they grow with it in harmony with their own maturation. By means of linking one successful experience with another, they need never feel overwhelmed at any point but can progress smoothly on the solid basis of real self-awareness. This is what a teacher wants to happen. But sometimes, whatever a teacher or parent may wish, a child is left too abruptly and is panic-striken. Then the teacher moves quickly into the mothering role, comforting the child through physical closeness, the most primitive and direct way. This links her in his mind at once with his absent mother. Next the teacher can use a toy as a link from her to the world of play which

he is entering at school, and by means of play he can work the problem out.

● Three-year-old Kenny was left almost immediately on his first day
   because his mother had to get to a doctor. He was crying and
   shaking. The teacher picked him up and held him close, sitting
   down with him on the floor near the toys and saying, "I know. You
   want mommy. She'll be back soon. And I'm here. But it's scary."
   At first Kenny resisted her holding him, but she rhythmically
   worked the large toy crane up and down, saying, "Up it goes, and
   down, down it comes," and thus distracted his attention until he
   got used to her closeness. When a teacher holds a frightened child,
   he feels her lack of tension and is reassured by it, as he is by the old
   familiar body warmth and contact or the hand stroking his back. In
   spite of himself, Kenny would relax and nestle when he forgot the
   teacher was a stranger; then, each time he remembered, she had
   herself become a more familiar person. He got to know the feel of
   her skin, the sound of her voice, her movements, size, shape, and
   even her scent. She asked one of the children to bring a small
   crane, and she put it on her lap too. This he soon picked up and
   held. After a while, he slid easily off the teacher's lap and went to a
   nearby table to eat a cracker, carrying his little crane, the link from
   him to her and from her to his vanished mother. He kept it with
   him all morning, and it was saved for him in his locker to greet
   him the next day.

● If there is a baby in the household, a child's idea that now he can
   no longer be a baby himself may be uncomfortably confirmed by
   the suggestion that he is ready for nursery school, and he may be
   concerned that the good old days will be lost forever if he allows
   himself to like it. When Suki came for her first visit, she sat on her
   mother's lap throughout the time she was there, keeping her face
   turned in toward her mother, her eyes tightly closed and her arms
   wound around her mother's neck. She was making a clear statement that she wanted her mother and rejected school. At that time,
   the teacher reflected in words her feeling of not wanting to have
   anything to do with school, and an appointment was made for her
   to return in about a month. When she came for the second time,
   Suki peeked out now and then as though she couldn't help re-

sponding a little, and she was enrolled on a trial basis, her mother agreeing to stay with her as long as needed.

With Suki comfortably established on her mother's lap in the waiting room on her first day, the teacher said, "You want me to go away," when Suki drew back from her, but she brought a small teddy bear (hand-size) and laid it, too, on the mother's lap. When she returned later, Suki made a hitting gesture with the bear. (It is always easier for a child to show hostility behind the facade of a toy.) When the teacher responded, "That bear doesn't like me!" Suki did it again, saying "No!" "He certainly tells me," the teacher said. For several days "No!" was all the bear said, but now Suki sat bolt upright on her mother's lap, watching for the door to open. The bear was kept in Suki's locker, and the teacher would bring it in to her as soon as she was seated on her mother's lap in the morning. Very soon Suki began to accept it directly from the teacher's hand. One day it appeared dressed in a jacket and cap. "Does he like those new clothes?" the teacher asked, and Suki nodded. Then, with a twinkle in her eye, she hit out with the bear again. "But he doesn't like *me!*" the teacher responded, and Suki twinkled again and said, "He says, 'No!'" — her first words admittedly in her own person. The teacher went on then, "I wasn't sure what kind of clothes he'd want, because I didn't know how old he is." "He's two," she replied, and her own behavior had certainly not been beyond age two, prior to this.

The waiting room had a Dutch door which opened into the office, and just around the corner from this door, in the office, was a low sink. Since Suki had been identifying with age two, and twos love water, the teacher put some water-play materials in readiness on the sink, saying, "I can see you don't want to go very far from your mother, so I thought this could be your special place." And she left them alone awhile, closing the doors to the big playroom. Suki put the bear on her mother's lap and went to peer through the open door. Water is an almost irresistible magnet, and soon she was washing a baby doll and feeding it from a bottle. When a washcloth, spoon, and cup were brought, she accepted the teacher's presence and produced some "Yes" answers. "The baby's getting really clean." "Yes, he is." "Do you need some soap?" "Yes." "You have a baby at home, but he's too little to come to school, I guess." "Yes," she said, suddenly sounding quite grown-up; "He can't do much; he spills his food." And she threw a little water on the floor quickly. "Like that?" "Yes," she agreed.

After a day or two of this play, when Suki needed a towel the teacher offered to show her where they were, holding out her hand. The two of them went, hand in hand, all the way down the playroom to the bathroom at the far end. A child spoke to them. "Why doesn't she play in here?" "Because she doesn't want to get very far from her mother," the teacher answered, as Suki turned her face away. (Weeks later she was heard telling someone this herself, only then she said, "I didn't used to want to get very far from my mother.")

Picking up the feeding idea from Suki's interest in using the doll bottle, the teacher had prepared herself with a small stuffed alligator with a large mouth that opened and shut. Having seen the sandbox through the glass doors near the bathroom, on returning Suki whispered to her mother to go outside with her. The teacher offered to go instead, showing her the alligator and saying, "We could feed it some sand," and they went out, again holding hands. Then followed days when large quantities of sand were fed to the alligator by both. Here was a symbol Suki could use. The teacher, too, was a feeding person, like her mother. The bear who was "only two" was left in her locker, and now the alligator, strong and fierce, but also an insatiably hungry baby, represented herself in transition.

The sandbox always contained other children who were interested in the hungry alligator. A motherly little girl, Dody, began making cakes for it. Like the bear who said no, at first the alligator rejected these by breaking them. Dody accepted this as a joke, and then Suki, in her own person, invented a game of slowly cracking sand pies by kicking at the underside of the board on which they lay. This game was played by a number of children for several days, with Suki's mischievous, smiling face surrounded by them. And now she began to make some spontaneous remarks, such as "Give him some more"; "Let me do it"; "I'll make one, now." As often happens when they realize that special attention is being given someone, Suki became a center of the children's interest. Many asked her to play, and when she left for home a chorus of "Good-bye, Suki" always arose. With a little delay she would then wave and say, "Good-bye," a moment everyone waited for.

Progress was now steady. Next Suki tried the swing. At first just pushing against the ground with her feet, soon she began pumping high, to everyone's admiration. Now, too, she had no trouble opening the door to go in and out, though in her two-year-old phase she had been unable to do it. Soon she was a busy, independent group member, bidding her mother good-bye at the door on arrival. Some time before Suki's mother really left, however, Suki had parted from her psychologically, going to the playground early in the day and not even returning for a visit. She kept her bear and her alligator in her locker as long as she attended nursery school, but rarely played with them. In these two symbols the two sides of her, the angry child and the symbiotic baby, had found expression, and now she was free to be the competent four-year-old she was.

● How a father can help is shown by Norman's transition experience. Norman, a four-year-old, was used to being alone with his mother all day in their secluded, tree-surrounded home. She had first felt he needed school, though she "hated to part with him," when she realized he could never go anywhere without her. But separation was no nearer after she had stayed at school with him several weeks; in fact, as Norman grew jealous of the other children he stayed in the waiting room with his mother more and more, closing the door to hide them from her. A conference with both parents revealed that the father felt rather shut out by the relationship between mother and son, and a plan was made for him to bring Norman to school on his way to work.

The long ride to school with his father all to himself pleased Norman and from this point on, the father played an increasingly important role in Norman's life. Various projects related to the school were soon undertaken by father and son, such as painting the toy trucks, collecting nature materials on Sunday afternoons for collages, and bringing wood scraps for the workbench. Coming to school and sharing his son's interests made it possible for Norman's father to enter his life, whereas at home he had not been able to compete with his wife because of her single-minded devotion to Norman's affairs. As Norman and his father grew more companionable, his mother began to find interests outside the secluded home, and her need to keep Norman to herself lessened. This is a natural way out of an overly strong mother-son relationship, if a father is, or can become, sufficiently interested.

IV

Sometimes, after an easy adjustment at the beginning of school, there is a relapse later, and the child wants to stay at home or have a parent stay with him at school. Perhaps the child may realize that he has less of his parents' attention now—that the baby, or other siblings, will get his share while he is away. If either parent has started a new job or hobby, a child may also be jealous of that interest. Relapses like these usually tend to pass as children find out that the family situation remains stable whether they are at home or not. In another case, perhaps going to school has been so built up in anticipation that a child is at first too excited to feel comfortable and relaxed there and needs some days off. A child may also acquire the idea from older siblings that any day now a good deal will be expected of him in school. Still another child may belatedly realize that there are really a lot of strange children at school, and, if he has been accustomed to sharing the attention of an adult with only a few others, he may feel insecure when he becomes aware that at school the attention is divided among many more. A socially sensitive child may also discover that others have friends, while he hasn't any yet. Taking detailed notes on what a relapsing child does at school can give insight into both what he has on his mind and where he stands, socially, in the group.

Another reason for a relapse is a change in the school environment to which the child is just getting accustomed. Small children are very sensitive to such changes. Coming in, expecting to see his teacher, and finding a strange adult just inside the door might be a shock for some three-year-olds. (This is one reason why it is a good idea for extra adults, such as mothers staying with children, to remain in another area.) Other changes might be an altered arrangement of the room, a toilet overflowing, a strange dog near the front gate, a new teacher in the playground, a child crying loudly, or even a small difference in one's favorite teacher, such as a new hair style; any of these could be enough to cause a child to have what might be called a "double take" about school.

Relapses may also occur because something happened which, for the first time, made the child miss his mother. Perhaps there was a tumble. Maybe after a toilet accident he didn't know how the teacher would react or whether she could help him get clean and dry again. Or, after intensely concentrating on play, the child might at some point have become a little disoriented, thought it was much later, couldn't remember the door his mother would come in on her return, and wandered around with a panicky feeling growing inside him. Perhaps, for the first time, some child he didn't know said, "Go away!" crossly. Or the child might have been angry at the teacher for not letting him do something and suddenly have come to the conclusion that she didn't like him any more. (If a child is angry at a teacher, he sometimes assumes she must be angry at him for having such feelings.)

For any of the above reasons, or others, a child may balk at coming to school soon after entering. Then the mother may need to come in and stay for a while, even though she was not needed at first, to help the child over the hump. If she knows what the problem is, she can pass her information on to the teacher, or the teacher, if she cannot recall any reason from the previous day, can give the child some openings. "You didn't want to come today. Something happened, maybe? Something about school? About me?" (with a smile). "About the children? Or maybe about mother or daddy?" She will do this in an easy, unpressuring way, and unanxiously, and whether the child can explain or not (he often can, and only needed the opening), at least he learns that such feelings can be talked about. Most children will rule out some of the suggestions by shaking their heads, then respond when one has hit it. "Something about the children?" "Mark doesn't like me." "Mark did something?" "He said, 'Go away!'" "Oh. We'll go talk to him." It's important for a child to come back to school and work things out. If he stays away, it will become harder and harder for him to return.

Sometimes even after a child has been in school and happily adjusted for a long time, one day he or she may not want to come because of an uncomfortable social situation at school that needs working out. Perhaps he wants to stay home to punish either the teacher or another child; he may have said, in an angry moment, "Then I won't come to school any more!" He may feel unable to settle a disagreement, protest unfriendly treatment, or join a desired group. With any of these problems, the stay-at-homes can be helped if encouraged to return and talk things over with the teacher's support.

Most apt to cause a child to want to stay at home are disturbances in his home relationships; these are of more importance to him than any he has in school. Is there a visitor who is getting a lot of mother's attention? Is someone sick at home? Is father away? Has the family moved, or is it getting ready to do so? A common situation is reluctance to part from mother when relations are temporarily awry. Penny, one day, was heard screaming at the gate, "I don't want to go to school!" Penny's mother said that Penny had wanted to visit her friend Dee across the street earlier in the day, but Dee had had another guest, and Penny had been fussing at her mother for refusing to let her go there ever since. "And now you say you don't want to go to school!" the mother said, looking exasperated. A hint from the teacher, out of Penny's hearing ("She probably can't separate until you're friends again") brought a warm response from her mother, and they made it up, Penny showing her things and her mother smiling and admiring them, particularly a painting of Penny's, which she said she would like to have framed. Soon, with a big hug, they parted.

V

It is natural for a parent to feel worried if a child seems unhappy at school. A mother might even say, "I don't want him to come if he's not happy there" (meaning, happy all the time). Such a mother may think of nursery school as a special treat she has brought the child, like a party or a trip to the zoo, asking him every day if he has had a good time. But, though most of the time the children do look thriving and buoyant, being happy does not seem to be their main concern. They tend to think of school as a part of life, in which one has all kinds of feelings—a place where one is learning about the real world.

● Jason is an example of a child's courage and determination in the face of what, at one point, were anything but "good times." Yet never did he object to going to school during that period. He was a passionate, dark-haired boy with a set of power fantasies that he was engaged in playing out, the meaning of which was probably the father identification so common in boys of this age. Again and again he ran into difficulties with the children because he demanded that no one else climb the jungle gym, which he was using as his "office." His teacher could not satisfy him with other "offices," such as a special corner with a table for his desk, because he wanted the second-story height. She was obliged to say that the whole jungle gym could not be reserved for him, because a climbing place was needed for the others, but she told him he could use one section at the top for his office. However, every time he saw anyone climbing about elsewhere in the jungle gym, he became furious and frantic. Each day, over and over, he pulled up his grimy white T-shirt to mop off his tear-stained face and started out once again to make everyone see things his way. At last he learned that his efforts were futile, but that nevertheless there were advantages in having other children around; often if you admitted them to your play world, they could even enrich it, as when they knocked on his office "door" bringing letters or telephoned him on a toy phone. (As with Suki, the teachers' interest in Jason was picked up by the children, and they soon began to help.) Jason was an only child whose imaginary playmates always did what he wanted them to do. His transition to school was very stormy, yet he seemed to know all along that something worthwhile was happening to him there.

For new children, a personal tie with the teacher is the natural way to become comfortable in the school's world. The teacher, whom his mother seems to like and trust, is his link with home. The teacher must make the child feel that she, too, cares about him; he cannot be left in limbo. But as soon as a child has found his way to the sense of separate identity he needs in order to take the step toward growing up that school can be for him, the development of different and deeply satisfying relationships with people outside his home can begin.

3 Group Climate

I was once in the sun
In the creek by the blue;
In the meadow were flowers and trees.

And yellow sunshine
Was over the trees,
And I was a little girl called Susan.

—Moka

I

The composition of any nursery school group needs careful consideration if the atmosphere is to be right. The best group has children of different personalities but is well balanced so that the world is not presented in a distorted form with too many members who are aggressive, passive, anxious, withdrawn, inhibited, or otherwise unusual. The group itself is the material used in learning about people, just as the musical instruments, the puzzles, the books, the toys, and the playground equipment are the materials used for other kinds of learning. Each child will need enough choices for friends, and also enough peace in the group to allow him to concentrate, to have conversations with other children, to talk privately with his teachers, or to rest. This kind of thoughtful group building will greatly facilitate social learning, individualized teaching, and group management. Twenty is probably a maximum number to permit group cohesiveness at this age; sixteen or eighteen might be better in many cases. In general, younger children need smaller groups, but if a group becomes too small the social learning becomes correspondingly limited. The number of teachers depends on the training of the teachers and on the ease of supervision of the physical environment. But hiring extra staff, if a group becomes too large, is not really helpful; rather, it adds yet another complicating and potentially overstimulating factor to the social situation. In addition, the individualized approach by which anyone learns best, but which is particularly important for these young children, becomes progressively harder to maintain as groups become larger. A teacher can only help so many freely moving children, each with his own needs. Yet if the program is not of this free kind, opportunities for the children to try themselves out in ways that really interest them and in which, therefore, the whole child is involved are seriously limited. If this is so, chances for the teacher to observe and study their interests, motivations, development, and relationships are just as limited.

II

Disturbances of group climate through the spreading of tension from a single child to others is one of the most puzzling aspects of group behavior. Why is it that almost all of the children in a group can become affected by a kind of hysteria at times, when they are not threatened in any way that one can see? To begin with, one child in the group, for reasons of his or her own, becomes anxious. Old, buried emotions may begin to assert themselves and find expression in the same ways they did when the child was a baby. Body activity and vocalization increase, the latter at a higher pitch and volume than the child's usual speaking voice. The content of speech becomes more chaotic, too, with words that resemble a baby's random repetitions of syllables. A baby early learns that laughing brings warm adult response, and many an anxious child laughs more and more wildly.

How is this anxiety communicated to other children, who certainly cannot understand it intellectually? This seems to come about by means of the small child's almost uncanny ability to empathize. As another child watches the anxious one's movements, he himself experiences the same movement impulses in his own muscles, and when he hears a certain kind of vocalizing, meaningless but with agitation behind it, his own vocal apparatus tenses. The next step is that when a child has these physical sensations, the emotions that were associated with them in his own past are revived, and he, too, becomes anxious. This is similar to the response of a child to another's crying. Why does this so often make him feel like crying himself? He is not the one who was hurt or made unhappy, and yet this response occurs even when a child does not feel sympathy and may even feel dislike for the other, and when he has no reason to fear any similar harm for himself. But, again, as when he observed the anxious child, the sound of the crying and the sight of the screwed-up face arouse empathic reactions, and when his own throat tightens and his own face contorts, the distress that has been associated with these sensations sweeps over him.

The tendency to empathize had its start in early infancy. It began when the baby, who as yet had no sense of himself as a separate person, saw his own hands clench, reach, and tremble, and felt at the same time the corresponding emotions. He heard his own wails and screams without knowing whose cries he heard, any more than he knew those hands were his own, and while hearing the cries, he was at the same time experiencing the feelings that made him cry; this is how the sound and the feelings became linked together in his mind. In the nursery school, children react sensitively to small cues of excitement and tension expressed in the sounds and movements around them, and the feedback among individuals leads to more and more intensity in the situation.

III

In order to maintain a helpful group atmosphere, a teacher needs to protect children from overexcitement, since they are so vulnerable to its contagion. When overexcited, children are unable to function well. Not able to use their minds to make the kind of judgments of which they are ordinarily capable, they may be swept into actions they will regret or which are harmful either to themselves or to the group. An immature organism can tolerate only so much stimulation; it must be paced to the emotional stability and maturity a child has achieved. This principle often does not seem to be well understood; children's excitement is frequently mistaken for pleasure. The screaming of children at parties, in swimming pools, on playgrounds, or while watching puppet shows or cartoons on television may thus be misinterpreted. Small children overreact to assaults on their senses.

The differentiating of enthusiasm and active, vigorous play from overstimulation and overexcitement requires sensitive awareness on the part of a teacher so that preventive measures can be taken early, rather than restorative ones later. Often children show indefatigable energy in running up and down or in circles, in jumping off boards again and again, in leaping and falling while dancing, in riding their tricycles as fast as possible, in sliding, swinging, throwing balls, or rolling hoops and tires. Noise is heard, too, in full-throated shouts, chants, patterned word repetitions, calling friends, telling somebody off loudly, playing the piano percussively at top volume, beating drums, crying in the role of a baby, or giving orders in the role of a fireman or policeman. Activity and noise need not mean tension. And if a child wants to try something new that is hard for him to do—perhaps climb into a high swing, jump off a top step, pound a nail in so it stays there, finish a hard puzzle, or button a doll's jacket, a degree of tension is useful to help hold him to his task. But there is another kind of tension that results in purposeless, random activity, and an inability to concentrate on anything; this type does the child no service. The outward signs of it are rapid movements (usually; more rarely there is immobility); a loss of motor coordination that leads to spilling, dropping things, falling, or stumbling over and bumping into things; a high-pitched voice, and laughter and scream-ing; or a loss of caution seen in a child's throwing himself about and pushing others on high places. All these are typical of regression to a more infantile level. In addition, the tension can be seen in raised shoulders and in the child's face, particularly his eyes, which seem to dart about and focus on nothing for more than a fraction of a second. He seems not to hear when one speaks to him, and if one touches him he may jerk away in a startle reaction.

It is this kind of tension that is contagious in a group. Even before they have themselves experienced any difficulty with the tense child, the sight and sound of him have affected the others. And soon his disorganized behavior may threaten them in reality, unless there is prompt action by the teacher. He may race about wildly, perhaps hitting the nearest child or kicking a toy. Sensing that the child has lost control, the other children feel threatened, even if they resist the urge to behave similarly, and soon he may arouse defensively hostile responses from them. This can only upset the child still more, and consequent actions for which he fears retaliation or which are de-structive to his own aims—as when he tears up his pictures and disrupts his own play—continue the downward spiral.

To help a child who is, or threatens to become, a focus of group excitement, one needs to understand the reasons for his tension. Certain causes can easily be seen because they are outward ones. The child might, for example, be in a situation which is making him anxious. One of the most common is the chase. What looks like ordinary play may really be a kind of scary pursuit to the child concerned, and he is beginning to fall apart. Another cause is the child's involvement in group play at a level for which he is not quite ready at his present stage of social maturity; he feels insecure and, finally, completely over his head, and so, asserts himself more and more frenetically to get attention from the rest of the group. Or perhaps he is overstimulated by a new relationship, and his excitement has mounted to the point where he can neither contain it nor leave the other child. The thoughts in a child's head when there are outer causes like these might go, "I'm out of my depth here; I don't know if I can cope with what's going on. I'll run fast and make a big noise; then nobody will know." Or he may think, "What's happening is making me feel inadequate; if I keep changing what I do, I won't be caught short." The answer to these dilemmas is a change in the milieu of the moment.

In another child who is the focal point of a group's overexcitement, tension is being produced by inner worries and fears. The thought here might be something like "I'm scared of my thoughts, and I need to drown them out now by shouting and screaming, or run away from them by dashing around." This child needs the teacher's help to come to terms with the feelings from which he is trying to escape. Then he will be ready to use the school's resources for activities and relationships, so that learning, growing, and experiencing in the real world can play their part in helping him to overcome his problems. The teacher acts quickly in situations like the above, to protect the rest of the group from becoming anxious or overstimulated, but also for another reason. She wants the children to learn to distinguish their own feelings from those of others, as a part of the growth of the self. She helps an overexcited child recognize what he feels and do something about it, both for his own sake and in order to aid the others to see that the problem is in him, at that moment, not them. Helping children understand other children helps them know themselves better, and this results in a back-and-forth process of insight that makes it possible for them to separate their feelings from those of others, so that, in time, they will no longer have to react automatically (as mobs do, for instance) to other people's emotions. "Binky is worried because his mother has gone. It's the first time she's left him at school. I think that's why he's walking around and around so fast. Do you remember when you weren't used to school yet?" And the tense watcher's face clears. "She'll be back at story time," he says.

Home television viewing is a common source of disturbed climates. If children are identifying with television superheroes, tensions are high, because each child, darting around in the cape or T-shirt that turns him or her into a favorite character, must be the one who comes out on top. Children all look for models, and the actions of grown-ups on television are particularly vivid and impressive. But the stories on television have frightening aspects; so many adults seem to be "bad guys" who must be dealt with in some way—by capture and imprisonment, by using fists or guns, or by otherwise overpowering them. Soon, a superhero seems the safest adult model, since real-life adults look so much less strong and invincible.

A small child is always aware of the difference in size between him and what seem to be the important people in his world; so he likes to play fireman, policeman, truck driver, cowboy, or soldier—all strong, masculine figures. Some of his ideas also come from stories. But those roles, many conceived to be helping ones, are less vividly presented than the television ones. And unfortunately a superhero must find victims; after repeated viewings, a child's identification is so strong and his own aroused feelings so intense that he is unable to keep from chasing other children or shooting at them with impro-vised guns. Some children who don't see the programs will imitate his play in a less driven way; others in the group, however, resenting being objects of aggression, are led to retaliate, and thus become "bad guys" in reality, requiring still more aggressive treatment. Thus the patterns of disruption become circular, and overstimulation and chaotic behavior become characteristic of the group.

Since the play is a result of one of the strongest motivations a young child has—his need to model himself after adults—the teacher knows it will not stop soon if it is being reinforced by con-tinued exposure to new shows on the superhero theme. He may be able to briefly postpone playing out these fantasies, but they will come out again, inevitably, in one form or another. The teacher will need to find ways he can do this without disturbing her group. One child might be able to pursue imaginary victims on a tricycle in a separate area, supported by a special friend. Another might be helped to make use of art materials or dictate stories to externalize the fan-tasies. Several might play together, using small figures and buildings made of blocks, and the teacher could supply the figures with capes or other identifying symbols as needed. One or more children might bring their own toy television characters or other props to be used in protected areas such as an adjoining office, where the teacher could look in and reduce tension by an occasional uncritical comment. But in any case, the anxiety that is beneath the surface in this play will result in its supplanting other activities. Eventually—sooner, if the child stops seeing the program—the play will lose its intensity, and other interests will take its place.

Many young children are also affected by the violence seen in television cartoons. In their efforts to release the tension these programs produce, they, like the characters, behave in frenetically clownish ways that are contagious in a nursery school group. Encouraging large-muscle activity often helps, but only temporarily. Television violence has a circular effect. Any small child has some violent feelings that are discharged through the viewing experience as he identifies with the aggressors, and the satisfaction this brings leads him to want more of the same. However, as always, part of him also identifies with the victims, and he feels helpless and overpowered. Sandy said of Saturday morning cartoons, "I get scared in my tummy." Then comes the need to turn things around again, so as to feel strong and invincible in the role of aggressor once more. Thus the need to express aggressive wishes results in fear and more aggressive wishes, and the original need is satisfied in a way that recreates it. Release of that kind can become an addiction.

A child is always drawn by powerful stimuli that excite his senses, and he can easily learn to feel bored, restless, and unsatisfied when life is not continously at that level. Then he demands, "What's on next?" "Where are we going today?" "Who's coming to play?" and "What can I do now?" I once observed a group of three-year-olds watching a television cartoon. One animal stamped with all its might on another one's foot. The children screamed and laughed, shouting, "Do it again! Do it again!" But there will never be enough. The more they see, the more they want; the need remains, and the dosage must be continued and increased as the shock is reduced through habituation. The answer does not lie there; in the end it is necessary to come to terms with the violence within oneself.

IV

Examples of disturbed group climates and the measures taken to deal with them follow.

● One group that seemed unusually chaotic was composed of young three-year-olds; the time was early in the school year. Conspicuous among them from the first day was Philip, called Pip. He was eager for playmates and toys, and easily stimulated and attracted by the sights, sounds, and movements around him. He was everywhere at once, no more than starting play one place than up and away at the opening of a cupboard door, with "What's in there?" Playing with one toy, he was drawn to, and soon clutched, the toy he saw in his neighbor's hand. If anyone said, "I want—" to a teacher, he hastened over to put in his bid, too, without waiting for the end of the sentence. In this state of continuous distractability, Pip was apt to carry around vestiges of his previous interests, and thus bits of puzzles, or pegs, beads, crayons, or paste brushes were dropped here and there as he went, and he always left a trail of cracker crumbs in his wake as he bore a fistful away from the table in pursuit of yet another appealing goal. If two children were involved in a disagreement, he enthusiastically entered in by pounding one on the head or throwing himself on top of them both. Thus, through his day, he would follow one impulse after another without pause. Coming inside to wash, covered with paint, he was drawn to a paper cup and washed it, instead; intrigued with filling and emptying the cup, he poured the water into the wastebasket; next he carried two full, paint-smeared cups into the doll corner, leaving a discarded one plugging the wash basin and the water running. Once at the doll corner, he emptied his cups shakily into the teapot and sat down in a puddle to have "dinner." Here he tangled with the two children already in possession of the table, but, laughing good-naturedly, he waved his splashing teapot at them and pushed them off their chairs. And so it went.

If one adds to Pip a number of other children even a little like him, one can see that it isn't so much Pip who has the problem—it is the teachers. In a school where the children are not all gathered together under the teacher's eye for one activity at a time, they roam freely and find their own interests. This requires a certain amount of ability to select from various stimuli and to structure one's own actions and materials toward a goal. But it takes time for children to develop this. As things were, in this rather young group, the teachers felt they were not helping the children progress toward self-direction, and, in fact, were having trouble even keeping up with Pip, to say nothing of the others. So measures had to be taken.

In the playroom a large table was set up by combining two smaller ones, and in the center of it was placed each day a large, flat basket which everyone could reach. In it there might be small building blocks, beads to string, plastic lids with holes punched so short sticks could be poked through them, a village set with houses, trees, and little figures, or other sets having many similar pieces. Also, outside, another large table sometimes had clay or playdough, or on it might be placed a large pan filled with water or wet sand, with paraphernalia to use there. The children who soon gathered around the tables were thus engaged in parallel play, and little supervision was needed. With the use of these large tables, which could hold up to eight children, the number circulating in the room or playground was quickly reduced. Those who played on the periphery alone, or in pairs or small groups, could now be supervised adequately and given help when they needed it. Pip learned where to go and what to do when he wanted to play with water. He learned where to keep and use crayons and paste, and where to eat crackers. When he became interested in something, his teacher could protect his play from interruption and prolong and enrich it. For example, she added a sponge, a drainer, and some soap when he was washing dishes at the doll sink, and, after he had scribbled on a paper and was passing on, she helped him find his locker and put the paper away to take home.

Meanwhile the teachers cut down the stimulation for the whole group. No extra supplies were brought out until the children had learned the contents of the open shelves. The morning snack was delayed until ten-thirty, when picking-up time started, so a fairly large number would be seated then. This transition is especially hard for young children. The bustle and stir, and the disappearance of most of the toys, owing to the impending arrival of parents or a change to song and story time, confuses many. Some then get into fresh difficulties, as though to try to draw the teacher's attention back to them. It is a time when shoes are pulled off, things are spilled, forays are made into others' lockers, and children get wet or fall down. In any group, if transition tension is not well handled, it leads to the toys just put away being pulled out again, with children milling about in an ever-increasing tempo. As usual with such young groups, there was a good deal of picking up to be done at the end of the day's activities, even with the teacher's doing it fairly continuously throughout the session, and only a few children were ready to participate in the process. So the teacher did the picking up as quickly as possible, and she talked and sometimes sang as she did it, to let the children know just where she was all the time. Those who trailed at her heels disarranging toys again and those still playing could be helped by special attention and explanation, because there were fewer of them. Food also helped to quiet this young group at that time, until they had learned what to expect. From snacks they could easily progress to play with new materials at the same table outside, and to songs and stories at the same one inside.

Gradually Pip, who had been the prime chaos-producer of the group, became stabilized. In his case, there was no need to look for trouble beneath the surface. All his behavior was the response of an inexperienced three-year-old, sensitive to stimuli, and curious and energetic, to a situation that was too complex for him. It was as though he had been given a puzzle with too many pieces; he was unable to see how it might be organized meaningfully, so he just reacted in a random, chaotic fashion to each separate element. The group Pip joined was an immature, unstable one, and he upset its balance. A more stable group would not have been as affected by Pip, nor would he have been as confused by it. But sometimes the effect of child on group and group on child produces a mushrooming problem for teachers. In the new, simpler milieu, the attention spans of all the children lengthened, and the jumpy group atmosphere changed. As the group relaxed, the need for constant help and attention diminished. Now that the teacher was no longer moving so fast from place to place, a child was able to look up from his toys, catch her eye and exchange smiles, then go on with his play, reassured.

● In a four-year-old group, symptoms of a seriously disintegrating group atmosphere arose from competition for the attention of one of the children. When the group was analyzed, it was found to be orbiting around Nan, its most popular member. Each of the girls, particularly, wanted to play with her first and foremost. Some of this was due to her own cheerful warmth and charm, and some, no doubt, to the contagion of the Nan-as-playmate idea. Lani, who was a little younger and followed Nan everywhere, was especially resented by the others. Lani often played with Nan at their homes, and a great deal of emphasis developed on who was invited where after school. "*I'm* going to play with Nan today; *you* aren't invited," to be countered with, "Well, then, I'm going to invite Betty, but not *you,* tomorrow."

When so much animosity springs up in a group and focuses around a particular child, one wonders in what way this child is

responsible. A socially mature child can usually manage popular-
ity so as to keep everyone happy; teachers have often seen this
happen: "You can sit across from me, and you can sit next to me,
O.K.?" Was Nan somehow contributing to this rivalry over her?
She was obviously a little uncomfortable about it. She felt self-
conscious and found it necessary to clown a lot and keep a table in
a mild uproar when the atmosphere became unpleasant. One day,
when she was being pressed on all sides to "play with *me*, now,
Nan," her teacher invited her to come into the office for a private
talk. Climbing into the desk chair, she seemed glad to get away
from the intensity of the scene. "Did you really want to play with
Lani?" (the most insistent), the teacher asked her. "No, but I'm
afraid I'll hurt her feelings if I say no," she answered. The teacher
then reminded Nan of a recent situation when she had said to one
of the boys, "Don't take that puzzle; Lani had it first," to please
Lani, though Lani hadn't really had it first, and how, on another
occasion, she had reported that she had "fooled" the teachers by
taking flowers from the vases home in her lunch box. "Those were
two fooling times, weren't they?" the teacher said. "I fooled my
mother, too," Nan responded. "I told her my green pants were
dirty and I couldn't wear them." "What did she do?" "She got
mad." The teacher asked if Nan thought Lani would like to be
fooled and think Nan wanted to play with her when she really
didn't. She looked thoughtful. "I wouldn't want to be fooled," she
said. "Then I wouldn't know if the person really liked me or not."

Nan then talked about how the children pressed her to play with
them and how she didn't know what to say. "Then things get
worse, and they start fighting with each other, and you're glad to
get away, like in here," the teacher said, and Nan nodded. She
accepted an offer of pipe cleaners and buttons to make "jewelry"
by herself, and enjoyed this very much, finding it possible on several later occasions to say, "I'm going to play alone, now," and
come into the office to do that, though she couldn't as yet face
having to decide between the children who asked her to play with
them. But her mother reported that she had said, "I feel like I've
done something wrong when I have to play alone." The teacher
took this up with her. "Do you think you'd like to play alone
today?" "O.K." "Is that a fooler?" asked the teacher, and Nan
laughed. "Yes; do I have to?" "No, it's for you to decide." "Well, I
thought it might hurt your feelings if I said I didn't want to play in
your office." "Like with Lani?" Nan looked thoughtful again.

"How is it really?" the teacher asked. "I think I do want to make that jewelry, but nothing else."

As Nan settled down in the office, the teacher said, "It takes a while to learn to say how you really feel, doesn't it?" Then this very intelligent little girl pulled it all together. Looking up from her untidy bracelet, she said, "I'm going to say, 'Yes, I do,' or 'No, I don't' to Lani." "Is Lani the hardest one?" asked the teacher. "Yes, because she's the littlest. But I don't say it to the others, either. And then they all fight about me. I used to like them to fight about me, but now it makes me feel like I've done something wrong." "Wrong—like fooling them?" "Yes." "It isn't so nice to have them fighting over you now, and you think not telling them what you really want makes the fighting worse?" "Yes, that's it. But I don't know what to say." "Would you like to practice? I'll pretend I'm Betty. 'Play with *me*, Nan—don't play with Lani.'" She laughed, but looked a little uneasy, too. "I'll say—I'll say—I don't know." "Do you *want* to play with Betty and not Lani, like she's asking?" "No—poor little Lani. No, Betty, I think I'm going to play with Lani now." The teacher went on. "Now shall I be Lani? 'Play with *me*, Nan.'" "I'd rather make some jewelry now, but I'll play with you after school. *I can't play with you all the time!*" Her face grew red, and she dropped her head over her jewelry, looking close to tears. "That was hard," the teacher said, and she nodded.

Bit by bit, as Nan learned to level with everyone, teachers and children, the group tensions eased. Once in a while she would again practice what she wanted to say and then bring it out to the child concerned successfully. The other children gave up their intense rivalry with each other for her attention when she became more than just an object to fight over and expressed feelings of her own. As some became annoyed with her and she grew less popular, she needed help to keep from feeling she had "done something wrong." But gradually her focus changed from trying to please everyone to trying to be true to her own feelings and let others know them.

● Group tensions can also develop around a child who becomes the scapegoat for a number of other children's hostilities. A child like this often seems to have something a little different about him or her—a strange name, an unusual way of speaking, an odd appearance, or something else that draws attention. Dale had a lot of whitish hair that hung below his shoulders. But a different appearance may also be a reason for special approval by young children. One child with very black skin was a great favorite in Dale's group. Before his name was learned, he was referred to admiringly as "the little boy with the dark face." So there was more reason than a different appearance for Dale's being made a scapegoat.

It developed slowly. "I don't like you," said Maggie, when he tried to sit at her table. "Why?" "I don't like your hair," she told him. For a while he bore this well, speaking of Maggie in a matter-of-fact way as "the girl that doesn't like my hair." But others began to pick up the idea of not liking Dale, also, and soon the friendly atmosphere of the group as a whole began to be threatened; people of all ages have a tendency to look for someone to pin hostile feelings on. Heard everywhere were "Go away!" "Don't let Dale sit here!" "Let's run away—here comes Dale!" "You can't play with us," and, again, "I don't like Dale." Help was needed for Dale, but also for the children who were using this destructive way of expressing their negative feelings.

The teacher watched any group in Dale's vicinity, looking for a chance to work out the problem. One day, high, shrill voices emanated from the jungle-gym climbers, who seemed to be scrambling round and round, and up and down, as though they were all being pursued. When the teacher asked, "What's happening?" Sandy said, "It's Dale! He's a wolf, and he's chasing us!" Since Dale himself was just standing nearby smiling, the teacher suggested, "You're pretending he's chasing you? Did you *want* to be chased by that wolf?" "Yes," was Sandy's answer. "I see. And then what would you do?" "I'd chase him back! I'd be a wolf, too!" "It looks as though some people are feeling kind of cross at Dale, lately," the teacher said to Sandy, Maggie, and Penny, all peering down at her from the top of the jungle gym. "How about you, Maggie?" "Yes, I don't like his hair." Well," the teacher said, "If Dale's doing something you don't like, you could tell him, and he might stop, but I don't know what he could do about his hair, do you?" "His mother should take him to the barber," she said, severely. Then she paused. Children of this age have a surprising sense of justice. "I think I'd better tell his *mother*," she said. "How about you, Penny?" "I don't like him. I hate him." "You feel pretty angry at him. Did he do something?" "He jumped the wrong way," she replied. Sometimes answers seem contrived, but teachers need to notice them; often they lead to the heart of the matter. The three girls had been jumping on the lawn previously, with Dale, as now, on the edges of their play. "Something about his jumping," the teacher hazarded. "He jumps backward," came from Sandy. "He's trying to jump like *us*," said Maggie, resentfully. ("And wear his hair long, too, 'like us,' maybe?" the teacher added mentally.) "It was a jumping for three. For three *girls*," Sandy said. "I see," responded the teacher. "There are times when you girls just want to be with girls, no boys — is that right?" "Yes!" "I expect he didn't know that," the teacher went on. "Perhaps he likes you and wants to be near you; is that right, Dale?" "Yes, I do." The teacher told the girls, "You might say, 'Sometimes we like an all-girl game. You could come another time.' Do you think you would feel like saying that? *Could* he come another time?" They said he could; "another time" is a long way off, and at the moment they felt drawn to Dale by the suggestion that he might like them and want to be near them. Sandy nodded; "We'll say that," she said, "and then he'll understand and go away."

Of course the problem was not solved immediately. In a day or two one of the boys said, "Here comes Dale; we don't want *him*." But Maggie, a strong group leader who formed her own opinions, said, "*I* like him." Penny still frowned upon Dale quite often, however, and the teacher brought the two of them together for a private talk. "You could tell Dale now what he does that you don't like," she suggested to Penny; "I think he'd like to know; is that right, Dale?" He nodded. "Why don't you like me, all the time?" he asked her. "'Cause you always come when we're playing alone," she answered. "You understand that?" the teacher asked. "Would it be all right with you to let them play alone?" "Sure," Dale answered. Penny looked surprised. "Now can I play with you?" he asked, hastily pressing his advantage. "O.K." Penny told him, and they built tracks for trains in the waiting room, remaining there for some time as a twosome.

Evidence that scapegoating had happened — that hostility in only a few had spread throughout the group — was seen in the fact that when the girls' attitude toward Dale changed, the boys soon seemed to forget all about not liking him. They appeared merely to have adopted a convenient victim, much as they used their big stuffed bear. The teachers, however, had learned something about how Dale contributed to the problem. As they watched, they could see that he did, in fact, walk into play already under way, eavesdrop, and trail after groups already formed. He didn't barge in obviously, but he edged in and was ever-present whenever others were especially enjoying closeness. Several children were helped to say clearly to him, "I'm playing with so-and-so now; I'll play with you another time," or "We have all the children we need here, right now; you can come when we're finished." It was of interest, too, to hear in a talk with his parents, "Dale will never give us any privacy. He has to be in on everything we do."

Learning of Dale's difficulty in allowing his parents to have their twosome suggested how the teacher might offer more help directly to Dale. She had a talk with him about Bill, who, though friendly to Dale, wished to be private with Alex sometimes. "He likes you too, though," she said. "A person can like two people at once. Even when he's busy with Alex, he can still like you. You like your mother and your dad, don't you? And your daddy likes you *and* your mother. And your mother likes your daddy—" "*And* me," he could hardly wait to put in.

One situation that occurs in almost every group and needs special handling in order to preserve a stable environment is the development of a kind of love affair between two children. With pairs who become chronically overexcited when together, there is usually an intense attachment that is probably somewhat stimulating sexually, whether it be between a boy and a girl, or, as is more common at this age, between two children of the same sex. The tension is expressed in noisiness, nonsense talk and giggling, tussling and pulling each other about, rapid changes of activity, and even an obliviousness to everything and everybody else that can verge on accident-proneness. There seems to be an uneasiness between the two, as though each feared the other might forget him unless continually stimulated, and also as though each feared the other's rejection if escape from the bond was temporarily contemplated. This lack of security in the relationship often leads to passionate expressions of jealousy and rage. Sometimes the pair may calm down if separated for a while from the other children. No need, then, to put on a noisy, hectic show to keep one's friend's attention off others. Another way to relieve the tension of their interactions is to offer new or interesting material for them to use side by side, so that their focus is not on one another and they can experience a more relaxed companionship. If all else fails, to protect the group atmosphere it is sometimes necessary to separate them from one another for a while, so that each can calm down by playing either alone or with a less stimulating child. Occasional separations are helpful to such a pair as well, since the more they play in an excited way, the more habituated they become to that kind of stimulation, and the harder it will be for them to play in any other way. The separation also helps the children learn to recognize in themselves a need to slow down and relax at times. Sometimes a pair shows an interest in investigating each others' bodies. The teacher can usually gain their confidence so that they will permit her to join them; then her presence reduces excitement, and she can answer questions and indicate by her attitude that such interests are natural.

● Chip had a very intense relationship with David, and in this pair it was he, particularly, who had trouble containing his excitement. Now and then he would grow very reckless and wild, dashing about, screaming with laughter, and falling down on the floor. One day he and David just couldn't seem to settle down to anything. The teacher invited them to "fall down" to music. They gradually worked off much excitement by using the floor space for running, jumping, and falling down, while the teacher played a drum and then a piano accompaniment. Sometimes it looked as though they were doing a primitive courtship dance, as they circled face to face, never taking their eyes off each other, and approaching and retreating without actually making contact. Later, alone with David, the teacher said, "You certainly are good friends, you and Chip. But sometimes his laughing sounds as though he can't stop, you know? It almost sounds like crying. Maybe you can watch out for that sound and say, 'Let's do something else.'"

V

The previous examples have analyzed well-established group disruptions for which restorative measures were needed. Much more often a teacher's focus is on the maintenance of a desirable climate already achieved. Her own relaxed bearing, quiet voice, and smiling calm help greatly. (Wearing rubber-soled shoes is a good idea, too.) She keeps the room and playground from becoming too crowded by providing separate play areas that small groups and pairs can use. Physical crowding increases social pressures, so when one group threatened to become overexcited, swarming over the slide and pushing, the teacher set up a number of small separate slides made from boards and standards. The activity then continued without the overstimulation, because the proximity to others' bodies, movements, and voices was reduced. The key factor, however, was stopping the communication of tension.

In another incident, the teacher also stepped in early to prevent disruption of the group climate. The children in the playroom were reacting one day to the loud, chaotic drumming of two boys. Some of the children were jumping about, others were running around the room, and several were shouting, "Be quiet!" The teacher picked up a drum, too, and then sat down beside the drummers and began to play along with them, but using a steadier, slower, more resonant beat. The rhythmic sound of her drumming, picked up by the boys, drew others to instruments, and the running, jumping children began going in a circle around the big basket of dress-up hats she had pulled into the center of the floor space. Sitting in the midst of the music-makers, she maintained a steady beat for a while; then, as new rhythmic ideas emerged either from drummers or dancers, she reinforced and underlined them by echoing them with her drumming or with the sounds of a tambourine or wood block.

In an outdoor play incident, rhythm of sound and of patterned movement, combined with a change in the environment, were stabilizing influences. The children were throwing cars down an inclined plank. Some began to run down it and some to climb up, at the same time. Conflicts were increasing, and pushing, shrill laughter and screams, and scrambling to get ahead would come next. The teacher expanded the board idea by adding more, placing them in a *U* shape, with one slanting up, one across, and one down. A little help soon started everyone going the same way, and a round-and-round flow developed, which she accompanied by singing "On the Bridge at Avignon." Rhythm helps organize children's chaotic impulses and steadies them, and the teacher's songs, chants, or made-up rhymes communicate her calm, as well as supporting the play. Disorganized, hectic behavior on a slide can similarly become a round-and-round rhythmic activity, as children climb up, slide down, run around, and climb up again, when the teacher emphasizes the design of the play by singing "Down comes Penny, down the slide" (or a monkey, Superman, or whatever is suggested). Children seem to feel more secure quickly as soon as they are aware of the repetitiveness of the pattern, probably because they know what to expect. Play like this is antichaotic; in chaos, of course, everyone becomes anxious because no one knows what to expect and anything can happen at any moment. All a child can do in that case is to hold himself in a state of tension, ready for who knows what. Rhythmic movement provides a framework for the safe discharge of tension, and the children return to normal.

In many situations a teacher can just move into an area where tension is increasing. Her physical nearness will lend support for wavering inner controls and reassure the anxious. Perhaps a group is becoming overexcited at the clay table, where toilet talk has developed and tension has mounted to a point at which children are beginning to push and pummel one another. The teacher could sit down and join the conversation, not changing the subject, as she didn't change the inclined board play, but adding to the theme. The fact that she talks about the subject of "do-dos" matter of factly calms everybody down. "So it's not so naughty and dangerous a subject after all," one child may think, while another forgets his physical tension by becoming interested in the facts she presents. She may say something like "Yes, 'do-do' is one word children sometimes use for bowel movements; there are other words for it, too; do you know another one?" Or she may say, "You know, it's very interesting—all kinds of animals, and even birds and fish, make 'do-dos' of some kind, and they all look different." A matter-of-fact response, though also appreciative of the clownish humor, could be made, as well, to "I'm eating the do-do" and similar talk if it threatens to become too stimulating. "Well, that would be a funny thing to eat, wouldn't it?" (smiling); "However, it wouldn't hurt you; babies taste it sometimes." One reason such talk becomes exciting is that, because of the efforts they make in toilet training, many children think feces are actually a harmful substance. Other misconceptions, perhaps about the sexes, may also be discussed at times, following the children's lead.

Methods like the above can be used when the group has just started down the road to disorganized behavior. However, the teacher can take many steps throughout the day to prevent children's reaching that point. If she is aware of what each child is playing, she can reinforce an activity by showing interest and appreciation or by facilitating and enriching it with new materials. For example, the children in one group were milling about outside on a certain day, unsettled for the most part, and just starting to pester each other. A germ of a play idea was seen there, however, in what Eric called his "train," a large box in which he sat, wearing his engineer's cap. Entering the situation as an imaginative playmate would, the teacher said, "This other box can be fastened to your engine; would you like that?" and she added other details — a bell, a seat in the back for his bear, and so on. Soon other children gathered around and offered ideas too. "Can I load in some food for you, Eric?" "Can I hitch my box on, too?" "Here's my ticket; can I get on?" until there was a long line of smaller boxes and a station where people waited, and train play had taken over the playgound. As this idea caught on, the teacher returned to the sidelines. Her function had been that of a catalytic agent, a role many creative children play, but one nobody at that moment was ready to assume. Here the train idea was a focal point, providing a pattern into which individual energies could flow. Order and plan, appearing in a clearcut design, draw random, unfocused behavior like a magnet. But because the teacher is not another child — is really an adult, with an adult's status — she is careful to make it clear to the group that she is picking up a child's idea, not offering one of her own. As a result, the other children's ideas, such as "Here's a caboose for you" and "Do you want some animals in your boxcar?" were all presented to Eric, not to the teacher. If this is a teacher's way of helping, the point is made for children that they themselves can be creative, self-directed, and self-organized toward their own goals, and that many resources lie within them.

4 Between Teacher and Child

I hate you,
I love you,
I never will marry
Nobody but you.
        —Jessica

I

What kind of person is the teacher in a nursery school, and what is her role there? Successful teachers have all kinds of personalities, but they all probably share an ability to form relationships with children. Because communication is so important, a teacher must be able to empathize with a young child if she is to understand and respond to him. Yet she remains herself, and keeps an adult point of view. She helps, at times, as a mother would, with physical comforting and care, and she interprets and explains his world to him, at his level and as he seeks to understand it, in the role of all teachers. In addition, she is a special kind of friend. She helps him to do what he feels it is important to do; she backs him up. She often lets him know she likes him by saying, "Hi!" and smiling at him, as well as by showing her appreciation of his ideas and achievements. She shares his pleasures and triumphs, enters into his interests and curiosities, and sympathizes with his troubles. She protects him from both his own and others' destructive impulses, and she makes it clear to him that she will always do this. She gives him as much help as he needs, but is ready to let him use self-direction and self-control as much as he can and as soon as he can.

One of the most important things a teacher does is to respect a child, by assuming that he has good reasons for what he does and

51

trying constantly to understand these. Her focus on understanding rather than on changing him makes him able to change himself. A persistent attempt to understand will win through to almost any child. He is aware of the earnestness of this effort and the honesty of the adult in not pretending omnipotence and can scarcely help responding by letting her into his thoughts and feelings, if she keeps judgment and censure out of the process. These attempts assure him of her respect and faith in him as nothing else does. They also help a child learn to be honest with himself, in order to do his part in making the bridge between himself and his teacher. Through these interactions in which he experiences her respect, his self-respect inevitably increases.

Honesty is essential in any relationship. It follows that the nursery school teacher would not manipulate a child, ask him rhetorical questions to make him perform intellectually, or take advantage of his ignorance. She lets him in on what she is trying to do, rather than maneuvering behind his back or fooling him. She might not think it wise to answer all his questions, but she is opposed to telling him untruths, no matter whether he will ever find out or not. She will want to make a continuous effort to find the words that explain her beliefs and decisions honestly, in terms he can understand. And perhaps most important of all will be a consistent acceptance of a child's feelings, even though she is not able to permit some of his actions; to this end, she works to resolve any negative feelings she may have toward him and tries to be always ready to listen to him.

A teacher whose aims for children stress independent learning, which they will engage in both inside and outside the classroom and which will continue throughout their lives, will keep herself in the background. She offers a stimulating environment, then is quiet and supportive, responding to each child's interests. She makes no effort to charm or involve the children through becoming the center of their attention, though she is always ready to help when needed. Nor does she amuse herself with them or attempt to make herself important to them. A child may sit on her lap if he wants closeness, and then she will respond warmly, but when he has had enough, she lets him go; this is equally important.

Although a nursery school teacher values children's needs and purposes and fosters these all she can, she avoids establishing a relationship of self-sacrifice with them. This means that she keeps an eye on her own aims. She must see that the school's atmosphere and environment are right for everyone, and that her work is not impeded by too much noise in the room, too much disorder, or too many demands for her attention. Her teacher's role will not include waiting on children unnecessarily or making herself into their entertainer by pushing swings, pulling wagons, and so on. If she prefers not to do something a child asks of her, she says no. If the idea of cleaning up after more finger paint seems too much late in the day, she ends that activity, and if loud drumming, usually acceptable, bothers her on a certain day, she says so. This kind of honesty is essential for a good relationship between any two people.

Probably the most important element that goes into making a nursery school teacher is a good self-concept. If she believes in herself and her work and has confidence in her feelings and judgment, children will pick up her attitude toward herself. If she has respect for herself, she will give an impression of strength and integrity that will make children feel secure with her. If she likes herself and enjoys her work, she will be cheerful and fun-loving; this, too, is very reassuring to children. The sound of a teacher humming in the room or her smile when their eyes meet helps them to feel that the world of adults is a good place to grow up and enter. If a teacher can respect and like herself enough, she will have no need for children's accomplishments or their love to make her feel admirable and lovable. Only then can she really let children be themselves; also, only then can she really see them as they are. When this basic attitude of acceptance of oneself is there, the most desirable attitude toward others, including children, follows. Many problems concerning what to expect and what not to expect, or when, where, and how to set limits on children's behavior then seem to solve themselves.

Ordinarily children have a good sense of their limitations, but adults are often apt to confuse them with their own ideas of what children can or should do. A sensitive kind of awareness is necessary for a teacher to meet each child where he or she is — "big" one day and smaller the next — while maintaining her faith that the child will surely continue to grow and learn if she does her job of providing the right environment. Sometimes this environment may include an especially close tie with the teacher for a while. In helping a child who has trouble separating from his mother or in controlling too impulsive behavior, for example, such a relationship might be needed. But she is always ready to loosen this tie and let the child turn toward others and toward independence. The tie is a helping one — a means to an end.

Remembering how vulnerable young children are to feelings of rivalry, a teacher always tries to avoid such a predicament as being surrounded by dancing, begging children shouting, "Me, too! Me, too!" Their drive for any new experience is so powerful that even the best of friends become alienated at such times. The same rivalry situation also exists if a group is engaged in an activity that cannot proceed without a teacher's aid or attention, and cries of "Help me!" "I can't!" "Teacher!" then arise, so it follows that such activities are best avoided.

II

If a teacher thoughtfully considers the words that she uses in speaking to children, she may realize that many of them communicate disapproval, disappointment, criticism, impatience, and other negative attitudes, even though her general attitude toward children is a positive one. If this is the case, her words will make the children feel that they need to watch her state of feeling. Therefore, they will be unable to focus on her words with full attention to their meaning and react to them with their own thoughts and feelings intact. Also, because a young child is so dependent on love and acceptance in order to form a healthy self-concept, he or she is very vulnerable to words that do not carry this message. Better results, both immediate and long term, can be secured if teachers' words are well chosen.

A teacher who wants to work on her manner of speaking to children can set herself some exercises. She can, for example, observe what proportion of her verbal contacts are directive. "Put your apron away, if you're through painting." "Sit down here by me, now." "Pick up your toys, now; it's story time." "Wash your hands. Use lots of soap and wipe well." "Move over a little, please." She can then practice straight information-giving as a substitute. If a child is given the information upon which a directive would have been based, he will usually change his behavior in line with that information, thus experiencing self-direction. The substitute words could be: "It's a good idea to hang your apron up for the next child, if you're through"; "Here's a place for you to sit"; "It's picking-up time. We're going to have stories when it's done"; "Your hands seem to need some washing"; "That place is getting a little crowded."

The directive "Don't" can be eliminated almost entirely. When a change in behavior is desired, suggesting what a child *can* do opens a door, rather than closing one; "You can do it this way" would replace "Don't do it that way." By avoiding "Don't," a teacher also avoids suggesting that a child is doing something wrong or foolish, being inadequate or clumsy, or making a mistake, and his self-esteem is not diminished. Another reason for avoiding "Don'ts" is that they emphasize the act to be avoided. A child picks out the vivid words of the sentence and hears those. Thus "Don't *throw* the *sand*" is a suggestion to do just that. Since a teacher's real function is to show a child what he can do, rather than what he can't, information-giving is a logical replacement for "Don'ts." For example, instead of "Don't leave the blocks scattered all over the floor," she might say, "The floor needs to be cleaned up to make room for new buildings," and, instead of "Don't hit children," she might say, "You can *tell* them what you're angry about."

Information-giving takes a little more time, but since it results in a faster, smoother response from the child, the extra time may well be made up. This better response occurs partly because information-giving arouses less negativism, but also because if one gives a simple imperative, such as "Hang up your jacket," a child often may not know the steps to be followed in carrying out such a general direction. Information-giving (such as "Your locker is the red one, remember? And here's the little loop on your jacket to hang it by") starts him off. In addition, if one thinks of time-saving, with the information kind of guidance the adult is less and less needed each time the situation comes up, whereas the reverse is true with teacher directions; the latter will need to be gradually increased as children become more and more dependent upon them and less and less capable of thinking for themselves and making their own decisions. Since a child has had no chance to develop an understanding of what is involved, he forgets directives as soon as he has more or less automatically complied. With a teacher who tells him what to do all the time, why, it will follow, should he remember? Another unfortunate result is the number of things done in opposition to directions behind the teacher's back, since the imperative form "Do such and such" leaves no room for discussion, disagreement, or compromises.

Information-giving statements have all kinds of subjects — people, materials, events, customs, feelings — anything about which more knowledge will help the child in his day to day living. Here are random examples. "If you go and play with something else, I doubt if she will want to save your swing so long. Children get tired of just holding something; they want to play themselves. Saving works best if you're coming right back." "If you keep your toy near you, people can tell you're still using it, but if you go away and leave it, they won't know." "It works best to put your pasting in your locker as soon as it's done; that way it won't get mixed up with other children's at the table." "Your ring would be hard to find if it came off while you're playing in the sand." "Before you take her toy out of her locker, you'd better ask her. She might not want you to." In all of the foregoing, the idea implied is "This information might be useful here, judging from my experience with this kind of situation." The statements contain advice and suggestions, without requests or requirements. A child is free to make his own decision.

Some information carries with it limits on behavior. Statements about school customs or group needs are examples. "These puzzles are just for the table. They get mixed up on the floor, and it's too hard to sort them out again." "The paper cups are just for drinks. The plastic ones are for sand play." "When there are several children eating crackers, the basket needs to stay in the middle so they can all reach it." "Right here is where the trains and trucks turn around, because we need the place beyond that for people to walk." "Water stays in the bathroom. For water play, you would use the play sink." "Boots need to go on at story time, so mothers won't have to wait so long when they come." "The gate and fence aren't strong enough to bump with the bikes, but you can bump the steps if you like." "Those painted trucks get scratched if they're crashed. We have some rubber ones to use for that." "Just one child at a time at the water sink, remember? Just one." All of these limits are presented as they are required, with the reason built in or closely connected with the statement. "Need" and "just" are limiting words, and when there is no time for explanation, they make the limiting character of the teacher's information-giving clear. Sometimes, of course, the content itself makes the limit clear, as in "That board isn't steady enough to climb on."

Changing one's habits of speech takes time and practice. It helps, if one has launched a negative or directive sentence, to change it in mid-flight to information-giving by the use of words like "if" or "you can." ("Don't sit—if you sit at the end of the table, you'll have more room." "Let go of—you can let go of the fire hat; I'll hold it, while you two talk it over. Pulling it is hard on the hat.") Probably more difficult than changing one's words, however, is being clear about when to use which ones. For example, a teacher might ask, "Do you want to wash your hands?" to find out how a child feels about it, but she would not use those words if making a suggestion; then it would be, "I think you'd better wash your hands." But a child can still disagree with a suggestion, and if the teacher's reasons are not convincing, she would settle for that. However, if the washing seemed really necessary, the words "You need to wash your hands" give the child no choice, though "Why?" questions would be willingly answered. These questions become fewer, incidentally, unless there is an actual interest in the subject, once a child learns that "you need" means the teacher will not change her mind and that she has a good reason for anything she requires in this way. Honest and complete explanations pave the way to such trust, as well as the thoughtful and sparing use of limiting words.

Somewhere between advice or suggestion and definite limit-setting are the requests a teacher makes, usually in the form of a question. "Can anyone help with this picking up?" ("Can," here, means not "Are you able?" but "Are you willing?") "Will you stop a moment, so I can tie your shoe?" "Could you just use your little trucks in this part? He wants to ride a tricycle where you are." "Would you move your pasting to the other table, so more children can have lunch here?" "Could you please play the piano very softly until I'm through telephoning?" "I wonder if you'd finish water play as soon as you can? I'd like to use the sink soon." If a child refuses a request, the teacher might ask what solution would be more acceptable to him. But the many requests made in this form all leave the door open for him to say, "No, I don't want to," and while a discussion of the wishes of both can follow, his reply needs to be considered, since the form of the request has asked for it.

A teacher's verbal communications with a colleague are usually in a form to which no one could take exception, and in most cases they could take just that form with children. The essence of her approach to the other person is respect. If she feels this for children and can demonstrate it by her way of speaking to them, her attitude will permeate her group. Not only will the children's self-concepts improve, their relationships with each other will also, as they identify with the teacher and speak the way they hear her speak. Inevitably they will begin to say such things as "This piece fits in here," instead of "You're not doing that puzzle right"; or "I just got off the swing to get the other strap; I wasn't really through," instead of "Give me back my swing!"; or "We're playing alone in here right now; you can come in when we're through," instead of "Get out!" — all statements that give needed information without a single negative or imperative.

Is it really necessary to give so much attention to the words one uses? The answer is the same as to questions regarding other techniques or ways of relating to children. One can say that a few mistakes will not matter, if, on the whole, the teacher's relationship with a child is a good one. But it is more desirable that a teacher's behavior consistently communicate the kind of feeling for the child that is most helpful. Realizing that with the best we can do, we still will not be able to completely protect a child from untoward influences and that he or she may in the future have to face many of which we can have no conception, we cannot afford to ignore any chance for positive experiences in these early years. They, too have their cumulative effect.

III

An important reason for special concern about a nursery school teacher's relationship with her pupils is that children of three and four are going through a difficult time. They are full of strong feelings. Their love of and dependence on their parents, their jealousy of siblings and of their parents' closeness, their feelings of smallness, the confused concepts of the real world which intermingle in their minds with fantasies, and their lack of control over impulses all combine to make them many problems. While it is true that these stresses will ease after five or six, many concerns are only pushed below the level of awareness when children begin to orient themselves in reality and their focus is less exclusively within the family. But the past is still there. Adults who have emotional problems often find themselves reacting in puzzlingly inappropriate ways in the present because their emotions in similar situations in the past have become rearoused and have overwhelmed them.

Because the emotional associations made in the preschool period are so important to a child's future, the nursery school teacher has a significant part to play. She can offer direct and immediate help in the school milieu, rather than merely providing a secure and loving temporary environment, manipulating situations that arise, and trusting to time to do the trick. A teacher is in a different position from a child's parents or other family members. She can become a kind of neutral sounding board for him. The quality of such an uncluttered relationship is delicately portrayed in a brief incident described in a novel called *Morning*, by Julian Fane (1957). A home-loving little English boy is to sent away to school. His nanny's standards require manly behavior. His mother's anxious questions either hurt his pride or appeal for his reassurance. And between the boy and both his father and older brother is an unbridgeable gap, because they must defend themselves against feelings like his. But the maid listens. With her he feels no need to be anything but what he is, a grief-stricken little boy, and he can gain the strength to go.

A teacher's verbal reflections of a child's feelings are one of the best ways she has of letting him know that she understands and accepts what he tells her about himself. The secret of her success is her basic attitude toward this process. She believes that if a child has a strong feeling, there is always a good reason for it; she believes that the child can tell her in some way what is troubling him and that she will be able to understand him; she thinks nothing is too "bad" or "scary" to talk about and helps him feel this way too; and she is convinced that talking about problems helps to resolve them. In short, she projects a faith in communication, and it is catching. Children must discover the value of sharing feelings through their relationships with adults who believe in it. From the teacher's response to a child when he makes efforts to explain himself, he develops the faith that talking things over with other people will really help. And he passes this faith on to a child with whom he has a conflict, implying by look, tone, and gesture the basic trust in other people that he has developed.

As the teacher practices her skills in listening and reflecting a child's feelings back to him, her sensitivity increases. When she has hit it right with her response, there will be that quick, clear eye contact that says to her "We two have met." The abstracted gaze off somewhere else or the puzzled look show her that she is not quite on the track. A response that accurately restates the child's feelings with no distortion shows him that the teacher has been listening to him carefully and understanding what he said, as mere parroting of his words cannot. This leads to more talking on the child's part, just as the wrong response slows down or ends it. Sometimes one has been right, but one's response was incomplete. More needs to be added to get things going again. "And you were scared, too, besides being mad; scared that *he* was mad at *you*." Or perhaps just "And there's something else? That's only part of it?" Sometimes one needs to say, "Shall I guess a little?" when a child slows down, because his verbal capacities are under a strain to express what he has to say. One can make some good guesses, at times, if one is familiar with the kinds of things that upset a young child. But it is very important, when making a guess in this way, not to put something into a child's head that was not there before, or make him aware, too fast, of a feeling he is not yet ready to recognize. It is best to be general, and let the child fill in the gaps. To give a name to the feeling a child's face or actions express can start things off: "You're angry, I guess" or "You're pretty sad." Then, perhaps, "You want someone to do something, or maybe not to do something?" One speaks slowly, letting pauses develop. It is also safe to start with something that has just come up in school. "I expect you were mad at me for bringing you inside." "You miss Alex, today, I guess; he didn't come to school, did he?" "You felt cross, I remember, when Cecily said to come and swing and then just went away and left you." Opening up one area of feeling sometimes leads to the expression of others, but the incidents need to be ones in which the teacher was sure of the child's reactions, and also sure that he was aware of them himself. A child can recognize his own thoughts if well expressed by someone else, though he may not have been able to state them himself, but sometimes it may be necessary to say something several ways until it sounds right and he claims it.

During these talks, a nod, an "mm-hmm," and a listening look can all help to encourage speech. Sitting down near a child so he can look into the teacher's face, holding him on her lap, or taking him into a private room or corner all impress him with her readiness to give her full attention to him. Efforts to comfort, argue a child out of his feelings, point a moral, criticize his attitude, or make up with him if he is angry have no place in this situation and end confidences. The best response communicates both understanding of the feelings and acceptance of them. Next teacher and child can consider what action is possible. Perhaps, if fearful, the child might go, with the teacher holding his hand, to meet the object of his fear, or, if he is angry at another child, he might go to him and let him know.

Acceptance of a child's feelings also means acceptance of his wish not to talk about them. The teacher can verbalize that wish. "You don't want to talk about it; I see how you feel." But even if a child is unable or unwilling to tell in words what is disturbing him, the teacher's response has at least indicated that it is all right to have feelings and that she would be interested to hear about them. She will also take note of what the child talks about if he changes the subject and, if he goes away, what he does immediately afterward. Sometimes an answer comes that way. Many times, too, he will come out with his problem later, after he has thought it over.

Another time an appropriate reflection of a child's wish not to confide might be, "You're so mad at me you don't want to even talk to me, I guess." In this case, something about a child's relations with the teacher needs to be cleared away first. What follows then might be "Yes! And I'm never coming to your school again!" The teacher might reflect this with "You don't want to have anything to do with me or the school." (Or perhaps, if she gets a feeling of the child's wanting to punish her in this way, "You won't let me see you ever again.") "Yes, and I'm going to smash your school all up!" "Just wreck everything that belongs to me. You really don't like me at all, not a bit." All these responses are made in a serious tone of voice; none of this is a joke to the child. But feelings come around from negative to positive when expressed, and something then comes out like Jamie's "Well, I only like you one inch." After the angry feelings have been discharged and accepted, the talk could move on to what had made the child angry. This, too, the teacher would accept, without any attempt at self-justification, apology, argument, or consolation. The important thing is the chance for the child to get his resentments communicated and accepted. It is usually guilt-producing, or at the very least distracting, for a teacher to change the focus from him to her own feelings by saying something like "Well, I like *you*," "I'm sorry you feel that way," or "I didn't mean to make you angry."

It is hard to make clear the tone and inflection of printed words. "I see how you feel" or "You're very angry at me about that" are not said in an offhand, too matter-of-fact way, as though what the child had said was not very important. They are not said mechanically and absent-mindedly. They are not said soothingly or reassuringly. And naturally they are not said reproachfully, or impatiently, either — "I *know* you're angry," as though the next words should be "so stop going on and on about it." They are not said in a resigned, martyred tone, as though one were waiting for a child to get over his problem and wishing he would hurry. Nor are the words dramatized, as though the matter were of tremendous importance. And they are not said in a manner that emphasizes the intimacy of the revelations — "*I* understand, darling" (even if nobody else does). Probably most helpful is to gain real acceptance within oneself of the feelings one is reflecting and then speak to the child calmly and quietly, with confidence that what is happening is a step toward emotional maturity that he will be able to take.

Some examples of teachers reflecting children's feelings follow.

• Dropped off at school by his father one day, Bo sat miserably on the outside stair, huddled against the railing. When his teacher went to him, he began to wail, "I want to go *home*, I want to go *home*," over and over. She said, "You really want to go back home." He went on, "But there's nobody there to take care of me." "No one at all; that makes you *very* sad." Crying, he said then, "My mommy is sick." "I see," the teacher responded, "You miss her especially today, and it's very upsetting." He sat on her lap awhile; then suddenly he looked up and said, "She'll be better soon," and back came his smile as he ran off to play. After a real expression of grief comes a real recovery.

● Kathy's sit-down strike against going home occurred at a time when the teacher was too busy to give her much attention. She brought Kathy just inside the door, so her feelings would not be further confused by the audience of arriving mothers, and said, "There isn't any way you can stay at school, Kathy, but I can see how you feel about it; you really don't want to go." A little time and a chance for Kathy to pull herself together helped, and after a short wait, watching others leave, she went quietly out the door to her mother. Next day the teacher told her, "I didn't quite understand why you got upset about leaving yesterday. Do you want to tell me now?" Kathy told her then that she had wanted her father, not her mother, to come; he had said he would. The uncomplicated reflection of feeling on the day before had paved the way to the confidence the next day.

In stating the reality of a situation, it is most helpful to follow this with a reflection of the child's feeling, and then stop. If, instead, one says, "But Kathy, you *have* to go home. I know you don't want to, but your mother is here, and it's time. You can come back tomorrow," the reflection of feeling is buried by the reality statements and the attempt at consolation. Results are better if, after the reflection of feeling, no "but" follows. A reflection invites expression of feelings, whereas the "but" clause only invites another "but" from the child and starts a circular pattern of "but you have to," "but I don't want to," with mounting tension until "*I don't want to*" is finally heard and receives a response.

● A reflection of one feeling often opens the door to others. Hoddie, running across the room, tripped on the toy train. Fearing he would fall on it, the teacher caught him up. He retreated to his locker and sat holding his bear. "Was that pretty scary when I moved so fast and grabbed you?" the teacher asked. He nodded, not looking at her. "It was to keep you from falling on the train, but I can see how it felt," she said. But still he wouldn't look up. "Maybe you're kind of angry, too." "Yes, I'm mad." But there was another look on his face, as well; discouragement. "And a little sad." "Yes." "You didn't *like* almost falling down and having to be caught." "But I learned to tie my shoes," he said, perking up. Later he offered the teacher a birthday cake made out of sand. "This is for you," he told her. "Don't spill your coffee."

- With David it was necessary to focus on his feelings when something interfered with his good relationship with his teacher. On being called for at dismissal time, he was infuriated because his mother had sent the baby-sitter, instead of coming for him herself. He ran off and hid behind a bush, refusing to go to the gate. When the teacher went to him, he turned a furious face on her and tried to kick her. In such a situation, feelings need reflection imperatively. The teacher told him, "I guess you're pretty angry because your baby-sitter came, and now you're mad at me, too; I expect you think *everybody* is mean to you." He smiled a little and looked at the teacher. In a moment he said, "I'm just mad at my mother." Now his anger had returned to its first object, and the spreading of it to his baby-sitter and then to his teacher had stopped. Meanwhile he had learned that a friendly person can understand and that this helps, even if one can't have what one wants. He also learned that even if one feels very angry, others won't necessarily be angry back—they needn't be kicked away—and that running away and hiding isn't of much use either. But perhaps something else might help. "I think I'd like one of those fuchsias to take home," he said. As he was opening the gate, the teacher suggested, "When you see your mother, perhaps you might talk to her about it, if you're still angry," and he nodded.

- Mikey's feelings were more violent, and the teacher's reflection of them revealed a deeper cause. He had been tickling children's faces with a feather duster. He had been told, "Dusters make some children sneeze or can get in eyes that way, so you'll need to keep it away from faces." But he had ignored this. At length he approached one child, and as he quickly thrust the duster toward her face, the teacher as quickly took it from his hand and put it away. He flew into a violent rage. "I hate you! I'll kill you! You're bad!" he screamed, flinging himself at her and trying with all his might to land a blow. He was making a great deal of noise, but whenever he drew breath the teacher reflected, "You're very mad at me!" Then he said, "You don't like me! You don't like me!" To the children, who watched fascinatedly, the teacher said, "Mikey is feeling so mad at me he thinks I must be mad at him." Angry children can often hear what is said about them better than what is said to them, and the other children can also learn a lot about feelings this way. "You are too mad! You don't either like me!" Mikey shouted. He began to try to overturn chairs and throw toys. Silent messages passed between the two teachers ("He is building up"; "I'll take over the others"), and the teacher carried Mikey, struggling, into the office. Inside the room, she set him down and seated herself quietly in a chair. His eyes blazed, but he looked rather afraid, too. "What will she do now that we're alone?" he probably wondered. "Tell me more, Mikey," she said. "I can listen better in here." "I hate you," he sobbed. "You're very angry, and unhappy, too, that I took away the duster," she said. Crying harder, he said, *"I don't want to go home!"* She thought, "What has this got to do with what I said? There's some connection; listen." "I don't like my new bed. Mom gave my crib to the baby. And she cleaned my old toys out of my closet!" "Oh, Mikey," she said thankfully, "I see, now. You feel like you've lost so many things, and I took away your duster, too!" Then followed a teary, rather incoherent account of the way things were different at home and his bitter feelings about the new baby that caused all the trouble. Nothing more was needed after Mikey got to his main problem. When a child can talk to someone about what is wrong, he is already on his way to dealing with it. As a matter of fact, Mikey's mother reported that his tantrums at home diminished from that point and that he stopped waking in the night as he had done ever since the baby's arrival.

● For a child to move from the expression of feelings in acting-out behavior to the expression of them in words often first requires the teacher's understanding of the symbols he is using in play. Though usually friendly, Barnaby was knocking down everyone's block buildings one day. The teacher said, "I wonder what's the matter? Is something bothering you?" Barnaby was quite wild when she said this, and he giggled and threw himself about, saying, "A mouse, that's what bothers me — *mouse!*" They went off by themselves into the office, and he used some rubber blocks to build and knock down several structures. "You're mad at those buildings," the teacher offered. Then he said, "I'm mad at my house." (She noticed the rhyme with *mouse*.) "I want my old house to be where my new house is." After he was a little calmer, he asked for a cot and a blanket. "I live here," he said. "This is my pretend house. I'll go away, now." He went outside the office door, stood there a moment, and returned. "And now I've come back." He took off his shoes and socks and went to bed awhile, as the teacher sat quietly by. He began to look much better. "You were pretty bothered about moving," she said. "Yes. I didn't want to move. I just like my old house." She nodded. "Children often feel that way." Then he said, "Can this be my house any day I want it? This room?" She agreed he could use it whenever he came to school and set up the cot for him there for a while, but in a few days he seemed to have accepted the move and did not need the room anymore.

● A symbol was used by Vivienne, too. One day she settled down in a businesslike way to draw what she called "dragons." When she had finished, instead of putting her pictures in her locker she threw each in the wastebasket, mashing it down well with many stamps of her foot. "You are really getting rid of those dragons," the teacher said. "Yes," she replied. "I want to make them all dead. I'm afraid of dragons. I saw them on TV." Vivienne might have done all that entirely on her own, but the sharing of her fantasy with the teacher enabled her to experience a relationship in which there could be meaningful communication, and the smaller the load of private worries carried by a child, the freer he or she is to learn and grow.

IV

Setting limits is probably the most difficult part of her job for many a teacher. Children need to be prevented from doing some things, and they need to be required to do some things. But in either case, more important than just what limits are set or what is required is recognition of a child's feelings about limits and requirements. Teachers can make mistakes in judgment if they are willing to let children have and show their feelings. "I guess you're pretty mad at me because I won't let you do that." "Cry some more, if you want to, or scream a good scream; sometimes that helps. You're really angry at me!'' But if a teacher denies children the right to their resentments, she may do them deep damage.

Many factors complicate the setting of limits. Some issues are between the teacher and the child alone. Like any two people who are in conflict, each must make his needs known. If two children are quarreling, the teacher must keep clear which issues are between the children and which are between a child and herself. In the first case, she is neutral, acting as a moderator in the children's discussion of the problem; in the second case, she deals with the child alone. For example, if a child is throwing sand, hitting or chasing someone, or pushing another on the slide or bars, this is a matter between him and his teacher, first; she could not expect the other child, in the midst of that kind of predicament, to talk anything over. But afterwards, when her limits have been set, she will help the two children work out the problem together. The order might be the other way around, too. A single sand-throwing incident might result in a discussion between the children, revealing why the thrower was angry. After this, however, there is still unfinished business between him and his teacher, and this needs to be taken up, because on no account does she want him to throw sand at anyone, for reasons of her own that have to do with keeping everyone safe and unthreatened.

Examples of a variety of situations in which limits were set follow.

Even when a problem seems to offer no chance for compromise, as, for example, when a child does not want to go home at dismissal time, limits need not be altogether arbitrary, as a rule. The child can have a chance to present his own ideas, and it may be possible to give him a choice at least as to how he complies. A teacher, in offering to get his things from his locker, and a parent, in proposing to carry them (or him) to the gate, or halfway there, both demonstrate a flexibility in the way one can approach the inevitable and make it more tolerable. In time a child develops this flexibility, too.

● Leo, for a period, resisted stopping his play at dismissal time day after day. Finally the teacher had a talk with him. "You've been having trouble going home, lately, haven't you? I wonder what would help?" No answer. She started the ball rolling by saying, "Do you think it might be a good idea to be at the story table, instead of playing, when your mother comes? Stopping in the mid-

dle of stories might be easier." "No, I don't want to hear stories."
In these talks each must first rule out what is unacceptable. The
teacher tried another possible solution. "Well, I could call you a
little early, and you could be ready then, waiting in your locker."
"No, I don't think *that's* a very good way." "Do you have an idea?"
"No, I just don't want to go home, that's all." "How so?" "I just
want to play all day." "I see; not enough playtime. What would
help?" "You could let me stay." Now the teacher had to rule out
what was unacceptable to her. "I can't do that; I'm sorry. I have to
close the school and go home." (Pause.) Responding to Leo's
frown, the teacher said, "It makes you angry that I have to do
that?" "Yes." "I see." (Pause.) "What can we do?" she went on,
since he seemed to have no more to add about being angry. "I
think I can just stop." "It might be kind of hard; suppose you're
doing something you like very much?" "Oh, no, I can." "Shall we
pretend it's happening?" A play drama helps a child understand
what his solution implies and also reviews the solution reached.
The teacher called, "Leo! Your mother's here!" He smiled and
jumped up from the sandbox where both had been sitting, "I go to
my locker" (he ran inside). "Now I go to the gate. And I open it.
Goodbye!" He turned to grin at the teacher, and she said, "Well!
That worked fine!" At dismissal time, she said to him, "Remember how you showed me the way you were going home today?" and he carried out his plan, amused that he and the teacher
had a private plot.

- To Moira, limit-setting was synonymous with conflict. She usually responded as though all set for a battle in which someone
would win and someone would lose (but not Moira, if she could
help it). She would say, "Well, can I or can't I?" all ready to take
issue. But little by little, care in explaining the teacher's reasoning
and listening to Moira's brought her to the point of suggesting her
first compromise. One day she was still wearing a lace cap from
the dress-up bin when the time came for stories, and the teacher
reminded her that all the inside playthings were put away then.
"But I want to wear it at the story table!" she said vehemently. The
teacher replied, "The trouble is that when your mother comes,
you'll be busy collecting your things from your locker and putting
on your coat and won't have time to put it away then. And the
teachers won't either; one will be reading stories and the other one
will be at the gate." Moira looked thoughtful, and the teacher

waited. Then it came—a plan that met everybody's needs. "I could just wear it for the *first* story," she said.

- A teacher may need to share experiences and express opinions of her own in setting limits. When Chuck brought his toy gun to school, he was told, "At school I've always found it best if guns were left in the lockers. When children see a gun in someone's hand, it can be a little scary." "But I won't shoot it at anybody," he protested. The teacher answered, "Sometimes, though, they think they *might* be shot at, and even if they know it's not a real gun, they're not sure the child is friendly." "I'll keep it in my holster," he told her. But she told him, "Chuck, lots of children I know have tried to do that, but it's too hard to do. Would you like to play alone with it?" "No, I'll keep it in my locker," he said. If a child has a toy gun at hand, the temptation to use it, either to dispose of imaginary enemies at a safe distance or to show power, like flexing one's muscles, is irresistible.

- For some children whose out of bounds behavior requires limits, only a minimum of attention is desirable. Kiki, three years old, climbed on shelves, calling, "See? See?" threw paint about, pulled coats out of lockers onto the floor, and pushed over the doll-corner screens, always with an eye on the teacher. To avoid such issues completely would result in even more exaggerated behavior until she would have to be given the attention sought, so the teacher responded in a matter-of-fact, relaxed way: "We'll wipe up the paint"; "We'll need to hang the coats up"; and "Here's how the screen goes." She then talked to Kiki about something else and showed her some play materials. In this phase, Kiki would climb the jungle gym at the end of the day, although she knew that the time for climbing was over when the teacher was near the gate dismissing children. She would say, "See me up here? I'm climbing," and the teacher would say, "Yes, I see you. Pretty soon you'll be ready to come down; no hurry," and without the reward of attention, Kiki would soon descend.

  Behavior like this is often seen in children who resent the attention a younger sibling gets. It satisfies several of the child's needs at once. It keeps the adult's attention focused on her; it gets even with the adult for notice bestowed on a rival (or, at school, a number of rivals); and it makes the child feel powerful and important, especially if an adult's anger or feelings of helplessness are stirred up. Many children have some of the same needs, in less obvious form.

- With Max, acceptance of limit-setting was helped by an expression of warmth from his teacher. He kept getting on his knees in the wet sand on a cold day. The outside teacher explained that his pants would get too wet that way. But his argument was that he needed to get down that way to dig. She offered him a mat to kneel on and also suggested he might squat instead of kneeling. But he continued to take no responsibility for keeping dry, so the teacher brought him to the door, telling him he needed to play inside. "I'll throw a stone at you!" he shouted angrily. She said she could see how angry he was and could understand why; he'd been having a good time outside. Kneeling down to talk to him, she took his hand in hers and made her own position clear, saying, "You see, you need to remember about your knees yourself, because I won't have time to keep watching and reminding you. So you'll need to stay inside until you feel ready to do that." Then she returned to the playground. Max changed the subject abruptly, saying to the other teacher, "I'm hungry." She gave him a small basket of crackers and he ate them, sitting in his locker. Then he announced that he could keep off his knees by himself. He studied Bix's squatting technique through the glass doors, then, outside, carefully placed some rubber mats and took over for himself. It is impressive to see the resoluteness of a young child when, fortified by friendly acceptance, he is motivated to control his behavior or learn something new. "*I will*," he says, not so much to the teacher as to himself. And he does. But it was the clear setting of limits for Max that brought about the change.

- Some children, especially early in the school year, may make tests of the limits in order to find out exactly what their relationship with the teachers is. Toby, a new child, was like this. He had to provoke a crisis before he could become oriented in the school environment, a crisis that would determine the teacher's strength relative to his own. Toby began his testing by tossing handfuls of sand in the air in spite of nearby children, grinning. The limit was set for him, followed by information as to the ways he could use the sand. "It needs to stay low, away from faces. But you can use it for digging and filling things like buckets and trucks." But Toby continued to toss it, looking at the teacher expectantly. "Well," she said then, "Since you aren't keeping it down, I suppose you'd better play inside. There are things you can do in there." "No," he told her. "I don't want to play inside. I want to play in the sand." "Well, it isn't safe to use it that way." "I'll keep it down." "Oh. If you did that, of course it would be fine." But in a moment he threw it up again experimentally, his eye on her. "Time to go in, now," she told him. "No more sand." "I'll keep it down." "We did try that, and it didn't work, did it?" she said. He protested, refusing to go in. The teacher then carried him to the door, walking slowly, and the inside teacher greeted him. After about half an hour, he reappeared at the top of the stairs. "Before you come down," the outside teacher said to him, "do you think you are ready to be careful with the sand?" "Oh yes," he told her. Preparing a child before temptation fortifies him.

● Another tester, Bobby, scattered the workbench nails on the sidewalk, then ran away. The teacher followed, moving slowly but persistently. Soon she came to where he was. She picked him up, holding him firmly but gently, and patted his back soothingly as she carried him back to the workbench. He squirmed, saying, "Let me down!" "I'm just taking you along to help pick up the nails," she told him. He relaxed at that, but told her, "I won't pick them up." Some children are interested in picking up, perhaps because they enjoy knowing where things go, want to be helpful in a really meaningful way, appreciate the attractiveness of a setting, or identify with a teacher's activities. But others are resistant, feel inadequate or bored, and see no reason to bother about picking up. Since most find sorting and separating objects very difficult at this age, all picking-up jobs must be preorganized by the teacher herself, and she must usually participate throughout. Even so, some children only watch, or perhaps respond to the suggestion that they select just one toy to pick up. Most children are less ready to put away toys right after using them, having played until they need a change, and a general time for picking up is more acceptable.

But when Bobby made chaos and confusion on the sidewalk, he probably felt a little anxious and guilty; if he could help make order again, his chaotic internal feelings would subside. The teacher put him down and started picking up the nails herself. "That's all right," she said to him. "You can wait until you're ready. But they need to be picked up; we can't leave them there." In a moment or so he started off, but she said, "You're not quite ready to play yet; there's this job to do first. Can you reach some of those under the table?" And he did.

Teachers make mistakes; this is inevitable. But making mistakes is one way by which they learn.

● Charles, at four and a half, thought of himself as big and strong, which in fact, he was, for his age. He was furious at a mistake in handling him that was made one day when a quarrel developed between him and Richard at the swing. Both children ran to get an empty swing and, as far as anyone could tell, arrived there at the same time, with Charles putting his hand on one chain and Richard on the other. But each insisted that he had been there first, and a fight developed. Both began hitting — Charles, because of his strength, quite hard.

The teacher moved in to stop the blows and ask them if they could think of a solution, but none was offered and neither would give in, so she said that, since no one could tell who had been first, she would put up the swing and they could try later, when it might be easier to tell. This often is accepted as a fair solution. Richard left, but Charles forced his way into the swing and refused to get out. Then the teacher, having gone that far, decided to take him out, which she did, although he put up a protracted struggle and kept trying to run back after she put him down. Finally she picked him up and took him inside, then returned to the playground. A teacher who is uninvolved in his problem is often used by a child as someone to whom he can pour out his feelings. "Why did *I* have to come in? Why didn't Richard, too? Why blame *me*? I did too have it first!" he complained bitterly to the inside teacher. At length he calmed down and was encouraged to take his grievances to the outside teacher. She came across the playground to him, and they sat on the steps.

Meanwhile the outside teacher had been thinking. She felt that the usual way of dealing with children unable to decide who had had something first — putting it away until later — had been wrong for Charles, now that he was older. He was so proud of his strength that a way of handling him that used strength would be a challenge. But afterward, when he lost the battle, he would feel angry and humilated. She wanted to find a better way to settle the problem, with his help if possible.

The first requirement was to be honest. "Charles," she said, "I think I made a mistake taking you out of the swing. I think there must be a better way to settle the problem when two children both think they had it first. Let's try to figure one out." Charles responded well to her admission of a mistake and appeal for his help (as most children of any age do), and a plan was worked out between them. Two children who seemed to have equal rights to the swing would stay there until they settled it themselves, no matter how long it took. Finally (Charles agreed this was so) one of them would get tired of waiting and go away. It might be because he was not as interested in swinging as the other child, or, the teacher suggested, because he really knew that the other child had been first to get there. "I wouldn't be able to let them hurt each other, though," she told Charles. "Stop them at the swing if they fight," he answered, and that is the way it was left between them. But although there were some incidents of waiting it out when similar situations arose, Charles never again came to blows there, and, since young children are not able to wait for anything very long, soon one of them would leave, for whatever reason.

But more had been accomplished than the working out of the swing dilemma. Charles had recovered his self-esteem, and, pleased that the teacher had considered his feelings enough to consult him, he went, looking important, to share the new plan with Richard. The outside teacher learned from her mistake, as teachers always do if they are willing to take the first step and admit that they have made one. And Charles and his teacher moved to a new level in their relationship.

V

Examples of some personal qualities that can be of inestimable value in a teacher follow.

● Empathy is always a resource. If a teacher pauses to experience empathy before taking action, not only is her own way smoothed, but the child has yet another encounter with an understanding adult.

One day the teacher noticed that Pete was in the jungle gym wearing the school's dress-up clothes, kept for use only indoors. Just seeing this from the corner of her eye and busy with other things, she called to him, "The clothes stay inside, remember?" "No!" he shouted, and, dressed in his idea of a Superman costume, "You can't catch me," he said, scooting rapidly around the upper bars. The teacher realized that she had spoken too fast, without getting the feel of his involvement in play or of his current mood. If she had taken time to empathize first, she could have indicated her approval and support of his play theme (and thus, of course, of Pete) and then reminded him about the clothes. Abrupt interruption would have been avoided, and he would have been given a chance to terminate the play more at his own pace. Now she needed to get him off the hook quickly. She said, clearly, "That's all right, Pete. I didn't see you had already started your play. When you're finished, then you can climb down and take the clothes in. Of course you don't want to stop in the middle; I know how people feel about that. Just finish as soon as you can, O.K.?" "O.K.," he answered. (When a teacher has asked something of a child and then changes her mind about the wisdom of it, to protect their relationship it is important not to just leave the child alone to feel guilty and out of contact with her, but to tell him she has changed her position, so he can feel all is well between them.)

Another teacher moved in slowly, with empathy, when three-year-old Nina took a long-stemmed flower from a freshly arranged vase and began carrying it around with her. She watched a moment, avoiding saying, "The flowers are just for looking" or the pedagogic "That's a narcissus." Instead of these, responding to Nina empathically as she held the flower before her and seemed to drink it in, sight, scent, and all, she said, softly, "*Beautiful.*" Sharing such moments makes an experience deeper and shows children a relationship at its best. The time for putting the flower back "for the others to see" could come later.

Empathy helped Benny's teacher understand why he was pestering Oliver on the swing one day by catching at the chains. Oliver was protesting, but Benny didn't stop. What was going on? Did Benny want the swing? Was he angry at Oliver about something? The teacher watched Benny's face. He certainly didn't look angry; he was laughing. His eyes weren't on Oliver; where, then? On Annabel and her friend Kit, hanging over the bars at the top of the jungle gym, watching him. He was showing off. "Say his name, and tell him again, Olly. I don't think he's listening," the teacher said. After Oliver did this, the teacher said to Benny, "Could you think of another way to make them laugh?" And Benny did a dance with a bucket on his head that they found hilarious.

Empathy also helps a teacher to know when a child is immobilized by a flood of feeling and guides her in finding a way out for him. Nigel, at the end of a school day, saw his father pass the side door of the playroom on his way to the dismissal gate and started to depart that way, instead of going out through the back door to the gate as was customary. The teacher didn't have the information then that might have helped her understand Nigel's need to exit the quickest way—the fact that he and his parents were to leave that day on a plane trip. (That they might leave without him could perhaps have been dimly in his mind.) So she said, "The back door, remember?" But once at the back door, he wouldn't go out. Swamped by anger at the teacher and his dad for changing his course, excited about the trip, and a little anxious, too, he threw himself on the floor in desperation. With no time to sort out all these feelings, the teacher had to find a solution. All day he had been acting "big," proud, perhaps, of making this important trip with the grown-ups, and now this humiliating collapse. The teacher said, casually, not looking at him, "Nigel, would you like to ask your dad to come inside the gate to see your big picture that's drying on the line?" This way out was gratefully seized, the father admired the picture, and they went off together.

- Ingenuity is another valuable trait. It makes a teacher flexible enough to meet ever-changing demands. It helps, too, when she must consider the needs of an individual and the group at one and the same time.

Zeb was just beginning at last to believe that the teachers at school were on his side. One day he filled a bucket with water and carried it to the sandbox. What to do? The experienced teacher knew this would not be the end—not with anything so fascinating as water. He would be back in a moment for more, and other children would follow his lead. It was a cold day. Did she want the sandbox full of puddles and a stream of water by the dismissal gate? Did she want splashed pant legs, shoes, and sleeves right now? And was there time to take care of all that? It was nearly going-home time. What to do? The teacher had to think what "No" would mean to her new friend Zeb. She decided on a compromise and asked Zeb to limit his water play to a tub on a table. He couldn't have sand there, but the water had the stronger pull, so he was happy, especially when he was given some soap powder to mix into it. The spreading of a problem to the group had been stopped.

While the teacher would not want to avoid an issue that needed to be faced, much of her ingenuity is used in devising solutions that make issues unnecessary. Amy liked to take crackers from the snack table to the doll corner, but once there, they were broken into little pieces and mixed with water from the doll-corner sink, wasting food and making a cleanup job that was hard to manage. The teacher explained the problem of sweeping up crumbs and washing the doll dishes and suggested that they work with real food only in the place where snacks were prepared and use play food in the doll corner. She also offered an idea that they might have crackers on a "front porch" instead of inside the doll corner, turning chairs around to make the porch. From then on the children made a "porch" whenever they wanted to eat at the doll corner.

Sometimes a child needs extra consideration, and ingenuity is needed to help him or her get through the day without falling apart. Little Ruth's parents were out of town and she was lonely, wanting to be picked up and held every few minutes. The teacher did this as much as she could, and also sat down and held her, but eventually it became necessary to move about and do other things. Ruth found it hard to let her do this, whining and demanding to be carried. The teacher then told her the story of a child who had wanted to be picked up when her mother was unable to do it; she said that the child's mother had sung to her, "Polly Perkin, / Hold on to my jerkin, / Hold on to my gown; / That's the way we go to town." Ruth followed the teacher around, holding her skirt as she sang, and with this game as an occasional resource, she held up all day.

● A sense of humor in a teacher is especially appreciated by children. When she responds to their kind of jokes and goes along with their verbal play, they feel a special kinship. Mark tried one teacher out. "I'm going to throw you out the window," he said. "And maybe I'll flush you down the toilet." But there was a twinkle in his eye, and the teacher played up to it. "Oh dear, oh dear, what *will* I do?" she said, twinkling back. By receiving this kind of talk undisturbed and even seeming to enjoy it, a teacher makes friends with a child.

A light touch helped in a conflict between two children, its humor relieving the tension. Alex came to the teacher, saying, "I'm cross with Bill. He says he won't let me come to school." Bill was nearby, and the teacher asked, "Is that right, Bill?" "Yes," Bill answered, "I'm going to tell his mother not to bring him." "You won't see her," Alex countered. "I'll call her on the phone," Bill said. "Oh, I see," the teacher told him. "You'll say, 'Hello, Alex's mother, this is Bill. Don't bring Alex to school.'" (They both grin.) "And she'll say, 'Oh, I can't? You won't let me? O.K., Bill, if you say so.'" (General hilarity.) But then the teacher went on. Alex's vulnerability to Bill's threat had been eased by the humor, but she still didn't know why Bill had made the threat. "You were cross with Alex about something?" she asked him. He answered promptly, "He wouldn't give me any people." "But I'm using them," Alex told him, "I need them for my train." Bill accepted this. "O.K., I'll use animals in mine."

All children are delighted when a teacher joins them in their fantasizing. Angus and Patrick were enamored of the things at school. "You and me'll take these dress-up clothes home," Angus told Patrick. "Yes, and then we'll wear them all the time, instead of our real clothes," said Patrick dreamily. "You'll take them all home? And the toys, too, that you like?" the teacher said. "Oh, yes!" they told her. "And all the crackers in the cupboard?" "Yes, we will," said Angus, the cracker lover, "All of them." "And the piano? You'll help each other carry it out and put it in your back seat?" They nodded, grinning widely. Then they whispered together a moment and produced, "And you, too. We'll take *you* home." "Hm-m-m," said the teacher. "I think I'd like that!"

It would be sad if, in her concern for all the other things she does, a teacher forgot to enjoy the time she spends with the children. These sensitive companions of her day can tell whether she likes their company, and, if she does, it makes them feel valued in a very special way. The sharing of a private joke can make this compatability especially clear to a young child. "You're not Mrs. Griffin," says Dody, her eyes dancing. "I'm not? And here all the time I thought I was. I feel just like her." "That's because you have a fever," says Dody, and they both roll over on the grass where they are sitting, doubled up in laughter. Moments like this are treasured by friends, whatever their ages.

5   Between Child
and Child

Emmy laughs,
And she wiggles when she laughs.

Emmy likes me.

She just laughs
To tell me that she likes me.

I like Emmy.

          —Constance

I

A nursery school provides special opportunities for children's social learning, since it presents a wider variety of other people than a home or most neighborhoods would have. But more is needed than gathering together children of the same age and providing playthings. Of primary importance is the help that teachers can give, in order that a child may progress toward warm and comfortable relationships with others. From the point of view of mental health, too, social play deserves special consideration. Emotional health depends basically on adequate relationships in infancy; later, as life progresses, it is almost defined by the presence of successful group associations and satisfying intimate ties. And it is in the preschool years that foundations are laid for the kind of relationships — or lack of them — that will be characteristic of a person later on. What this means for a nursery school teacher is that when she is aware of a situation involving a child's relationships with others, she needs to give it her first attention and concern, allowing other duties and interests to wait. Because feelings are strongly involved and the child needs this immediate help for practical use on the spot, intellect, body, and emotions are all united toward one end, and all factors for learning are present at that time.

A primarily unstructured program, with free choice of activity, permits problem situations to arise and be handled immediately. It also lets teachers see what kind of help individual children need in their social relations, because they are able to observe how and where each child is adequate or inadequate and the intricate ways in which he solves his problems or creates them. They can also judge the level of a child's inner security and stability by observing his undirected play choices. Does he need to do so much playing out of feelings that he can hardly get around to social play? Does he show so much dependence on the presence of playmates that he can never be happy alone? Does he tend to sabotage his relations by too chaotic, disruptive behavior, so that sustained play or interactions rarely take place? If, instead of treating others in a friendly way, a child usually makes trouble for them, the teacher can see in what kinds of situations he feels impelled to do this. She notices, too, in the behavior of a child who is not well accepted by others in the group, what he himself does to bring this on—why he is rejected or ignored. A day that is broken up into periods when children for the most part have preplanned activities under teacher direction will not leave enough time for this kind of careful observation or for working with children in the midst of the situations where they need help.

A bottleneck in the establishment of good relationships is an emergency requiring attention without delay. But more is needed than responding only after someone has been hit or frightened, or has had to hit or frighten someone else. It means being alert to much earlier signs of trouble, recognizing them by sight or sound. A teacher needs to be so responsive to the atmosphere in the room or playground that unfriendliness, discomfort, tension, or rivalry is sensed at its very beginning, before it has spread and multiplied. She also needs to be so aware of individual faces and expressions, of voice tones, and of postural and movement cues that she knows, at any time, who in the room or playground most needs help. The advantage of small groups for these young children is thus very obvious. As a teacher listens in her room or playground, she may hear a scolding voice saying, "No! Go away!", a shrill tone or a whining one, complaints, name-calling, shrieks, wild laughter with tension in it, or an argument that is leading to blows and the rupture of a relationship. As she sweeps the room with her glance, she may see tension in the pose of shoulders during an interaction, a child cornered by another and appearing alarmed, a child looking lonely and sucking his thumb, or angry faces.

The teacher first of all moves close to the trouble spot. Her nearness helps worried children feel more secure and helps children who are losing control to maintain it. "Something's the matter?" or "Can I help?" is a good general opening; then she listens, and as the quarreling pair talks out the problem, the children pick up her interest and nonjudgmental efforts to understand both points of view. Perhaps this is all that is necessary, if each child now understands the other. But often it helps if a child states his grievance alone to the teacher first, to get his thoughts and words straight, helped by her questions—"Is this what you mean?" Then they can go together to the other person concerned, where, with the teacher beside him, the child feels safe enough to try to get his point across and she can help him if his words get stuck.

Often it takes a while to uncover the grievances in a conflict involving two participants. If the quarreling children are already involved in a physical battle, that needs to be stopped first (without judgments). No child can talk while trying to avoid blows, but children are remarkable in the way they accept one another's expressions of genuine feeling if these come in the form of words rather than blows, and if the words don't attack. Once the fight is stopped, the teacher responds with reflections of feelings, such as "You didn't like—? You wanted—? You meant—?" keeping an angry one's focus on his or her own feelings. When a child says to another, "You're bad! You hit me!" she reflects that with "You're angry about the hitting." (It is much more natural for children to talk about themselves than about others' failings; adults are prone to do the reverse, and this sometimes irrevocably damages relationships.) These talks may just be ended with a nod and an "Oh," or perhaps go on with "I didn't mean to" or "Well, I was mad at *you* because—" Nor do children seem threatened at hearing how others feel; rather, they appear relieved at the clearing of the air. Often one will say spontaneously, "I won't any more," or be noticed making amends later: "I'm fixing her block building for her." The teacher can help, too, sometimes, by indicating ways a child can show friendliness, if she is sure that he feels it: "Want to get him a Kleenex?" "Maybe he'd like his bear." "You're feeling sorry?" (if his expression shows sympathy). "Then you could say 'I'm sorry, Bill,' or maybe pat his back." She can also add, after things are explained, "He knows, now; he understands how you felt. You told him very well."

Just as the teacher can help a child stay with his own feelings in two-way discussions such as the above, she can give similar aid when name-calling occurs. To "Dummy!" the teacher might respond, "You're mad at her?" and proceed to specifics with "You don't like something she's doing?" Again she starts the child off with "I didn't like" or "I don't want you to," and so on. Similarly, when he says, "Don't," "You can't," or "You shouldn't" to someone, she brings him back to expressing his own feelings about the other's behavior. She helps a child be clearer, too, when he says, "Shut up!" "Don't mess with me!" "Get out!" by suggesting that he can explain himself with "We need quiet; our babies are sleeping"; "I don't feel like wrestling"; or "We're using this place right now." With suggestions like these she is strongly indicating her faith that other children will be reasonable and friendly if approached in this way, as, in fact, they usually are. When a child complains that someone did something he didn't like, often the teacher's words "I see; you can tell him about that" make the same point.

Feelings in a young child can mount in intensity fairly rapidly to a loss of self-control, and when this happens a child's playmates may lose their trust in his friendliness and sometimes will retaliate. Loss of self-control is hard on the child himself, as well; he may feel guilty, and he may be frightened at having been swept away by anger into doing something he regrets. His confidence in himself is shaken; also, at the very least, his relationship with another child is often disrupted, even if the hiatus is brief.

The teacher would try very hard not to let hostile feelings accumulate during the day to the point of explosion, and, instead, would deal with each conflict as it arises. If a child is angry at someone at ten o'clock and is not helped to say so, when the next and the next incident are added on, he may be very angry indeed by noon. This is why teachers find it a good idea to say "I guess you didn't like that" or "That probably made you a little mad" without delay, if a child seems annoyed by someone's behavior to him, and follow this by "You can tell him," adding, if needed, "I'll help you do it."

Sometimes, in spite of everything, so much negative feeling has built up between two children, perhaps when they played together at home in addition to meeting at school, that the relationship has badly deteriorated. The pair seems unable to play together at all any more without bickering or outright quarrels. Though separation of two children may sometimes be necessary when the pair becomes over-stimulated or too fatigued by their play, separation of two angry ones does no good; they need to be reunited, rather than divided. But helping them discuss a conflict sometimes fails to end their hostility. In this case they are brought together later for another talk, and they go on, "And *I* didn't like it when—," "And *I* was mad about—," until finally the teacher's question "Is there anything else you're mad about, Bix? Earl?" brings a "No, that's all!" from each. After this, protected play in another room or private corner is helpful, perhaps with interesting special toys that can be easily shared, to reestablish their trust and help them find each other again.

II

Children learn about other children by watching and listening to them, and even more by interacting with them. But much of this information comes too fast, and sometimes at moments of too much personal involvement, to be really understood. Because their relationships are of so much importance to them, they eagerly welcome the teacher as interpreter, especially if the explanations are given when they are not preoccupied with an interaction at the moment.

- Livy, a new child, approached the other children too abruptly in her eagerness to play with them. When she walked into the doll corner uninvited, those already there saw her as an invader of their privacy. The teacher interpreted her behavior for them, saying, "She wants to have friends, just the way you do." The children's response was a warm one, and later Janie was heard to say, "You can play with *me*, Livy." "Does she want me to be her friend, too?" asked Patrick, ready for a new playmate anytime.

- Daniel needed some interpretation of Bobby's early school behavior when the latter was running about and overstepping limits. Hearing him call Bobby "that bad boy," the teacher felt Daniel was threatened by the presence of this stormy child. She told him, "A lot of things here are new to Bobby, so I'm going to tell him just one thing at a time; I think if I tell him too many things, he might get mixed up about school and not know I'm friendly." Later, when Daniel came again to report a deviation, she said, "I think it's better, today, not to try to help him learn about staying off his knees in the wet sand; I think I'd better just change his jeans for him. He probably has as much as he can learn, keeping the sand off other people, don't you think?" And later she added, "You know, Daniel, I'm not sure he knows what *keep the sand down* means. I'd better show him." At one point, when Bobby hit Daniel, she interpreted this, too, saying, "Bobby's angry, but I think he doesn't know how to tell you instead of hitting. Let's go ask him what's the matter." When Bobby later began to show he was attracted to Daniel, again interpretation was needed, because Bobby expressed this at first by becoming upset and brandishing his fists whenever Daniel withheld the attention he sought. The teacher offered, then, "I think he's cross because he wants to play with you and you're busy. But he's learning."

- Newcomers often take toys away from other children. When Frederic did this to Penny, she was indignant. After helping Penny reclaim her toy, the teacher took her aside to try to interpret Frederic to her. "Remember how you felt that day I brought the new doll stroller to school? You told me, 'I just love new toys!' You wanted it so much; you felt so wiggly, and your fingers wanted to reach right out and try it. You thought you knew just how; you could hardly wait for your chance. Just think, Frederic feels that way about lots and lots of things, because all our toys are new toys to him." Later Penny ran to the teacher, saying, "He waited! He waited! He put his hand out like this, and then he stopped!"

- An example of considering the needs of both children in a conflict situation involved Seth, a child who often tried to take others' toys away from them. When he snatched the toy rabbit that Kathy was using and ran away with it, the teacher suggested that Kathy follow him—not running, lest he should be scared by pursuit, but persistently going after him. She also suggested that Kathy put her hand out for the rabbit, saying, "Pretty soon I'll be through," with the teacher's tone, as she made the suggestion, indicating reassurance and encouragement, as well as confidence in Seth. Such words communicate to both children her expectation that the aggressor will understand and respond. Thus a calm confidence also comes into the voice of the explaining child and has its influence. since young children usually respond to our expectations. Had Kathy just said, "Don't!" in a distressed tone, or "That's mine!" in an angry one, her voice would have indicated a lack of that confidence in Seth's reasonableness, and the response would probably have been continued unreasonable behavior. The teacher made no attempt to take the toy away from Seth, since to do that would arouse Seth's resentment against both her and the other child, and in addition Kathy would feel, "I'm little. I had to have help."

Kathy continued to follow Seth until he came to a corner, then put both hands on the rabbit, holding it (but not pulling at it) as she talked to him, so Seth couldn't get on with play anyhow. The other things Kathy said made it easier for Seth to identify with her need, such as "I was just going to put it to bed; it's nighttime." And he was helped toward having more trust in Kathy by the teacher's saying, "She'll give it to you when she's through playing with it, won't you Kathy?" to which Kathy readily agreed.

● In a sharp conflict involving Paul and Johnny one day, the need to consider both of them was urgent. Only one swing was free, and both the children hurried toward it, with Paul arriving barely ahead and sitting down on it. Johnny snatched at the chains, jerking angrily and screaming, "No! No!" Paul called, "Teacher! Teacher!" as he held on grimly to keep from being unseated. But as the teacher approached, Johnny turned on her, hit at her, and ran away and crawled under the big bush at the far corner of the playground, from whence, a moment later, shovels were seen flying out in the direction of the swings. It was obvious how Johnny felt about Paul; he'd have liked to hit him with a shovel and would try to get back at him somehow, whenever he could. He was also hurt and angry that the teacher didn't take his part; probably he felt that if she hadn't come over just then, he could have jerked Paul off the swing. At that moment, all relationships were disrupted. Johnny's aggressive behavior had frightened Paul and angered him, too. "Johnny is mean," he must have thought. "He tried to take my swing. I couldn't stop him . . . he's pretty rough . . . I'd better keep out of his way. But anyhow, I can make him feel bad." And he began to sing, "Ha ha, I've got the swi-ing." There had been a complete breakdown in communication and both children were suffering from it.

All this needed to be worked out. The teacher went first to the bush and reflected Johnny's feelings, as he stayed there out of sight. "You must be pretty mad that you didn't get the swing. And disappointed. You ran as hard as you could, but Paul got it." Johnny crawled out then, grimy and tear-stained. "I'll help you talk to Paul," she said, holding out her hand. When they got there, she placed her hands over Paul's on the chains and tightened his grip, saying, "Hold on, Johnny wants to tell you something," reassuringly, since Paul looked a little anxious on Johnny's approach. Johnny, too, took hold of the chains, and now the two were back as they had been. "You can talk to Paul, now," the teacher assured him. "He'll listen." "*I* want to swing," Johnny said. "I got here first," was Paul's reply. The teacher suggested, "You might say, 'You can have it when I get through,'" and Paul added that. Johnny was still hanging to the chains, and she went on, to confirm Paul's friendliness in Johnny's mind, "And will you come and tell him, when you're through, Paul?" (A nod.) "He says, yes; did you see him nodding, Johnny? And I'll help him remember." By then Johnny was looking much more relaxed, and in a moment or two he went off to play elsewhere.

Some things were probably learned by both children from this experience, without the need for further discussion with them. Paul had seen that calm persistence could make it unnecessary to call, "Teacher!" Johnny had found out that force and temper don't convince someone who feels he's in the right, that "No" doesn't mean "Never," and that it also doesn't mean someone hates you. But to help them gain as much as possible from the incident, the teacher spoke to each of them separately a day or two later. To Paul she said, of Johnny, "He has a very hard time waiting for things he wants, right now. He wants them so much. But he's learning." Paul must have felt friendly and sympathetic in response to this, because soon afterward he went to tell Johnny that a swing was free. In a similar conflict that Paul had with someone else, she added to his learning by telling him, "When we just say, 'No,' children sometimes think we mean they'll *never* have it; that's why it helps to say, 'You can have it when I'm through'; remember Johnny?" And when Johnny was all set to begin one of his extensive block buildings, she said to him, "You won't want to stop building until you're through, I expect. That's the way Paul felt about the swing. He was all ready to start, and so he didn't want to stop then and give it to you—not until he was through. I think everybody is like that."

III

When a damaged relationship has been repaired, it is helpful to end the experience by focusing on the future, pointing out what a child can do "next time." Hearing this, he thinks of himself as a success (tomorrow), rather than a failure today. Here are some examples.

- Cindy innocently took the doll Helen had brought from home out of the doll bed where it lay unattended, and Helen snatched it away. Cindy shrieked, "No!" and grabbbed it back. Helen, in desperation, then hit her. Cindy cried hard, and Helen, upset at this result of the incident, cried almost as hard. The teacher comforted them both and said to Helen, "*Next* time you'll say, 'That's my doll that I brought from home,' and then she'll know, won't you, Cindy?"

Focusing on "next time," of course, does more than help a child feel better about himself. It serves as a review and a preparation and is thus real teaching.

- Once when Bobby hit Daniel and then ran away, the teacher took advantage of a quiet moment to discuss what had happened with Bobby. "You're angry at Daniel?" she asked him. "Yes!" shouted Bobby. "He won't play with me!" The teacher said, "Hitting him just made him run away; I wonder if there's something you can do so he'll want to play with you next time?" There was a thoughtful pause. "Maybe if you asked him to play something he likes, he would." "Yeah! I'll bring my truck, and I'll say," (relishing it) "'lookit!'"

- Emphasizing "next time" is particularly helpful for a child who has just experienced a consequence of overstepping limits, moving the problem on to a learning situation. Molly threw sand directly at Tom, and at first the teacher led her away from the sand without comment. Molly sat down at a table inside, pouting. Her expression said, "I'm misunderstood." The teacher seated herself beside her, saying, "Hi." Molly turned her face away, mumbling something. "You're feeling pretty bothered about that sand business, I guess," the teacher told her. She nodded. "You didn't want to leave the sand and are cross at me for taking you in, maybe?" This was clearing the decks so Molly would feel more ready to talk to the teacher. "Yes," she agreed, but the yes sounded more sad than angry. "And you're sad, too? I expect something happened that made you feel like throwing sand at Tom." It came out violently, then, with tears. "He said, 'Let's throw her out!'" "Oh, of course! That must have been really upsetting. Let's go find out about it." The teacher held her hand, and they returned together to the sandbox. Tom was with his friend Gerald there. The teacher started Molly out by saying, "You can talk to him now about what you told me." "You said you'd throw me out," she told Tom. "Why did you say that? It makes me scared." (With help of this kind, children come to know many feeling words: "cross," "mad," "scared," "lonesome," and "worried," as well as "loving," "friendly," "happy," "cozy," "comfortable," and the like.) Tom answered with feeling, too. "You're bad; you threw sand at me!" Bringing Molly back was important for him, too. He and Gerald had just classified Molly as "that bad girl" and were surely going to "throw her out" somehow, whenever they had a chance. Thus do incidents snowball.

To help Tom move from a judgment statement back to an expression of his own feelings, the teacher responded, "It made you very angry when she threw the sand. Is there something more you didn't like?" "We were playing here alone," he said. "And you didn't want anybody else? And when she came near, you were afraid it would spoil your twosome?" (a favorite word in this group). "Yes!" And "Yes! Yes, we were," put in Gerald. "So it wasn't really about Molly exactly; it was about anybody who might come in." "Yes, that's right; we didn't want anybody." Molly was feeling much better by then; she knew that they hadn't been rejecting her personally. (This is so often the case in a conflict; a child stands for something else, such as the disruption of a twosome or interference with a project.) Now Molly understood and was ready to offer a solution. "But the sandbox is for everybody," she said. "You could play over there, under the bush, in that sand. That's a good play-alone place, and then I could play here." The suggestion was accepted. "Yeah! Let's go over there!" and off they went.

It was not necessary to discuss the sand throwing with Molly; the teacher had made her point by removing her. Molly had had the experience, however, of using words, instead of action, to express feelings; she had seen that she was understood and that talking things over also helped her understand Tom better, so that she ended up not being "scared" of him. As preparation for the future, the teacher only added, "Next time you can say, 'What's the matter? Why are you mad at me?' And they'll tell you, just like they did now, and you won't have to feel scared and throw sand at them."

- "Next time" can also be presented in the form of a small drama. When three children seemed threatened by innocent intruders on their doll-corner play, the teacher suggested, "Shall we play I'm a child coming into your house, and see if you know what to do about it?" She roamed in without ringing the "doorbell" and wandered about, fingering their things. They were delighted with the game. "You can come when we're through," said Lucia. "But where can *I* live?" asked the teacher, plaintively. "Outdoors in the playhouse," said Agatha, firmly. (Janie was so charmed by the new "child" that she almost upset the drama by saying, "O *let* her come in and play, Agatha!") The teacher went on with other familiar ploys, such as "But I didn't play for a long time," and "When *will* you be through?" and Lucia thought out her answers carefully. "Never mind; you'll have a chance later," and "I don't know, but we'll come and call you." The doll corner is a scene of many such conflicts, but rejection of a child there is not often on a personal basis; it is more apt to occur because children prefer their own friends who can be relied upon to take certain roles there as mother, sister, baby, or father.

- Focusing on "next time" at the end of a complicated discussion can tie it up for the children and direct their attention to the central issue, which sometimes gets lost in the proliferation of feelings. Maggie was sitting at the pasting table, and Candace gave her a hit as she walked by. "Don't do that!" said Maggie, angrily. Candace said to the teacher nearby, "I don't like her face, that's why I did that." "What kind of a face, Candace; do you mean an angry face?" "Yes." The teacher said to Maggie, "Are you angry? Is it an angry face?" "Yes, 'cause she hit me." "Any other reason you're angry at Candace?" "No." "I see. Your face wasn't angry until she hit you. And how about you, Candy? Were you angry before?" "I'm mad at Maggie because she talked about her big cousins," Candace said. Maggie protested, "But they *are* big — bigger than me." Candace, now talking directly to Maggie, said, "I don't like you saying they're bigger than *me*." "Oh," said Maggie. The teacher asked, "Can you think of anything now, Maggie, that made you feel like making an angry face at Candy?" "Yes; she said my cousins weren't either big." "Anything else?" "No." "And how about you, Candace?" "Yes. When I was at your house, your baby hit me." "That made you mad at Maggie?" "No; I didn't hit her back, but you did, Maggie, and that made me mad, 'cause your baby didn't know no better. I like babies. I don't like you messin' with her." "Anything else?" "No, that's all." "Maggie?" "No, I'm done." The teacher then used "next time." "You both did a good job, talking over those things. Maybe next time there won't even need to be a hit to start with, Candy. You could tell Maggie what you're mad about right away. At her house you'd say, 'I don't like to see you hit your baby,' and explain about their not knowing any better. And at the table you might say, 'I don't want to hear about your big cousins any more, Maggie, O.K.?' if it bothers you." "Yeah, I talk good."

IV

Basic communication skills necessary for discussion of disagreements are learned in children's confrontations, with teachers' help. The examples that follow show how lines of communication were kept open.

● Norman hit Tom, and the teacher said to Norman, "You're mad at Tom?" Then, to help him be specific, she went on with "He did something you didn't like?" Norman said he had been too crowded by Tom at the top of the slide. "You were angry and afraid?" "I was afraid I would go down too fast, or I would get all squeezed over the side and fall right down." Now Norman was ready to cope, and the teacher said, "You can tell Tom, just the way you told me." Looking earnestly into Tom's face, as he clung to the ladder, Norman explained, "I don't want you to get so close when I'm up there. It scares me." "Oh."

The benefits of this kind of communication, even as brief as this was, are many. Tom, if hit by Norman, might have learned to stop pushing him, out of fear of being hit again. But he might also have felt, from that point on, that Norman disliked him and begun to wonder what was wrong with him, Tom, to cause this. He might also have felt abused and ready to take revenge on Norman when he could and even less trustful of others, since it seems that people may sometimes hurt you out of a clear sky. But when Norman explained how he felt, Tom took a step in learning about other people—that they, too, can get angry or feel afraid, and that such feelings may be the cause of their aggressive actions. Hearing about others' feelings might also have helped him be more comfortable about his own. (Tom, for instance, would not so easily have admitted to being afraid.) And one of the most important gains for children from such incidents is the chance to use their ability to empathize. It is practiced awareness of others and their feelings and needs that in the end will prevent Tom from crowding and pushing Norman and others on the slide and help him to move from self-centeredness to socialization.

Sometimes it is hard for children in conflict, just as it is for adults, to sort out what really happened from what they feel. In this difficult task, the teacher keeps everyone's focus (including, most importantly, her own) squarely on communicating and understanding. The aim is to teach children a way to resolve conflict by talking things over—to reestablish communication in a disrupted relationship, not to discover who is in the right or wrong or to make other judgments. If a teacher maintains this focus, guilt, resentment of her interference, fear of her disapproval or of punishment, regret about having disappointed her expectations, and other relationship feelings involving her will not cause them to lose touch with their original feelings.

In keeping the focus steady for Gordon and Martin, in the conflict to be discussed next, the teacher had to avoid the side issue of who did what first (or, in Gordon's view, who was to blame) and help each express, instead, what he felt at the moment.

● Gordon was seen to hit Martin with his fist when the two were in the sandbox. Martin cried, and the teacher joined them. "You're angry at Martin?" she asked Gordon. "Yes!" "He did something you didn't like?" (This is always easier to answer than "Why?") "Yes," Gordon replied, "he hit me." "I did not!" interjected Martin. "You're mad, too, Martin?" "Yes, 'cause he hit me." Gordon said quickly, "He hit me first." "I did not!" Martin insisted. The teacher said, "You're both pretty mad. Who would like to talk first?" Gordon was silent; this was his first experience with such a discussion. Martin said, "I would. He grabs my things, and if I don't let him have them, he hits me." "Anything else?" "No, that's all." "Gordon?" Gordon said, "I'm mad because *he* hit *me*." "I did *not*! I did *not*!" Martin shouted. "Anything else, Gordon?" A pause ensued, and then Gordon said, "He won't let me have the shovel, and I need it." Martin protested, "But I'm not through! I'm still making my tunnel. Go get that one on the shelf!" "Oh— O.K.," said Gordon, starting to go there. "And don't hit me any more," finished Martin. "O.K., I won't," said Gordon then.

This talk moved through phases of violence, disintegration of the relationship, discussion and clarification of feelings, and, at the end, an agreed-upon solution ("Don't hit me any more") without the need for straightening out such facts as who hit first—or whether, indeed, Gordon was ever hit at all, which seemed unlikely. Had that argument continued, a comment such as "You two think differently about it" would make them see that the teacher could remain neutral, accepting a difference of opinion. A factual discussion would only have led to a stalemate or, at best, would have cluttered up the important movement aimed at the restoration of good relations.

- An issue can often be turned back to children for a resolution, after both have aired their points of view. Sandy was dissolved in helpless tears. "Maggie took my book. I want my book! I want it! I want my mommy!" Since she was working herself up more and more, the teacher took her off to the waiting room. There Sandy was soon ready to say more. "Maggie said she would get the book from the shelf for me, but then she didn't give it to me," she said. They went together to ask Maggie to come and talk it over. Sandy spoke first. "You said you would get my book, but then you kept it." "I changed my mind," Maggie said. Sandy began to cry again, and said, "But *I* want it!" Maggie, sounding a little whimpery also, said, "But I want it, too." "What can we do?" the teacher asked. "Two girls are unhappy, and it looks as though we need to think of something." There was a silence. "What can we do to settle this problem?" the teacher asked again. Then Maggie said, "Sandy, you remember that book about the pumpkin you liked?

You could have that, maybe," and turning to the teacher she asked, "Could you get it down?" Sandy said, "Oh, yes, I know that one. I'll take that one." The teacher found the book, and the two girls went back to the playroom together, Sandy saying on the way, "But next time don't change your mind, O.K.?" "O.K.," Maggie agreed. "Because it made me cry." "We *both* cried," Maggie said, and they looked in each others' faces and laughed.

Another way in which a teacher keeps the lines clear in a conflict is to avoid at the time setting any limits that are not necessary to protect the discussion, bearing in mind that neither she nor the children can focus on more than one thing at a time with the concentration needed.

● Felicia and Kathy were swinging, with Betty sitting on the extra swing strap she had hooked between the two swings they were using. Felicia was making Betty's swing jerk, ignoring her cries of "Don't! Don't!" The teacher might have talked with Felicia about using the swings carefully when three children were on them together. But this would distract everyone's attention from the conflict, so it was left for later. (In any case, if the relationship problem was not solved, even if the swing problem was, Felicia would find another way to pester Betty.) The teacher said to Felicia, "You are cross with Betty about something?" Felicia answered, "Yes. I told her we didn't want the other swing on, but she put it on anyway. I just wanted to swing alone with Kathy." "I see," said the teacher. "I think you could explain that to Betty." "I want to swing alone with Kathy, Betty," Felicia said then. "That's because she's my best friend, see? That's why. You can come later. O.K.?" Betty said, "O.K.," and climbed down.

If a child will speak clearly and openly of his emotional needs to another, making a bid for understanding and giving the other child a chance to show it, there will usually be a response. Appealing to someone implies a faith in his or her friendliness, and children rise to the occasion. Felicia was grateful to Betty and later asked her to sit beside her at the story table. And Betty, having given in not by coercion but by choice, felt more friendly, too. Felicia had now become, to her, "the girl that likes me."

V

There are some conflicts in which positive feelings need recognition as much as, or even more than, negative ones. It is well to keep this possibility in mind in children's quarrels. Some examples of interactions involving mixed feelings follow.

● Jewel was very fond of Donavan, a boy who was liked by several of the other children equally well. They had been playing together a lot, but one day she was heard threatening Donavan, "If you won't play with me, I won't ask you to my birthday party." Donavan told her, "I won't ask you to *my* party, then," and went off angry. She sat alone, disconsolate. The teacher sat down by her. "You're upset about Donnie?" "Yes; I said I wouldn't ask him to my party, and then he said he wouldn't ask me to *his* party." "Saying that made him angry, and now you're sad." "Yes; I wanted him to play with me, but he's playing with Jocelyn" (tears). She cried a little and then began to feel better. But the teacher wanted to bring the two children together. Even though Jewel seemed to be clear about the part that her threat had played in alienating Donavan, she might not know how to repair matters. And Donavan must be having some troubling feelings too. He had probably been hurt and angered by Jewel's threat, and he had seen her crying. What was he to do about his very real warmth for her, short of being possessed by her, as she wanted him to be? Though outwardly busying himself in the doll corner with Jocelyn, he was giving Jewel some sidelong glances. The teacher suggested that Jewel tell him what she had just told the teacher, and she did so, across the doll-corner screen, adding, "Donnie, I don't want you to play with anybody else; just me, all the time." He answered, "Well, I want to play with Jocelyn right now, but I'll keep my *mind* on you." Later, as Jewel played alone at a nearby table, he looked over the screen and said again, "Remember, I'm keeping my *mind* on you, Jewel." No teacher could have reassured Jewel so well that a person can be involved in one friendship and still be able to keep his "mind" (feelings) for another. And Donavan had had an opportunity to show his affection, while still making the point that he wanted to be free for other relationships.

Being aware of children's friendships, such as Jewel's and Donavan's, and their need to keep these twosomes intact helps the teacher see the positive feelings that lie beneath many a display of hostility. At this age, children often find a first special friend outside the family, and many conflicts arise around this issue.

- Chip grabbed David's field glasses from Hal, who was wearing them hung by their strap around his neck. Hal grabbed them back, and Chip hit him hard. While comforting Hal, the teacher said to Chip, "You're angry with Hal?" "Those are David's!" Chip yelled. Hal interjected, "David gave them to me. He *said* I could use them." "No!" shouted Chip, trying to hit Hal again. "You're pretty angry; I can see that," said the teacher, stopping his blow. Chip looked ready to cry. "And you're sad, too," she added. Then it came out clear. "I wanted David to give them to *me*." "I see," said the teacher. "Then it's David you need to work this out with, isn't it? Let's find him." When they reached David, Chip asked, "Why didn't you give your glasses to *me*? You're *my* friend." "I know I am," David told him, "but I like Hal, too. I'll play with you pretty soon, and then you can have my glasses." Children respond with warm reassurances to the love that these jealous outbursts reveal.

- Discovering hidden positive feelings is sometimes difficult with teasers, who tend to disguise them by provocativeness. Sandor was a child like this. He grinned as he tumbled Betty's blocks down and ran off. To Betty, the teacher said, "You didn't want it knocked down? You were still working on it?" "Yes!" "We'll go find him." They went in search of Sandor, and, with the prompting words "I didn't want" Betty was able to say, "I didn't want my house knocked down." Sandor grinned again, turning his head away. "Anything you want to say yourself?" asked the teacher. "No." "I wonder if you felt like bothering Betty for some reason." But he knew just how to deflect the results of his actions. "I was just teasing," he said. "Perhaps she did something that made you feel like teasing her?" "No, I'm not mad at Betty." "At somebody or something else? Maybe you just felt like doing bothering things today?" (This was said in an unaccusing, unreproachful way.) "No, I'm not mad about anything." The teacher went on, "It was your hand" (she took his hand in hers, and they both looked at it) "that knocked down Betty's house, so there was some reason you wanted to. It's not mad feelings—something else? What did you want, Sandor? Can you tell us?" She held his hand while Betty peered fascinatedly into his face. (By now, usually all resentment is replaced by interest, on the part of the other child involved, and this interest plays no small part in helping someone like Sandor reveal himself. No one listens so intently and uncritically as a small child.) "*I wanted her to play with me!*" came out in a burst. "You might ask her to play . . . what?" "Bikes!" "Sure," said Betty, much flattered that this tough-acting boy liked her. "You know," said the teacher, "You don't need to tease her to make her stop playing and look at you. That way she doesn't know what you want. She thinks you are mad at her. It gets all mixed up, doesn't it, Betty? So you could say, 'Will you stop doing that and play with me, instead?'" "Or you could play *blocks* with me," Betty added, smiling at him.

● A confusion of positive feelings and other ones led to Bill's apparently hostile behavior in the sandbox one day. He hit Alex with his shovel, for no apparent reason, and Alex began to flail his arms, using that half-crying, half-scolding voice children sometimes resort to in emergencies. The teacher rubbed Alex's head where the shovel had hit it (but the hit was a very light one, more of an insult). As she comforted him, Bill watched. "Better now? Let's find out what's the matter," the teacher said. Alex spoke with indignation: "Why did you *do* that, Bill?" "You were bad," said Bill. "I'm not either bad," Alex told him. The teacher offered, "Alex doesn't think he's bad, but I guess Bill is mad about something Alex did." "You hit me," said Bill, surprisingly, since nothing like that had been seen. "I did not," Alex protested. "Alex says he didn't really hit you, Bill, but maybe you thought he was going to?" "Yes, he was. Alex doesn't like me." "You hit him because you were afraid he was going to hit you?" Alex burst out, "And *I* was afraid of *you!*" And suddenly the two little boys were rolling head over heels, laughing uproariously. When this frolic expressing their relief was over, the teacher generalized for them a little. "Sometimes when children don't know each other yet, they are a little afraid of each other, but when they do know each other, like now, then they aren't afraid any more." They both nodded, knowingly. Afterward they played together most of the day. Bill's "Alex doesn't like me" had meant, as so often, "Alex isn't showing any feeling of liking for me, and I want him to." It was upsetting for Bill to have Alex indifferently playing beside him, and his unfamiliar face and silent presence began to seem threatening.

VI

To protect relationships between children, a teacher needs to be especially watchful that hostility and aggression arising from other sources are not displaced and then acted out upon anyone who happens to be nearby. A child needs to communicate feelings to another when the feelings concern that person, but he needs to be prevented from taking out on someone feelings that come from elsewhere— perhaps from home, from a television-watching experience, or a visit to a doctor. This limit applies to his using another child as his "bad guy" or "monster," for instance, chasing or pretending to shoot the other child, his toy animals, cowboy figures, or puppets, or crashing into his trucks or tricycles. To do any of these things is equivalent to attacking the other child, as far as the latter is concerned. When relationships are protected in these ways, children can be of great assistance in helping each other to play out their hostilities and fears, often combining forces to shoot at, hide from, or imprison each other's fantasy foes. But this can only happen when they have cleared away any displacements.

● When Chuck kept bumping into Bix's swing, the teacher encouraged Bix to protest and then to ask, "Are you mad at me?" "No," Chuck said, "I'm mad at my baby brother," and his face vividly expressed the truth of his words. Bix responded immediately, "I'm mad at mine, too!" and this exchange of feelings led to days of swinging side by side, talking about the problems their baby brothers made for them and fantasizing about what they would like to do to them.

When children are engaged in playing out negative feelings—for example, shooting at a "bad robber"—the teacher would stop them from shooting at a child as the robber and would then consult with them about what they might use as their robber instead, such as a toy person, the big teddy bear with a rope to tie him up, or pretend robbers behind the bush. She would also end by suggesting that the child who had been their victim before, as the robber, could be their helper. Most children who are playing out what seem like dangerous themes are glad to have helpers. If the teacher offers encouragement and support, stays near enough to give them an occasional reminder to prevent the loss of control that would mean the end of the play, and helps by bringing materials or perhaps suggesting hiding places, it will be possible for the children to play out many of their aggressive themes together, with consequent deepening of ties of friendship.

Even when other children want to go along with a child's use of them as victims, relationships may be damaged in the end. At any moment the child playing out violent feelings may go overboard and scare or even hurt the "victim." In any case, a child always feels some sense of guilt about using other children in these ways, since fantasy and reality are not yet clearly distinguished in his mind. The teacher tries to help the child find a less destructive way to express the fantasy, using the same symbols he has chosen, if possible. So she might say, perhaps, "You need to keep the sand off Bobby," following this quickly with "but you could throw some sand on the rubber boy." Thus closing one door to action is followed so promptly by opening another that, in most cases, the impulse flows smoothly in the new direction with the same satisfaction; since the feelings have already been displaced onto real children, they can be as easily transferred to other substitutes. More examples of the handling of displaced feelings in interactions among children follow.

● Out of their own need to work through a fear, Agatha and Lucia enticed Melanie to chase them. When shrill screams were heard—evidence that they were getting excited and a little panicky—the teacher asked, "What are you playing here, I wonder?" "Melanie's a tickle bug, and she's going to tickle us," they told her. "Chasing doesn't work very well; could you play it another way?" the teacher asked the three. Children often find ingenious solutions. "I'll pretend I'm going to chase them, but I won't, really," Melanie suggested. She sat cross-legged in one spot. "And we'll pretend she's chasing us," the others said. But Melanie didn't enjoy doing nothing, so in a few minutes they said a "pretend tickle bug" was just there "by itself," and they all three went near it and dared it to chase them, then ran screaming to hide under the bushes. They did this several times with great enthusiasm.

The displacements that some children make onto playmates tend to damage their relationships, because the victims consider their treatment unjust. Before this goes on too long, the teacher tries to help the child face, and deal with, the feeling that is being displaced.

● Moira said to Gabrielle, "That's an icky picture you're making." Later the teacher said casually to Moira, "Were you feeling a little cross at Gabrielle at the table there?" Moira answered, "I'm not mad at Gabrielle. I'm mad about the picture." The reflection "Something about the *picture*" from the teacher brought out no more at the time. But later Moira said the same thing about Mark's picture, and the teacher took it up again. "I remember you told me it wasn't Gabrielle that made you feel like saying, 'Icky.' Is this the same? Or is it Mark you're cross at?" "No," Moira said, and "I'm mad about the picture" came again. Noticing that she had used the word "about" both times, the teacher said, "Something *about* the pictures seems to make you feel cross." Then Moira said, "My sister is in second grade. She makes *real* pictures. She keeps them in a Work Book." "Looking at Gabrielle's and Mark's pictures made you think of your big sister's real pictures. Something is the same?" Little children take surprisingly big jumps sometimes. Moira didn't bother with the next step—that both Gabrielle and Mark could also make "real" pictures, such as she herself couldn't make yet. She nodded and said, "The *crossness* is the same."

It is not unusual for a child to be unable at first to realize what is making him irritable, and to sometimes offer a delayed response in the form of a free association which may seem unconnected except for the fact that it, too, is involved with the same "crossness," as with Moira.

● When Tim hit his friend Mark, he could produce no reason at all for feeling angry. But, having had the question raised, a little later he volunteered, "My brother wouldn't let me play with his ball." In effect, like Moira, he had then disassociated the old anger from the present environment. His teacher could help him tie this up, after he had no more to say about his brother, by adding, "You were mad? Perhaps you felt like hitting him like you did Mark?" "Yes, I did! But he's too big — he'd hit me back." "I see. So it really wasn't about Mark at all." Sometimes that will end it. But at other times a child seems ready for more, looking thoughtful. Tim's teacher offered, "Maybe, even if you can't hit him, you could *tell* your brother you didn't like his saying you couldn't play with his ball." After anger is expressed, one can see the other side. Tim said, then, "Well, it's his ball. But I didn't like 'Cut that out!'" "It was the *way* he said it." "Yeah!"

● With Bo, it was necessary to wait awhile and let some silences develop while he thought. He was very irritable with his usual friend and companion Sammy one day. Yet it looked as though Sammy was trying very hard to be agreeable. If Bo said, "Go away — I don't want to play with you," Sammy went away and tried again later, patiently. Bo did things like bumping into Sammy's train and knocking over his cube tower, and Sammy looked bewildered. When this had gone on long enough for the teacher to judge that the hostility was only in Bo, she asked him to come into the office for a talk. She started by saying, "I wonder if you're cross at Sammy today because he did something?" (One can never be sure about this without asking.) "No, he didn't do anything." "But you're mad at him anyway? I wonder what makes you feel that way." ("I wonder" is easier for a child to consider than a series of questions.) "I don't know." Bo was silent for quite a while, slamming around in the little room, frowning. "Hard to figure out," the teacher sympathized, "but I can see you really do feel cross." Then Bo said, "My best friend, Don, is five. He's in kindergarten." "You like him best, but he's not in nursery school." "I wish *Sammy* was Don," Bo said, sighing, but on going back to the playroom, he stopped punishing Sammy for being himself. Later in the day, he had a solution. "I think I'll change my name to Don," he said. "And I'll change mine to Jimmy," Sammy added cheerfully, and for several days the pair reminded everyone to use these new names.

Children differ in the verbal ability needed to discuss their feelings. But it is possible that where their social relationships are valued children progress rapidly, not only because they hear speech constantly, but also because of the emphasis placed on talking about feelings. Sylvia Ashton-Warner, in her book *Teacher* (1963), makes the point that in beginning to learn to read, it is the word with emotional significance for a child that is most easily remembered. In psychotherapy with adults, even those who are quite uncommunicative in their daily lives often use language vividly and even poetically in their therapy sessions. Words are important in the nursery school because, although a child communicates in other ways—through behavior, dramatic play, art, movement, and facial expressions—with words, a different kind of communication, a two-way one, can be established. When a child tells of something in words, the listener can then respond in words that show understanding of what was said; then the child feels that the emotion behind the words was also shared. Often, when he lets someone know how he feels, a child finds that he and the other person are brought closer together, and this gives him the optimism and confidence to use that way more fully. A solution to a problem can also come from communication in words; sometimes it is a suggestion from the other person, and sometimes a child finds his own answer as he verbally explores his ideas.

- When Eric recognized that he had projected his own feelings onto someone else, he showed an ability to comprehend quite complex relationships and express them verbally.

  He had hit Marjorie one day. "Did Marjorie do something to you?" he was asked. "No," he replied, "but I think she did something to Jannie." (Children have an astonishing ability to understand each other's attitudes. Jannie had been resentful of Marjorie since Jannie's mother had started bringing Marjorie to school in their car.) "Something angry?" said the teacher, feeling her way. "Yes!" said Eric, emphatically. "You could ask Marjorie if she's angry at Jannie," the teacher suggested. Eric went back to Marjorie, by now imperturbably cutting paper at the table. "Are you mad at Jannie?" he asked her, peering into her face. "No," she said, looking surprised, and "Oh," he said, slightly dampened. The teacher then said, "Jannie's mother has been bringing Marjorie to school lately. Do you remember, Eric, when your mother brought Liz to school, and you told her you didn't like her to do things for Liz?" Wheels seemed to turn for a moment, then suddenly he burst into speech. "It's not *Marjorie* that's cross—it's *Jannie*, and" (smiling) "it wasn't *Liz*, it was *me!*"

This example illustrates something else, as well. Eric was not quite four at the time. True, he was bright and verbal, but in the beginning he had done more shouting and crying than talking when he was upset. His ability to work out the above situation did not just come out of the blue. At the time when he was having trouble with his own carpool group, feeling hostile toward Liz because of his reluctance to share his mother with her, he had no idea what was bothering him. But it helped him to talk about his feelings, and he came to understand them. Now he could use his own experience to help him understand someone else. His final statement was in the nature of a generalization, as though he said, "Jannie and I both have the same kind of feeling." First children learn about themselves, then about others. And when one accepts oneself, one is ready to accept others; this is the way it happens.

VII

Nursery school children learn much about relationships with little or no help. The dominant child learns that sometimes people follow his ideas and sometimes they prefer their own. The careless or obtrusive child learns from others' reactions that his ways are not pleasing to people. Most children soon learn that others will object if they intrude on their play, investigate things left in lockers, talk too much when a story is being read, or play the piano when they are listening to the phonograph. Many children show others how they feel readily and effectively, with sufficient confidence and control. Some only need help to find words that say what they mean. Others need some teacher support while they deal with another child, so they can keep their heads, rather than lose their tempers and futilely hit and scream, or withdraw from the situation. But whether without help, with a little, or with a lot, the children learn that people are usually approachable, mean well, will listen, and will respond to appeals. They are learning, also, to reveal themselves honestly, in the expectation that this will have a healing effect on a troubled relationship. This is a faith that cannot be simulated, but, if it is genuinely felt, others, of whatever age, tend to respond to it. Because the teacher's example is the most powerful influence she exerts in the school, if she herself has that faith, she will approach a child who hits, for instance, convinced that he must have had to do so, and expressing her acceptance and wish to help; children who observe this are then learning tolerance, nonjudgmental sympathy, and a belief in another's basic goodwill that is the foundation of all good relationships.

The fact that children (and all other people) have feelings of anger need not create relationship difficulties. The problem is how to handle and express these feelings. A child might annoy another and be told off by him, perhaps with a good deal of feeling. If this anger is expressed clearly — "I'm mad! I didn't like that!" — no help is needed. The emotion arose from an immediate cause and was expressed freely, without harm to anyone. Similarly, someone is bumped or jostled and shouts, "Don't!" A sand castle falls, and Bill stamps his foot and yells some swear words. Irene says to Joe, "I told you and *told* you, we're playing alone!" But "You're a bad boy," "I don't like you," name-calling, and physical attacks indicate that relations have broken down and that communication needs to be reestablished so that mutual trust can be restored. The child needs to bring out his grievance and have the experience of being listened to, understood, and accepted, as will never happen if he limits himself to mere attacks. And a child who can only cry or blow up under stress needs help to express himself more effectively, so that he can cope better with both his own and others' feelings. Perhaps he may even need his teacher to say all the words for him at first, checking as she goes along by saying, "Is that right? Is that what you mean?" and awaiting his nod or shake of the head, so that he is participating as actively as possible.

As the teacher helps the children, she always keeps in mind the time when she will not be with them. Her efforts are thus focused on helping children help themselves. Many school customs, such as that of allowing a child to keep a toy until he decides he is "through," have been established because experience has shown that without them, conflicts develop that children do not have the maturity to solve by themselves. Like traffic rules for adults, these customs permit a variety of activities, with a minimum of dependence and a maximum of self-direction. Children are helped to understand the reasons for the customs and sometimes start new ones; for example, one group devised the plan of checking the jungle gym for shiny raindrops so as to decide for themselves when the playground was dry enough to use after a storm. The two examples that follow show children's progress toward independent management of their relationship problems.

● A problem concerning Bix one day was solved in a way that enabled the children to deal with similar ones later without any aid from the teacher, although there might have been other solutions. He was holding everyone up on the slide by piling sand slowly up from the base of it. The line of waiting children began clamoring for him to "Get out of the way!" But he had been at his sand project before they came, and in many other situations children had learned to defend their right to finish what they had begun. The difference here was that he was one and they were many, and some began to call to the teacher for help, when, in spite of their urging, he went on stolidly shoveling his sand, saying, "I have to make it all the way to the top, first." The children who were waiting began to encourage each other to slide down and wreck his project.

What solution could be suggested that children could use later without a teacher's aid? If the teacher ended Bix's play, this would demonstrate a lack of concern for what he was doing, and, another time, the children would show the same lack of concern by sliding into his sand, angering and alienating him. So, regardless of the number that were waiting at the top of the slide, the teacher reminded them of what they all knew—that no one likes to be interrupted in the middle of something—and said that since finishing the sand project might take him quite a while, perhaps it might be a good idea for them to find something else to do meanwhile. Several children then offered to help Bix. He was agreeable, and this led to some amicable play, the sliding being forgotten. Some days later a group came inside, having handled a problem like that in the same way, leaving Lowell sitting at the top of the slide happily dangling his bare feet over. They felt no apparent animosity. "He wants to sit up there; let's build," said Dennis. That time the teacher was not needed at all.

● Sebastian, Martin, and Norah also managed their problem alone. The three were playing in the sand. Sebastian and Martin were together, and Norah was alone nearby. Martin took Sebastian's shovel, and Sebastian protested, "That's *my* shovel!" with considerable heat. "I know," Martin said, "but you laid it down." "I know I laid it down," Sebastian explained, "but I wanted to use my hand." Martin, accustomed to the kind of listening and reflecting he had heard the teachers do, said to him, "You weren't through?" Sebastian, accustomed to frankly expressing feelings with trust in another's understanding, said, "No, not really. I still want it very badly." "I want it very badly, too," said Martin, and he searched for a solution. "Maybe you could ask Norah for hers." Norah had a shovel, but she didn't seem to want it "very badly." (Children are quite good at judging this kind of thing.) Sebastian went near and looked in her face. The teacher had often demonstrated this intimate approach, as well as using a child's name, to establish contact. "Norah," he said, "Can I have your shovel? I really need one." In this situation a teacher would be ready to help, if necessary, by saying, "Do you really feel like giving it to him, Norah? Are you through?" If Norah gave Sebastian her shovel only out of a notion of the propriety of "sharing," because of a need to buy favor, or out of fear or submissiveness, she would later regret it and resent Sebastian. But having had this kind of help before, she gave some thought to how she really felt; she then said, "Yes, you can have it. I don't think I want to dig any more." "Good!" said the loyal Martin, when Sebastian came back with the shovel. Out of this small incident came an increase in the friendliness between Martin and Sebastian, and also between them and Norah.

When a child has the kind of teaching described in this chapter, he discovers that the frank expression of one person's feelings to another contributes much to their relationship. It can bridge gaps, clear away misunderstandings, communicate a desire for closeness and acceptance, indicate trust in the other's fairness and reasonableness, and most of all, demonstrate that the relationship means enough to the person to make him want to be rid of his negative feelings and go on with it. After all, he could just walk away—having things out is much more trouble. But relationships between young children become deeper and more meaningful to them when they learn not to just walk away, and each such experience increases their confidence both in themselves and in other people.

6 The Evolution of a Social Group

Pretend I was very tiny,
Growing inside my mother,
'Till I was big enough to come out.

Everyone came to see me coming out;
Then suddenly I became your sister,
And everyone started to love me!
—Kathy Jo

I

In studying a group's social configurations and the problems in so-cial learning among its members, the developmental stages through which young children pass in forming relationships need to be kept in mind. The aim of the teacher is to facilitate a child's progress from one stage to the next while maintaining basic feelings of security. She is not very concerned about what stage a child is in at a particular age. As long as his current stage is being well experienced, he will move on to the next, given the necessary social setting.

The first stage is peripheral play; the child is engaged in his own activities on the outskirts of the group. Because other children are in the environment, however, this is different from playing altogether alone, even though the child rarely looks at the others and seems uninterested in them or even negatively affected by them. During the stage of his peripheral play, he gradually becomes used to the sound of their voices, to their movements, and to the rhythm of their activi-ties, and learns to feel at ease playing in the same area they are using. As he becomes more comfortable, he will begin to show an interest in what they are doing and saying. The peripheral stage is being passed through well if the child is making use of the toys and other materials in a flexible and imaginative way, if his interest is high, and if his attention span is adequate and not easily disrupted by minor frustrations. It is important not to hurry a child through this phase. If it is made rich and meaningful, the child is developing many inner resources. These will make it possible for him to play alone when, later, his friend or friends at times perhaps turn toward others. And throughout his life, his relationships will be more sound if he does not weight them with too much dependence but can find sources of satisfaction in private expressions of his own nature and talents.

The second stage is parallel play. The child now plays side by side with one or more others, though not yet particularly caring which children they are. There is more awareness of the nearby playmates, and the child prefers being close to others to being in corners or on the edge of the playing space. Parallel players engage in side-by-side activity with little or no interaction. There is increased pleasure in the play if others are involved in it too; more verbalizing is one sign of this, though the child seldom listens to anyone else as he talks to himself about what he is doing. There is an increase, also, in "Me, too," when the parallel player sees that someone has material he would like; formerly he would not have particularly noticed. Learning from other children now begins, too; the child picks up others' ideas and imitates their words and phrases. This is a stage for conflicts over toys; the child sees a toy as more important to him than the child who may be using it. The parallel-play stage is being passed through successfully if the child finds pleasure in others' company without making demands on them, if he learns to accept their behavior and not be disturbed or distracted from his own aims by it, and if he learns to respect their privacy and protect his own.

The child then enters what could be called the twosome stage. He becomes aware of a particular person beside whom he has been playing in a parallel fashion and begins to follow him or her about. Toys are exchanged, and so are remarks, and the children use one another's names, sit together for painting or stories, go outdoors and indoors together, and eat snacks together. Now there is less talking to oneself and more listening to the answer, and "Let's" is frequently used. The twosome stage varies greatly in length among individuals. If a child has already experienced it at home with a friend close to his own age whom he enjoyed, he may not spend much time in it at school, forming shifting twosomes, or even attempting triangles, almost at once. With many children, however, the twosome may be the child's first close tie after those with his family, and provide him with a unique opportunity to grow in his sense of identity and feelings of worth apart from his home relationships. The stage is well passed through if the children's feelings for each other deepen steadily and their association is mutually satisfying.

It is important to help children strengthen these ties through home visits and, if at all possible, maintain them after they leave nursery school. Through caring about another child and trying to keep his friendship, real social learning takes place. The child uses his special acuity in regard to another's feelings; he learns to talk things over with someone, because he is strongly motivated toward communication and the resolution of tensions that may occur in the friendship; he studies and accepts differences between another person and himself. All these experiences lay a foundation for later friendships and for marriage. Group experiences help in other ways, but not in these one-to-one situations which make for so much happiness or unhappiness later. For these reasons this stage, too, is not to be hurried; the child will move on to the next one when he has consolidated enough growth and may well enter it along with his friend, carrying the twosome relationship gains with him.

The next stage is that of shifting pairs and triangles. The child now has more than one relationship in the group, but at the beginning of the stage he still plays most comfortably with only one child at a time. As he makes a second friend, he has a resource when his first companion does likewise, and the two pairs can play together in what is better called a double twosome than a group. Triangles are sometimes formed too now, and this is the last and most difficult hurdle before true group play. Because the child at this age is probably involved in triangles at home, they are hard to bear. But as the third member of the school triangle also becomes familiar — not a rival and stranger but a possible friend for him, too — the child can begin to be comfortable in a threesome. This is the same process that is taking place at home; his deepening relationship with his father is helping him give up the exclusiveness of the twosome with his mother, and his discovery of his sibling as a possible playmate for himself helps the child to accept him or her in a threesome with either parent.

The last stage is that of the group. Once a new triangle becomes bearable, it becomes stimulating (sometimes overstimulating), and many new activities can take place. The shifting triangle, in which the third member was now a child's own second friend and now that of his twosome partner, merges into an acceptance of both their alternate friends at the same time, to create a foursome. From then on, the link from one stage of security to the next is easily seen; each arrival is a friend of a friend of a friend. All these people can be accepted because the feeling of social comfort with the first friend carries through to the outer rim of the circle. In true group play, four, five, or six children play together in a highly interactive way, with every member having his own role and much cooperation, feedback, discussion or argument, assistance, advice, compromise, and input of ideas. Learning is proceeding in all of these areas for the group. The "we" feeling that this group play produces makes possible more organization and planning of their own activities, as well as more self-direction. If all goes well, toward the end of the nursery school period children have developed enough security in their relationships with other group members to cease spending most of their energy on interactions and turn their attention outward toward common goals.

The child is moving well through the group-play period if he is able to maintain the independent, creative thinking that he used in the peripheral stage, the enjoyment of others' closeness without too much overstimulation that he experienced in the parallel-play stage, the ability to work through disagreements for the sake of maintaining a relationship that he learned in the twosome stage, and the tolerance of competition and rivalry that he developed during the triangle period. The group stage itself can then give him a chance to learn how to remain himself and to speak and act as such without being overwhelmed by group opinions or group emotions, making his own unique contribution.

II

A group of nursery school children is always composed of a wide variety of individuals. They represent not only many stages of social development but also very different personalities. In spite of this, the emergence, little by little, of a social structure can be seen, as in the group of eighteen three- and four-year-olds in their first semester of nursery school described in this chapter. Of these children, Hal, Janie, Alice, Patrick, and David, the first of the group to be discussed, needed little or no help from the teachers and were themselves of help to others socially.

● Fair-haired, smiling Hal contributed to the group from the moment he entered some time after the others in the fall. A friendly four-year-old, he was unusually free from competitiveness and interested in everyone. Of all the children, he was the only one really ready for group play at that time. His favorite words were "we" and "us." He liked a group around him; in fact, he was apt to invite more children to join him than could really play together, and sometimes this made problems for him. It was "come one, come all" for Hal.

- Four-year-old Janie remained from first to last a comfortable little person to be around. She had a good deal of insight into other people's feelings; all such learning seemed to come easily to her. In fact, Janie appeared to take life easily in general. Wherever she was, Janie, with her dark braids and chubby red cheeks, projected an aura of peace about her, whether playing contentedly alone or with her special friends.

- Though most of Alice's play was still parallel, at three and a half she seemed to be on the border of the twosome stage. A long period when she and her older brother Miles played only with each other at home had perhaps held her back; because of his own need for companionship, he had taken her over and made their play decisions. Miles and Alice were enrolled together. At first they spoke only to each other, and in whispers. Apparently not as dependent on him as he was on her, Alice was able to remain steady while Miles gradually emancipated himself, and as soon as he left her free to do so, she moved into parallel play with other children. Through her interests in painting, sand and water play, swinging, and doll dressing, she became more aware of the younger girls and they of her. Her flexibility and agreeable disposition made her a resource for them; they often moved their toys close to her, or sat by her at story time.

- Patrick, a sturdy three-year-old, was usually happily busy, singing and talking in the charming monologue style of the parallel-player. He loved toys, and it was hard for him to wait for a favorite one; the play materials needed some replenishing to keep his progress smooth and satisfying in this period. Gradually he began to notice Angus, whose name he frequently used in talking to himself. A transition from parallel play to a warm twosome with Angus was harmonious, and they began to follow each other about, indoors, out, and back again, with contented play in a variety of forms. Patrick's good-humored sociability made him acceptable to the older boys, too, who were often building with blocks near where he played. They sometimes asked him to bring them loads of blocks in his truck. But he was happy just playing beside them, either alone or with Angus, never trying to work his way into their play or intrude upon them. He seemed to know his own needs, and, if a group became too large or the play too complex, would depart.

● David was a highly intelligent, verbal, imaginative four-year-old. He was always doing something interesting, and everyone admired him. He was very soon involved in a twosome with Chip, which then became a magnetic center for group play. He was especially interested in boats, and a "sail" was attached to the jungle gym where he and Chip, with Babette and Hal, in a double twosome, spent much of their time for a while. David possessed the information and vocabulary to make his dramatic play rich, but he also had the problem many very bright children have; he was not mature enough emotionally to handle some ideas for which he was ready intellectually. Some care was needed in answering his questions: for example, to "Do sharks bite people?" the teacher just said, "That wouldn't happen to *you*, David, because your mother and father take very good care of you" (which they did), and this satisfied him, because his real question had been "Am I safe?" With Melanie, Roddie, and Miles occasionally joining the boat play as swimming fish, divers, people needing "rescue," and fishermen, David became a very important member of the group. He was devoted to Chip. He also liked Hal, whose easy good humor was sometimes a relief from the mercurial Chip. Melanie and he seemed to have a private bond, and Miles and Roddie were always ready to join play sparked by David.

III

There were other children in the group who needed help initially from the teacher before they could move ahead socially. All of them were potentially capable of contributing a good deal to the group, and not much time passed before they were on their way.

● Three-year-old Rosie looked and acted younger than she was. She was chubby and rather resembled a doll. When sought out by Livy, as often happened, she responded with a shy smile, then dropped her head. It took Rosie a while each day to let her mother and baby sister leave her. When her mother was there, if the teacher spoke to her, she would hide her face in her mother's skirt. But after she was left, she would climb into the teacher's lap and say, "I like you." She was unable to handle the two relationships at once, apparently.

As time went on, Rosie let her mother go more easily, no longer requiring the teacher's lap. She would suck her thumb and stand around watching for a while. It seemed important to allow her this time and not to hurry her or take the initiative away from her by offering suggestions. She had begun to bring a snack from home in a large lunch box, and she made a little ceremony of eating it. This, too, was a parallel activity at first, but soon she began sharing her food with others at a table. As sometimes happens when a child seems smaller and younger, the other children enjoyed petting and helping her, and Rosie warmed to this. Perhaps it helped her feel less envious of her baby sister. Each day she seemed less shy, and she was often surrounded with children on all sides in the sandbox, leaving, one would think, scarcely room enough to play.

- Tad, at three, was a child who, with everything hitherto in his favor, was temporarily delayed in social development because something happened to him that he had to work out first. Some traumas, especially those involving the loss of a loved person, will cause a child to hold back from forming new relationships. A cousin of whom Tad had been fond, a boy near his own age, had been killed in a car accident. In his play at school, Tad kept on the periphery of the group, playing with the toy people. He had them be killed by cars and in other ways, carried away in the toy ambulance, brought back, and killed all over again. He was not withdrawn, however, and would often look up at the teacher and explain what was happening, and the presence of other children did not disturb him. The teacher continued to be aware of and responsive to his play, and eventually there was no need to have the favorite little wooden boy brought back again. One day it was carried away by the ambulance to the toy shelf, and Tad left it there. With the end of his preoccupation, Tad left the peripheral-play stage and moved ahead to parallel play, with steadily growing interest in being near others.

• Melanie, four years old, began with a bossy manner toward teachers and children. At home she was the youngest of four girls, accustomed to being waited on, it seemed. She would say, "Get me the bucket!" "Bring me a green crayon. Didn't you hear me? I said a green one!" "Here! Hang up my jacket." The teacher rephrased these demands, making them into requests: "Would you get me the bucket?" "I wanted the green crayon, O.K.?" "Will you hang up my jacket for me, please?" Immediately after the rephrasing, the teacher answered her own words, "Yes, surely, Melanie." Similarly, to "Come here!" shouted at the teacher across the playground, she demonstrated calling her name, then answered that with "Yes, Melanie?"

As Melanie became accustomed to speaking to the teacher in a different way, an opportunity arose to help her transfer this learning to her dealings with the children. David had told Melanie, "Get out of here!" when she approached the swing. "Melanie," the teacher said then, "Does it make you feel like doing what he says when he tells you that way?" "No!" David caught on. "Please go away, Melanie," he told her, "I'm not through with the swing." "How about now? Do you feel more like doing it now?" "Yes, I do." "I guess most people would rather be asked, instead of told, to do something," the teacher said. And another time she said, "Melanie, I wonder if you think people won't do anything for you unless you yell at them." A thoughtful look came over Melanie's face. "Do you know," the teacher told her, "I think lots of times they would; I think they would *want* to."

This last idea proved to be true. Melanie spent many a peaceful Indian summer day making tiny gardens of sand, decorated with twigs, pebbles, petals, and leaves, all by herself. Perhaps there was little privacy at home in her big family and shared bedroom. Her gardens were like a miniature kingdom of her own, and she received much attention and admiration from the other children for them, which, like a little queen, she seemed to accept as her due. As time went on, she began to look more and more like a true introvert, for whom few friends are needed. She gave up her bossy manner and began to show an affectionate concern for the children she liked. "Taddy's face isn't happy," she might say to the teacher, or "I think David needs you," and she took it upon herself to tie shoes after barefoot days, since she could do this with her clever fingers and most of the other children couldn't. She also began to give away some of her gardens in boxes as presents and was provided with tissue and ribbon for this purpose. Melanie thus became a member of the social group in her own personal way, after she was given a little help with her way of speaking and her need for privacy was respected. Though, as with all introverts, Melanie's inner life was still of most importance to her, she was capable of relating warmly to a few friends — David, Lucia, and Roddie — and she felt protective toward Tad.

● Three-year-old Angus needed help to make a smooth transition from his close tie with his mother to new relationships. The teacher provided a little initial assistance, and his own readiness for parallel play — and Patrick — did the rest.

On his first day at school, Angus's mother stayed in the waiting room within sight. He remained seated in one spot on the floor all morning. The teacher brought toys over, consulting with him as to what he needed, and he chose the fire engine. Whenever another child was nearby, she used his or her name — "Here's Tad; he's playing with the car he likes" — to give Angus a chance to begin to recognize a few individuals in what must have seemed an amorphous crowd.

The second day, Angus brought some animal crackers. At first he held them on his lap or kept them close as he played. His mother left as soon as he was settled in the spot where he had sat before, with his fire engine beside him. Later on, juice was served on a table near him. When the size of the group was reduced to only two, he joined them to eat his crackers. Asked for some, he doled them out, looking important. Again, the teacher used names: "Here are Angus and Tad and Patrick, all eating crackers, like a party. A party for three."

The following day, Angus chose a new toy, a train. However, like himself, it didn't go anywhere. To help him extend his spatial range a little, the teacher, guessing that he now felt secure at the snack table, put a basket of small cars there. Small toys sometimes help a timid child feel big, and perhaps he also feels that what he does with them can be more private. He stood by a chair awhile, fingering the cars, then sat down to play. If anyone stopped to watch, he looked distressed, and the teacher helped him by saying, "You want to play by yourself?" to which he would nod.

The day after that, when Angus arrived, he opened the outside gate by himself, waving his mother away rather peremptorily. Coming in alone, he went at once to the table where the small cars were waiting. While the teacher sat near, he took a car and hid it from her, smiling. "Where can it be?" she said, smiling too, "Is it coming back?" With many chuckles he brought it out, then hid it again, over and over. "See, it came back," he said each time. Realizing that on this day Angus had taken a new step in making the separation from his mother, the teacher picked up a second car and said, "This orange car wonders where it's gone." Angus seized upon this idea enthusiastically. "He'll be surprised," he said, "Here it is back! And now here they *both* are, together again." During this day Angus took several important steps. He spent a long time in parallel play with Patrick at the table and on the floor, and when music was being played, turned solemnly round and round in the middle of the floor. He was also able to go out to the playground, holding the teacher's hand, and settle himself in a new security spot in the sandbox. Having let his mother go, trusting they would soon be "together again," he could apparently begin to move toward other relationships.

As time went on, the true Angus appeared—busy, animated, and very talkative. Like Tad and Patrick, he loved all trucks, cars, and trains, an interest that always makes an easy bridge from parallel to twosome play. Gradually Angus and Patrick had been progressing in this direction. Now each often talked about the other at home. They spent most of their time at school together, with Angus playing and chattering, and Patrick playing and listening, nodding his head and saying, "Yes, Angus, you do!" or "Yes, you sure are!" as Angus talked about what he was doing.

- Livy, three and a half, was eager and outgoing. She seemed to be playing the role of mother or teacher fairly consistently. She always smiled at shy little Rosie, and she promptly took Miles and his little sister Alice under her wing; she used to try to gather them up and "read" to them or tell them what to play. The four-year-old girls, often playing mothers in the doll corner, particularly interested Livy, but her attempts to join them were usually unsuccessful because she was inclined to walk into their play uninvited and then stand about and get in the way, at her younger age not really ready for their complicated social interactions, in spite of her interest.

Livy had high standards for everyone's behavior. The teacher assured her that they were all learning, and she seemed to find this reassuring. That her high standards also applied to herself was soon seen. One day, in imitation of the teacher, she tried to move a tray and spilled juice over her dress and the floor. She turned very pale. The teacher helped her clean up, then held her awhile, saying that everyone, even grown-ups now and then did something that turned out to be a mistake. "My mommy and daddy don't," Livy said. The teacher replied, "Well, I put Rosie's doll in Mary Ann's locker, and that was a mistake." Then Livy offered, "And my mommy forgot to iron my panties that go with my striped dress." At story time that day, M. M. Green's book, *Is It Hard? Is It Easy?* (1948) was read, in which some things are shown to be hard and some easy for everyone, and the teacher added that for her, ice skating was very hard. This opened the way for several children to offer similar support for the idea that no one found everything easy.

Gradually Livy's high standards became more realistic. When she failed to do something—climb into a swing that was hooked up too high or put together a difficult puzzle—she would sometimes catch the teacher's eye and say, smiling, "I think that's too hard for me," and try something easier. Along with more self-acceptance, as one would expect, came more acceptance of others. Now, in hindsight, it was clear why other children so often failed to satisfy her behavior requirements, why she tried so persistently to join the older girls and thus prove herself their equal, and why, with Rosie, Miles, and Alice, she liked to play in ways that made her feel superior. As she learned to accept herself better, she began to find ties with those of her own age. She enjoyed three-year-old cooking play with Rosie and later formed a bond with Mary Ann, because they shared unusually good physical coordination. Now more relaxed, Livy showed her sociable nature successfully, and began to be an occasional third in a triangle with the older children, in addition to enjoying her shifting twosomes.

IV

Three of this group of eighteen children needed a short period of more concentrated, intensive help.

● When Chip first started school at four, he was very excited by the children and attracted to them, but also very uneasy. He would dash in among them, scattering their toys or blocks, laughing wildly, then run away again. His behavior was both a greeting and a provocation. He was, at all events, certainly bidding for their attention. The teacher's limits on Chip's behavior at that time were combined with suggestions of other play outlets. When he threw toys, for instance, a "throwing place" was arranged for him in the waiting room, cleared to permit him to use Ping-Pong balls, a soft wool ball, and some plastic airplanes. Throwing, however, had been to tease, and, like much of his other behavior, after being permitted, it soon dropped out. The teacher also drew his verbal teasing toward herself, away from the children, so no one would turn against him during this period. When Chip upset Patrick and Roddie by saying, "*I'm* Patrick," and "*I'm* Roddie — *you* aren't," she would say, smiling, "And are you also Mrs. Snoochick?" (his teasing name for her), and this helped to show the children that one needn't take such jibes seriously. The teacher often responded to Chip's sudden lashing out at others by picking him up and reassuring him, realizing that he might feel very frightened of his own loss of control, or of possible punishment or retribution. She would hold him and say, "It's all right, Chip. I'm taking care of you. I won't let you hurt anybody, and I won't let anybody hurt you, either." He sometimes seemed near to panic at such times.

Chip's excitement seemed in part due to his need to test the teacher — dangerously, he thought — in order to find out about her. "What would you do if I broke all the toys, and things like that?" he asked her. "Would you get angry at me?" With the question out in the open finally, the teacher could give him the answer quite simply. "If I didn't want you to do something, I'd stop you, and then I wouldn't have anything to get angry about." She felt that Chip was afraid he might go too far some day, and wanted him to know that she would take care of him and keep him in bounds. He went on, then. "But what if I tried to do it again?" "I'd stop you again," she told him, "But here's something else about that. I'd go on liking you." Weeks later, Chip was heard explaining to Hal on his first day, "You won't do anything bad in this school. The teachers don't spank, they *stop*."

Shortly after Chip felt assured of protection and acceptance by the teacher, David, who was looking for a special friend, came into his life. Chip's social seeking was now satisfied, and his needs for power and dominance were expressed in the rich dramatic play that blossomed between the two of them. Teasing of other children dropped out as soon as Chip had David. One of the ideas behind his behavior had probably been "Any kind of attention is better than none"; fearful and lonely, he found it devastating to be ignored. A new baby at home had been part of his problem, and exclusive attention from David was balm, restoring his feeling of being lovable and important.

Chip had always been easily overstimulated, even as an infant, but when he felt more secure with the teachers and grew accustomed to being with children in school, he was less excitable there. He continued his solid twosome with David, and as time went on a third was sometimes added, usually Hal or Miles. Chip had trouble accepting these additions; he needed to find some security with the intruder himself if he was not to think of him as a threatening and unwelcome rival. Miles usually waited to be invited by David before approaching their twosome, but Hal, who made many friendly overtures to everyone, was more and more often in the picture. The teacher tried to find opportunities for Chip and Hal to play undisturbed with some kind of interesting material easily shared, so as to give Chip a chance to see Hal as a possible friend for him, as well as for David. This can help such jealousy in much the same way as a boy's resentment of his father's relationship with his mother is helped by more intimacy with father. As little boys often do, Chip had fallen in love with David, his very first friend, and the possessiveness he felt was passionate. Some attention to shifts of the various pairings was leading to more periods of unconflicted triangles, however, and when Chip wanted to have David to himself on occasion, someone else was always ready to play with Hal, and he, outgoing as he was, with that person. Double pairings were also common, as Hal and Babette combined forces with Chip and David. Gradually, with David's support, Chip too began to move toward true group play.

● When first seen, Miles walked like a little old man, with fingers extended and stiff, and with tense, jerky movements. He looked at the teacher when she spoke to him with mouth open and eyes blank. He was four and a half, but still needed help at the toilet and with wraps, and he used crayons and paints at almost the same developmental level as his three-year-old sister Alice. Miles never sought help from the teacher, however. He even looked a little anxious when it was offered and got away as soon as he could. Most important, he never spoke, although he whispered to Alice.

Though in some ways Miles resembled a retarded child, there were inconsistencies that made one discount that impression. Miles learned which were his and Alice's lockers the first day and took care of both their possessions. And obviously he could talk if he wanted to; his whispers to Alice were apparently complete and meaningful communications. It seemed probable that his having had only Alice as a playmate had deprived him of opportunities for social learning at his own age level. At school he stayed close to her, but play that he soon began suggested that he resented this dependence and the way it limited him and sought to free himself.

When Miles and Alice were in and around the swings one day, he buried a rubber girl doll in wet sand over and over again. The teacher, noticing his frown as he did this, said, "You're making her go away; you don't want to see her." To this he nodded, his first direct response. Then he pulled the doll out, smiling, "Now she can come," said the teacher, and he nodded again. Then suddenly he threw the doll over the playground fence and ran to the swing. "All gone! Now you'll play," the teacher said, and he nodded and smiled. For some days he focused all his play around the swing, ignoring Alice placidly playing nearby. He would hide the doll in the bushes before swinging, or, taking it with him, he would throw it over the fence when his swing reached its highest point. Sometimes he would sit under the swing, burying and dirtying the doll, forcing sand into its eyes and mouth, then digging it up again and pounding it with a shovel.

The competence with which Miles used the swing now began to develop by leaps and bounds. Steadily he outdistanced his sister. He learned to pump, then to raise and lower the seat, then to hook a second swing seat above the first one and climb up into it. Finally he was able to climb to the standard itself from the high swing seat, then to work his way from there to sit atop the fence by the swing set. Great admiration came from the other children at this feat. He spent all his time for many a session in and around the swings. Next, linking his successful swing venture to a new experience, he began leaping from the moving swing, each time coming closer to the jungle gym. Then he began to play there as well. He climbed, swung by his hands on the bars, slid down the attached slide facing frontwards and backwards, and drew up buckets of sand with a pulley, meanwhile surrounded by children. And now, at last, Miles's voice was heard. First he spoke aloud to Alice, then he called to her across the playground, then he talked to the teacher in a soft voice, and finally he spoke to other children, too, sometimes even noisily. At length, one day, he told Alice that he was "going to play with Babette, now," and from then on he left her for longer and longer periods. At that time he said he only liked girls, but soon afterward he began to watch David's play, hovering about his group with the greatest interest.

Miles continued to grow socially as he grew in self-assurance. A child without a father, he seemed to look on David as a masculine ideal. He was still not very self-assertive, waiting to be asked to play; however, though David was Miles's leader in dramatic play, Miles could do much more with his lanky body. He climbed a rope to the top of the jungle gym and then slid down. And it astonished David that Miles could hang by his knees. "I'm scared to do that," he told Miles admiringly. Miles, David, and Hal or Chip would often swing in tandem style by adding an extra seat between the two swings, and the three of them would then see how far they could jump out.

● Most groups have a child like Mary Ann, who ignored the other children completely and followed the teacher around. She frequently said, "What shall I do now?" as though unable to get under way without adult suggestion or direction. She asked many questions of the kind that were hard to answer, because the answer seemed obvious: "What are you doing?" "Washing the glasses." "Why?" "So they'll be clean for next time." "Why?" What she seemed to want, rather than answers, was a cozy chat. The teacher tried to let Mary Ann into her own thoughts by answering as fully as possible. "Well, I thought I'd do the glasses now, because if I get them done early, then, in case people want some dancing later, I'll be free to play the piano for them." As the teacher's answers became more expansive, Mary Ann responded to their closer relationship by becoming more talkative herself. "I wanted to wear my Sunday dress today, but my mother thought it would be better to wear this one, because my Sunday dress needed a button sewed on, but I like my Sunday dress better, and I thought—" and so on.

After this kind of relating had gone on awhile, with Mary Ann standing around passively, the teacher offered her a sponge so she could help wash the tables before juice time. Mary Ann also helped pick up toys. For a while activity identified with the teacher was all she engaged in, but, as she was drawn into putting beads back in their basket, sorting doll clothes for the drawers, washing paste brushes, and so on, she became familiar with the school materials and their possibilities. However, she had no play ideas; in fact, she was unable to play.

Gradually, helping prepare art materials drew Mary Ann into using them. When she and the teacher were trying out felt pens, she achieved some markings and put them into her locker. In scraping excess paste from brushes, another time, she said it was "too sticky," and she and the teacher experimented with thinning it, testing their mixture for pasting tissue, feathers, ribbons, and other materials. Mary Ann kept some of these results, too. Then she moved ahead another step. "What shall I do?" was answered one day by "Let's look around and see what we have," and she made her own choice—to do some art work. Choosing the medium requiring the fewest decisions, she stamped neat rows of circles with a printing block, using one color only. But her progress was steady—more shapes, then more colors, then crayoning and pasting around the shapes, then, some days later, the printing discarded for free drawing. Her first paintings were done on very small papers at the same table, using small brushes and a paint box. Then, interested in going outside to use paints on larger pieces of paper, as well as clay, she no longer followed the teacher about.

For Mary Ann, art activity became a special pleasure, but, in addition, it helped her at this time to develop a sense of her own identity. It was she who made the choices about how something should look, and "I decided" became a favorite phrase. Further relaxation, as in the use of finger paints (when she allowed her hands to get dirty and even needed more washing up afterward than anyone else) indicated still more readiness to be herself, not holding back. As she began to experience herself as a person separate from others in this peripheral play, she could let her impulses go with more confidence. "I chose green because I felt like it" could lead to readiness to choose a doll, a toy, and eventually a child as playmate.

Outdoors, Mary Ann discovered that she could pump in the swing like Livy. Parallel play there led to other experiences in climbing and sliding. Since she and Livy shared these physical skills, they often found themselves in a parallel-play situation, and Livy's eager interest in other children began to play a part in enlarging Mary Ann's sphere of social interaction.

V

Agatha, Lucia, Babette, Roddie, and Quincy all had difficult social development problems, causing the most teacher concern and necessitating the most attention. Quincy's difficulties, in fact, were not solved when he was withdrawn at mid-year, though he had made some progress.

● Agatha had a stormy social adjustment. She was a vivid, dynamic four-year-old who sought friends and could attract other children to her. Though she had been happy as a baby with her warm, responsive mother, when she became aware of herself, an only child, as one of a triangle at home, problems started. She became upset over her parents' quarreling, taking now one side and now the other. She also tried to keep their attention constantly focused on her and off each other, since the tension between them made her fear new conflicts might arise at any time.

In school, Agatha's first choice was Lucia, also four years old. When anyone came near them, she would immediately say, "*We* don't like *her*, do we, Lucia?" and push or pinch the intruder. But even when she had Lucia to herself, she would play in a twosome only briefly. It became clear that she really wanted two friends at once, just as she wanted to possess both parents, so she used charm and persuasion to attract other children. She would manipulate a triangle in all kinds of ways, inviting a third girl, then rejecting her, then suddenly leaving Lucia with "Now Janie's my friend, and I'm never going to play with you again." A cloud of unhappy feelings followed Agatha wherever she went. "*We* think *you're* ugly," she would say to someone, or "*We* don't *like* boys." Always she used her tie with one child to punish the third of any triangle by showing how united she and her friend were. "Don't we, Lucia?" or "Aren't we, Janie?" followed most remarks. A game in which she might have been expressing her resentment of the parents' intimacy that excluded her involved hiding something with Lucia and telling a third child, "*We* won't show *you* what *we* have," of course calling attention to their secret this way. Similarly she would often whisper something, then say, "I won't tell *you* what I told her." Her aim, apparently, was always to have an intimate twosome, but, to make it more enjoyable, two should exclude and arouse the envy or jealousy of a third — in fact, she continually reproduced a triangle exactly like the one at home.

Children are remarkably patient. They responded again and again to Agatha's invitations to play and went away for the most part philosophically when rejected, sometimes rubbing pinched arms. At length their ability to deal with her was demonstrated in a dramatic way. Agatha had again pinched Livy, who had approached her while she was playing with Lucia, and Livy had gone away hastily. Agatha had also pinched Janie the day before. The teacher felt Livy and Janie probably needed to express their resentment of this treatment and suggested they talk things over with Agatha. They went to her resolutely. Janie began it. "Agatha, you don't need to *pinch* me. You can just *tell* me what you want, and I'll do it. If I *can*, I'll *do* it. You can say 'I just want to play with Lucia,' and I'll go away. Of *course* I will." Livy took it up. "I don't like no more pinching — no more! It makes my arm red. No more!" Agatha listened seriously. Lucia, who had been hovering near, offered support. *"I'll* help you, Agatha," she said. *"I'll* help you remember not to do that." "How do you feel about it, Agatha?" the teacher asked, to give her a chance to defend herself. But no argument came. "I won't any more," she said earnestly to the children. "I'm all through."

Later that same day, for the first time a triangle—Agatha, Lucia, and Janie—played in the doll corner for a long time, with only one problem, occasioned by Chip's throwing a paper towel at them across the screen. Agatha and Lucia came to the teacher to report this. "Well, I expect after that talk about pinching you understand what helps," she replied. They ran back, Agatha in the lead, saying, "You don't have to *throw* things at us if you're mad, Chip. You can just *tell* us." And peace descended again. But no miracle had happened. At story time Agatha, wanting to sit next to the teacher, was heard whispering to Lucia, "Pinch Rosie, so she'll move over." "Oh, Agatha," Lucia said, smiling and shrugging her shoulders. "It's not Lucia who's feeling pinchy," said the teacher, smiling too. Agatha, having given up pinching, was trying to delegate it to someone else; hostility was still there and would have to be expressed in other ways for some time to come. But she was really impressed. Her first words when her mother arrived to pick her up were "Oh, Mommy—know what? I'm all through pinching!"—rather to her mother's bewilderment. But even more important than Agatha's overcoming this disturbing habit was her being able to take the first step in belonging to a friendly triangle. On that day, apparently, Agatha's past learning became consolidated, and her growth took a leap forward. That this could occur seemed a good augur for the future. Without such learning, Agatha would soon provoke counter-hostility; then her need to punish rivals and be possessive about her love objects could only increase.

At the same time, surely playing a part in the changing behavior of Agatha, there had been a conversation between mother and daughter. Her mother had rebelled at Agatha's demanding, manipulative, controlling ways, and had made her feelings about this clear. Then she had said, "And can't you just not get so upset when daddy and I fuss? It has nothing to do with you." Agatha, by now accustomed to sorting out feelings at school in many a "What are you mad about?" encounter, had gone further on her own. She had said to her mother, "And when I'm mad at you and you're mad at me, it has nothing to do with daddy, and when daddy and I are mad, it has nothing to do with you. Or the cat."

As the school term proceeded, Agatha played mostly with Lucia and Janie, usually in turn, in shifting twosomes, but increasingly in triangles. Sometimes she sought Melanie or Babette when the others were busy; she was not very happy playing alone. She still wanted control of her relationships, though there was less hostility in the way she managed this need. She would require some special help before she could move on toward group play. In her sporadic efforts to join groups, her efforts to control and manipulate them led to their division into factions and then to their breaking up. But Agatha was potentially a catalytic agent for group play, like David. The fact that, in spite of her occasional unpleasantness to them, other children would usually drop anything to play with her showed her social gifts.

To help Agatha move from her present stage, to which she was bound by emotional problems, the teacher developed a closer tie with her, so that talk and dramatic play with family dolls could relieve her social relations of some of their load. Agatha created vivid play dramas with the dolls, and also dictated stories that she could illustrate in her own way with crayons. Another gain from these activities was that, once started, Agatha learned to carry them on by herself, playing with the dolls or drawing and coloring. In that way she could return to the peripheral stage and develop what she had failed to find then—resources within herself. She was learning to manipulate and control materials, rather than people, for self-expression and would, in the end, be less dependent on her friends and less demanding in their company.

● Moody Lucia was sought out by Agatha at once, perhaps because Lucia was rather tall for her age and thus had status in Agatha's eyes. But Lucia was after a twosome tie. When Agatha left her, she pouted and withdrew, and Agatha soon learned she could control Lucia by her need, and would threaten "Then I won't play with you" if Lucia ventured to differ with her. Lucia seemed unable to reply to this ultimatum, as, for example, Janie did when she said, "But you see, Agatha, I want to *play* with you, but I don't want to be the *sister* all the time." In such a dilemma, Lucia always gave in.

It was felt that Lucia needed to work out a better relationship with an adult before she could have a really satisfying one with a child. With the teachers, too, she withdrew and pouted, attempting a kind of emotional blackmail, rather than dealing directly with any problems that arose. She had frequent upset times that she either couldn't or wouldn't explain; she would sit in her locker, then, with her face covered by her jacket. On some occasions she seemed reluctant to come in the door on arrival, and on others she resisted going home at dismissal time.

Each time the teacher found Lucia sitting in her locker pouting, she went to her. She said she knew something was bothering Lucia and she thought Lucia would be able to tell her about it, if not right then, perhaps later. Even though no answer was forthcoming, the teacher thought it would be helpful for Lucia to know she was interested; Lucia might then ponder the teacher's question "What is making you unhappy?" and be ready to answer another time. The teacher also tried to sit by Lucia or hold her on her lap when possible, so as to give her many chances to confide. Finally a breakthrough came one day, when the teacher, finding the swing beside Lucia's empty, began to swing with her. "Do you know why I was so unhappy yesterday?" Lucia asked her. (It had really been several days ago.) "My daddy went away, and I don't like him to go away. When that happens, I don't want to go to school, and I don't want to go home. When my daddy gets cross, I'm afraid he'll hit somebody or—, or—" "Something else?" "*Or he won't come back.*"

Lucia's father and mother could now help her understand the

realities of her father's frequent business trips. She learned, too, that feelings—her own and her daddy's, too—could be expressed without something terrible happening. For this highly intelligent four-year-old, verbalizing her worries and fears, and later her anger, proved to be the bridge to healthier social relations. How could Lucia, earlier, have let Agatha go away from her, since, like daddy, she might never come back? She had no choice but to agree to everything or become immobilized when threatened with "Then I won't play with you," but, understandably, she felt dominated and abused. Her pouting had been to get even in the only way she could. It had said, "Then I'll leave *you*" (withdraw).

Now progress was continuous. After clarifying with her teacher what she wanted to communicate, she was able to return, fortified, to any conflict. In this way she learned to deal directly with Agatha, and with others also, instead of retreating to pout when in a tight spot. Less fearful of permanent rejection, she could also accept a substitute twosome mate. Melanie's play outdoors interested her, and she would sometimes leave her difficult friend to sit by Melanie quietly or help her with her gardens. Livy, who frankly admired Lucia as "the big girl" was a help, too. Lucia needed a more secure twosome experience before she could progress much further. This might happen with Janie, her long-time sympathizer and supporter. Janie wouldn't woo Lucia; that wasn't her way. But neither was she a deserter; she was loyal, and that would be a helpful change for Lucia.

● Babette, a four-year-old, was an extrovert, but somehow an unsatisfied one. She seemed not to have a real friend, though it was evident that she certainly could attract children—she was on everybody's birthday party list. She would play gaily and charmingly with a child for a whole day, but to her there might always be somebody better around the next corner, and the following day she would pick up another playmate. She greeted all guests and knew everybody's name. Yet the essential superficiality of her relationships concerned the teachers. Already, because of her social gifts, she showed signs of being drawn toward group play. She liked to be surrounded by children. Would she be the kind of adult who is lonely without a crowd, yet lonely in one, too?

Gradually the children lost their initial enthusiasm for Babette; though accepting her as an occasional sparkling addition to their play, they seemed to understand that she was not to be counted on to maintain a relationship. No one showed hostility to her, but they appeared to have closed ranks as they began to find more lasting friendships within the group. Some visits of one or another child to Babette's home had no lasting results, either. One teacher tried to establish a tie with her, playing and singing to her, bringing costume material for the dancing she enjoyed, writing down her stories, and giving her other special attentions. But as soon as the teacher felt at all close to her, she was off and away. Even her stories, light, gay, and charming, contained no confidence and revealed no feelings. In spite of appearing so outgoing, Babette developed no real tie with anyone. Babette, like Agatha, with a need for people and the ability to draw them to her, was having trouble in the very area of most importance to her.

Just when the teachers were most discouraged and Babette seemed most lonely, flitting constantly from one child to another, Hal burst on her like a ray of sunlight. Immediately he broke through her guard. Joining the group late, he found her the most unattached and accessible and offered her his very considerable warmth. He gave her a new name, "Dorky Bird," and influenced any group he was in to include her. Often she was to be seen ensconced in the upper level of the jungle gym, while the boys' play ebbed and flowed about her, with Hal able to keep her content by his way of treating her like an honored guest. And her own feelings began to deepen to meet this bath of affection from Hal. She would go to the gate to wait for him if she arrived first, sitting patiently on the little brick step until he came, when they would hug each other. Sometimes, too, if he was busy, she would wait in her locker, where he would come to reassure her, "I didn't forget — I'll be back soon."

The teachers continued to work on their own relationships with Babette. Sometimes, when a little girl finds it easier to relate to a boy than to a girl or woman, there may be a tenuous tie between the child and her mother, or even an unhappy one. If warmth came from her father, she might naturally turn to males first. Babette's mother had always worked, and there had been changing household help. But sometimes, too, a deeply meaningful boy-girl friendship develops at this age, for no reason except a special affinity between the two. There was also the possibility that Babette had been slowly getting ready for a friend and that Hal, eager for one himself, found her at the right time. Thus each answered the other's need.

● Roddie was an extremely attractive three-year-old, with golden-brown, curly hair and an appealing look. Yet, from the beginning, he made difficulties for both teachers and children. Asked to put his sweater in his locker, he would start off agreeably and stuff it in a corner. He went home with a teacher's Eversharp pencil that he had plausibly borrowed "for a minute." Patrick's steam shovel was taken out of his locker, most pleasantly returned there on request, but taken out again. When it was suggested that it was not a good idea to do something, he smiled and nodded, and it seemed almost incredible that the other teacher had just finished telling him that, too. He had seemed to thoroughly understand and agree with all she said, but as soon as he was out of her sight he had done the same thing again. Each time this happened, he gave the impression of doing the best he could; nobody had told him, so how was he to know? A little boy with a sweet smile, Roddie was always amenable to reason when asked to do anything. The only thing was, he didn't do it, and it began to seem that he never intended to. In spite of his friendly exterior, his behavior resulted in more trouble for them than anyone else's. Was he not aware of that? Yet he always avoided a direct issue. What did he want?

As might be expected, Roddie's attitude toward other children was similar. He created problems for them, in a subtle, indirect way. When, for example, he walked too close to Chip's block building so that it fell down, what gave him away was the flash of a grin — almost too fleeting to catch — immediately followed by his innocent look. When Chip shouted, "You wrecked my building!" he said, "I didn't mean to; I'll help you fix it." with his best smile. What he wanted, it seemed, was to feel important.

The next step was to help Roddie, an inconspicuous middle child in his family, feel important in his own right, through acceptance as himself, a person with real feelings, not as the sweet little boy he pretended to be. Only when he could allow his feelings to show would he be able to have real relationships with adults and children. So his teacher began to suggest, in a friendly way, what he might really be feeling. "You didn't *want* to put your sweater away. That's why you hid it, maybe." "You liked Patrick's steam shovel so much you took it out again anyway?" Sometimes the right thing to say seemed to be "You know how it's usually done, but you wanted it special for you?" or "You wanted me to tell you lots of times?" Verbalizing his feelings like this would bring a direct look from Roddie when the teacher had hit it right, instead of the old side-long, flirtatious one, and he began to be able to say, outright, "I don't want to" or "No" to her.

As Roddie's feelings began to be displayed more openly, his jealousy of his baby sister and older brother became obvious. He pushed the younger children, and pestered the older ones by intruding on their play, whether welcome or not. The teacher reflected these hostile feelings, too, and offered substitutes such as stuffed animals. Soon, through play, he was able to feel powerful and important without alienating others. Finally settling on the big bear, he was often to be seen dragging it around, forcing it into "jail," "spanking" it, or "cutting it up" with a rubber knife. At last he took a big step. "Come help me tie up this bear!" he called to Patrick, who entered into his play enthusiastically. Now, instead of taking out his feelings on other people, he began to realize they could be allies. Slowly, as Roddie began to find acceptable ways to let his resentments be part of himself, he became more genuine and outgoing. The new Roddie was noticed by several children — David, Melanie, and Livy, as well as Patrick — and he seemed well on his way.

● Quincy, last of the eighteen, was the only child of older parents. He seemed interested solely in playing records and looking at books, and stayed on the periphery of the group, though he was four years old. He had a phenomenally long attention span, much like that of an adult, when engaged in these pursuits. He tolerated children if they kept their distance, but would shrink and complain to the teacher if they came too close. He seemed to have no interest in toys or outdoor activities. At this stage the teacher helped Quincy tell the others he wanted to be by himself, and he was learning that they would respect his privacy and were not to be feared. Because his relationship with the teacher was the only one he had at school, she identified with his interests and supported them in every way she could. With this help, he was moving from passive listening to music and looking at books to more creative ways of expressing these interests, which would help him develop more sense of self. He had begun by making music himself along with the records, using bells and rattles. This had led to his playing the drums and blowing on whistles and pipes, and he tentatively tried out the piano. Soon the sounds coming from the music corner attracted the other children's attention, and some of them began to play instruments with him in a parallel fashion, the teacher remaining as a stabilizing influence. Hal, for whom every child was an attraction, found a way to approach Quincy by echoing back his music on a harmonica and smilingly marching around him when he played the drum. When Hal asked the teacher to print his dictated story in a booklet, Quincy wanted to "make a book" too, and they were soon side by side at a table, illustrating their stories, Hall scribbling a riot of colors in his book and Quincy painfully making a row of Q's in his.

After this, Quincy made more books and even made an occasional remark at the story table. He also began to take books or instruments outside to use in the grass area there, and this usually brought children around him. Apparently he now liked their proximity and attention; he continued to do this, sometimes consulting with the teacher as to what she thought they might like him to bring. His play had now moved from the peripheral to the parallel stage, but he had shown no special interest in any one child, though Hal had helped break the ice. Unfortunately there would not be much more time, since his parents were leaving the area. There was a danger that when Quincy entered kindergarten he might establish a pattern of always remaining on the outskirts of the group. As the other children in kindergarten became more and more at home in true group play, his chances of progressing through the earlier social stages would become less and less, since everyone else would be so far ahead. Quincy's parents were making plans to enroll him in another nursery school as soon as possible, to help him prepare for the social challenges of kindergarten the next fall.

VI

The role of the teacher in the foregoing is seen to be important, both as she herself has a special kind of relationship with a child and as she helps him develop in his peer relationships.

In the peripheral stage, before the child has other ties, the teacher's contacts with him are meaningful in helping him gain a sense of his own worth apart from his family. She shows an accepting, interested, appreciative attitude toward his play activities. Like a child's art, his play is an expression of himself, and his teacher's attitude toward it is, to him, synonymous with her attitude toward himself. This unjudgmental relationship is the prototype of all good friendships and helps to motivate him to seek and recognize these. At this time the teacher avoids encouraging too much dependence on her for direction or help in his play, since his child friends to come will not meet such needs. She is just around, as his parallel playmates will be, busy with her own activities, not hovering or trying to keep the child busy or entertained all the time. Nor does she establish such a close tie, through charm, affection, or fascinating play suggestions, that his coming friends would have too high a standard to follow. As the child matures and begins to show more and more initiative in making his own play choices and decisions, and his sense of worth grows correspondingly, it is an easy step to move from his relationship with the teacher toward ones with other children.

In the more social stages of play, the teacher's most important role is again to provide a model. Her way of dealing with children needs to be one that they can use with each other, incorporating listening to another's point of view and expressing one's own as honestly and clearly as possible, having confidence in another's motives, respecting his feelings, and being resourceful and ingenious in finding compromises in conflict situations. As well as providing a guide in her own behavior, she will also demonstrate her basic attitude toward people in the words and manner that she suggests to them for their use with each other.

Sometimes the teacher's role is to provide social information—vocabulary to use in communicating with others, or interpretations and explanations of other children's behavior and feelings. Sometimes her role is to help in the differentiation between a child's own inner world and the reality of the relationship he is dealing with at the moment. One of her most important roles is to provide a child with enough social stimulation by seeing that others who share his interests are brought into his orbit. And often the teacher's function is to protect a child from the wrong kind of experience, or from one that is wrongly timed for him. Livy, for instance, in her earlier period of wanting to be a "big girl," would put herself into a situation where there was too much social pressure. When four or five of the older children were engaged in group play she was not ready for, she might become demanding of their attention, overexcited, or so tense and striving that she was near tears, or she might feel defeated and withdraw. She might bring the others to the point of rejecting her or losing their own controls, because, in her efforts to avoid feeling lost and anonymous, she was moving faster and making more noise than anyone else. To be in a situation one cannot manage tears down self-confidence, so here the teacher would step in, offering as a substitute some simpler play involving the same theme, so that Livy could regain her sense of social competence.

There are also other important influences on social development in the nursery school: the kind of social person each of the teachers is, the personalities and needs of the children in the group, the opportunities for play and for interactions, and, most of all, the strong inner drive in each child toward relationships. Much progress is made, because of these factors, with very little active intervention on a teacher's part. During the period discussed in this chapter, there were, for each child, long stretches in which social learning proceeded smoothly. Nor did the children who needed help all need it at once. It was thus possible to concentrate on one or two in the group, keep an eye on certain others, and give the rest only a minimum of play supervision for periods of time. The art of the teacher probably lies at least partly in knowing where and when to give her attention. Certain children will need to be left alone to expand and enjoy a breathing space; for them, the chance to be without an adult's attention and special concern is a real growth experience. And much is done, too, by merely controlling the environment—by arranging equipment and spaces well and by providing the right toys at the right time. Play-drama props are especially important in socialization; when another detail is wanted to keep the play rolling, a teacher can help by quickly devising something, such as the cot sheet taped to a broomstick that David used as a sail on his jungle-gym boat. Because of the addition of the sail, which made the play theme easily recognizable to everyone, new groups were formed and new playmates found on that day.

In most cases, children will seek what they are ready to experience, responding with a sensitive awareness of their social needs. The social stages blend together subtly, one into the other. Often a child will move back to an earlier level for a while. Sometimes he just does it to enjoy special pleasures each stage has to offer. Sometimes he does it to fill in gaps of experience or to get his feet on the ground in an easier setting and thus gain new confidence. Social learning, like all other kinds, does not proceed in a straight line, but with backward movement and plateaus, as well as progress along its course.

133

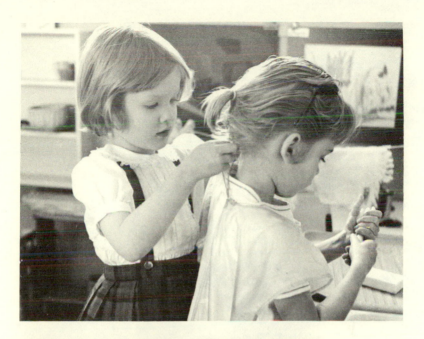

135

SELF-AFFIRMATION

7 Materials for Exploration and Dramatic Play

What do you think of a bucket?

A bucket
Is a bucket.
A bus
Is a bus.
A bus looks clean.
So does a bucket.
But a paintbrush
Is a paintbrush.
And a half a paintbrush
Is a half a paintbrush.

And you always have to have a mother
To take care of yourself.

—Anne

I

The nursery school provides a child with many encouragements for the growth of the self through all kinds of activities, both indoors and out. To achieve this end, the school environment contains a variety of stimulating materials selected to enable a child to find out for himself both what he is like and what his world is like. The teacher's role is to value these self-initiated explorations, promoting, protecting, and supporting them in every way she can. Whenever a child shows an interest in, and a readiness for, a certain kind of learning, she offers the materials for his own discovery of the facts he needs, and she also serves as a resource person who can contribute information, demonstrations, and interpretation to supplement his own efforts as required.

Since the teacher is in the background much of the time, and since, at this age, books are not the chief source of learning experiences, materials become of great importance. They are food for learning in the nursery school, being displayed for children to choose like food in a cafeteria. Each is used only until the hunger for that particular kind is satisfied. (There are times, too, when none are selected; instead, a child may talk with others, rest, watch, dream, wander about in a vague state of relaxed sensory awareness, or carry on a vivid internal dialogue. Passivity and activity are both necessary parts of the rhythm of living.) Materials, like food, are used with enthusiasm, approached in a matter-of-fact way, or rejected altogether, according to a child's own inner needs. But again, as with food, if this process is to go on beneficially, there must be plenty of well-chosen materials from which to select.

II

One kind of resource is materials that have been prestructured to permit a child to make discoveries about the properties of objects without the help of anyone. Examples are pictures to be matched; pegs to insert in number groupings or in holes of various gradations of height, depth, or circumference; forms to be placed in corresponding cut-out areas; different kinds of objects to be sorted by size, weight, color, or texture; rattles for sound comparisons; and similar problem-solving challenges. Whatever the prestructured material, the important criteria is that it be self-explanatory, or require at most only a brief introduction. In using a formboard, the child naturally proceeds to take all the pieces out and attempts to replace them, without suggestion or explanation. As he works, he begins to see relationships by himself. A piece that is placed wrong won't go in. When he finds a task too hard, he has two choices; he can ask for help or turn to something else. Sometimes these choices need to be made clear for a particular child. He may think he is expected to succeed, yet if he is not interested in the material for its own sake, he will become more and more incompetent, because his heart is not in what he is doing. Because he feels he must not fail, he can neither stop nor give his completely unanxious attention to the problem; he may then be led to constrain his own abilities, to dream and be pseudostupid, or to be intolerant of himself and react with self-punishment by destroying his own work. The suggestion that he choose something else releases him. Or, if none of the above applies, and the child can be made comfortable about his own limits and is able to ask frankly for help out of real interest in the problem, he and the teacher can work together until he is ready to say, "Now let *me*." While a child may sometimes tackle a job that is too difficult, the material itself would not be of a kind that requires him to go again and again to an adult for answers that he could not find out by his own efforts. His aim is self-affirmation, here by means of using his own intelligence, and if he is made to feel dependent on the large, all-knowing adult, especially in this period of his life when he is just forming his self-image, his purpose is subverted. Feeling less and less independent, and, therefore, less good about himself, the child may begin to block out the whole idea of learning, or perhaps turn compulsively again and again to the adult for help with his problem of self-doubt, a problem which such dependence only recreates for him.

Prestructured material, which primarily involves the cognitive faculties, is also occasionally sought as a temporary rest and relief from inner emotional pressures. Since all preschool children are passing through a period of problems and stresses, this kind of activity seems to have a place in their lives for that reason as well. To work for a time in a neutral area that is free from symbolic investments (if that can be so) may calm a mildly anxious child as occupational therapy or hard work does a tense adult. For some children this material even serves as a prolonged escape from emotional or social involvement, as well as from more expansive physical activity. It can at times be helpful when a group of children has been under social strain and a temporary return to the less complicated stage of parallel play seems indicated. In the use of this material, too, an interest is continued from the period when the baby touched, turned, poked, matched, inserted, dumped and filled, pulled and pushed, and otherwise handled objects in order to see what would happen. And there is a satisfaction of the child's need for order outside him, to lessen the discomfort of chaotic inner impressions and half-understood concepts. It is as though he said, "Oh, *I* know how *this* goes," and set about fixing up his own confusions as he put round pegs into round holes, and so on. As when hearing a story about familiar things, the child feels oriented in reality again. "I thought it was that way, and I was right!" can be very reassuring. His successes build self-confidence. Thus, prestructured materials have their place in the nursery school, and some children, for periods of time, show a special interest in this use of their problem-solving abilities.

As a really satisfying expressive outlet, however, the material described above is too limited and inflexible. More generally useful are those materials in which a child can invest himself more completely. For example, doll clothes and dress-up things teach the same skills as buttoning frames, but they involve the whole child in purposeful behavior at the same time. Activities which use a blend of all aspects of the personality, not the cognitive in isolation, appear to be the ones in which the longest span of attention and the greatest absorption are seen.

And there is a more subtle point which relates to the general aim of ego growth and self-affirmation. In all the above materials, there is, built in, a yes-or-no, black-and-white concept. A tendency toward polarized thinking is one of the small child's problems anyway. He loves or hates with such total commitment that he tends to feel "good" or "bad" and to label others that way, too, even without reinforcement from outside. "That's right," or "That's wrong," the material says to him, with no in-between shades, no tolerance of individual differences, and no room for the child to make any decisions or evaluations of his own. The material constantly stresses conformity, and every child's end product is exactly the same. The small child is already under pressure to conform and adjust in order to live in comfort with other people; the problem is to keep these necessary pressures at a tolerable minimum rather than adding to them, to help the child to judge himself and others less rigidly, and to allow opportunities for his own ideas to flower as much as possible, so as to do no violence to his maturing individuality.

III

Another type of material is only semistructured. It offers some of the same opportunities for small-muscle manipulations and size, shape, and color differentiations as structured materials, but includes, as well, an element of the creative. Examples are pegboards with a variety of kinds of pegs, mosaic tiles, construction sets (without models to follow), and assorted beads for stringing or fastening together with pipe cleaners—all to form into free designs. Material of this sort can be easily devised and inexpensively made. Cardboard geometric shapes with holes punched in them can be provided to fasten onto pegboards with cut-off golf tees, for example. Strands of yarn can also be poked into the pegboard with tees. Many household scrap materials with holes in them can be strung on cords or bootlaces, or made into mobiles with electricians' wire. Squares of variously-colored carpet scraps can be fitted into a box lid, as can discarded octagonal bathroom tiles. Plastic drinking straws, cut into different lengths, will serve as pegs to hold beads or spools on a pegboard or can be strung in combination with the beads, geometric shapes, or mobile objects. Children can also make their own designs from sturdy, bright-colored scraps of cloth ready to be snapped or buttoned together. The guiding principle is to provide material that a child can manipulate by himself, with a free design or pattern resulting. There is no right or wrong with these; the child orders his own world in his own way. The material is different, however, from that which is completely unstructured, such as paints, clay, blank paper, or scrap wood. The pegs must go in holes, the pipe cleaners through the beads, and the tiles will only fit together if properly aligned, whatever the pattern. In-between material like this can often serve as a link for a hesitant child to the use of art materials in which he is left to follow only his inner guidelines.

IV

Baskets containing special collections make it possible for children to discover, on their own, their properties and functions. When a child manipulates one collection kept in a "discovery basket," he might be encountering some basic scientific principles, for example. By experimenting, he learns how to bring about the result he wants, and then, by later repetition, he learns that the results are always consistent. The contents of this basket might be baby toys that demonstrate the principle of gravity, such as a plastic-enclosed waterwheel, a plastic hourglass holding colored dots in liquid, butterflies in a globe that whirl, fish that always remain on top of liquid when their ball is turned, birds that quiver with the slightest movement of the ball that encloses them, or swans that always swim in an opposite direction when their ball is turned. There might be magnets, a magnifying glass, a prism, color paddles, a kaleidoscope and teleidoscope, an open-faced music box, a plastic marble maze, and the like. Old watches and clocks, light switches, gears, and similar mechanical devices might be in another collection.

Some kinds of materials are especially adaptable and are thus suitable for both exploration and dramatic play. Examples of these are plastic irrigation pipes and joints, store scales, a cash register, a pulley, a toy telescope, field glasses, and a sand wheel.

V

Each item of the materials a school offers is seen by a child as something to which he can relate on many levels. His own way of using what is available to him is to employ many diverse elements, with his own creativity as the unifying factor. Thus, beads may be put into trucks, pegs used as cigarettes, cubes served up as play food, Lotto cards delivered as mail, pinecones in a nature display "sold," a paper cup used as a hat, or a puzzle piece given a doll. Thus, to prevent confusion and the frustration of missing parts, order is important, with materials consistently stored where they will be used, and substitutes readily available when dramatic play takes over. Logical spatial separations for materials help play proceed—

blocks, trucks, peg people in one place, puzzles and books in another area, art materials in their own spot, and materials for doll play in a special, screened-off corner. These basic things would be accessible to children, and extra ones kept on hand would be taken out as needed by a teacher. When area limits are clear, children enjoy being able to find the things they need and knowing where to put them away when it is time to pick up.

VI

Dramatic play is of special significance in the nursery school program. The inner world of fantasy and the outer world of reality are not clearly differentiated by the young child. Dramatic play provides a direct route to his inner life, making it possible for him to externalize his extraordinarily rich fantasies so that they can be communicated to others and also become more amenable to his own understanding. He learns to control the forms they assume according to his own choices, and dramatic play is then perhaps his most important medium of self-expression. In just the same way that a baby's need to recover a lost bottle or get to his mother through cries, grasping, reaching, and finally crawling leads him to exert all his forces and muster all his concentration, children deeply involved in dramatic play begin to do what they never could before. It is as though their powers all flowed toward the same goal. When a child is motivated by basic emotional drives, he is led to maximum mental, physical, and social functioning, and he summons up all his endurance of frustration, and his stamina, persistence, and patience in conquering obstacles. Thus it can be seen that the kind of materials which invite an initial emotional investment such as this can make possible learning that is both integrated and deep, because of the child's total involvement.

Why does playing fire captain in dramatic play help a child who feels small and overpowered more, in the end, than controlling the world as embodied in a formboard or a color-sorting puzzle? The answer seems to be that the dramatic play can move somewhere, ending up different from its beginning. Dennis played fire captain in many ways. In a fire hat, with himself in the role, he rode a tricycle and climbed the jungle gym to put out imaginary fires. Playing with the toy people, he called each of the men a "fire captain," and "chopped" and banged them all. When he stopped, the teacher said, "Those firemen have really been getting it," and he picked up the last figure, looked into its face, and said, "Yes, but he's a little bit good and just a *little* bit bad, now. I don't have to pound him any more." The formboards, graduated towers, and similar structured materials will never change; they are always either right or wrong, finished or unfinished. And, even more important, they are one step removed from the child's problem and remain there, so the child can gain no insight. Dennis, in contrast, after his fireman play, later talked about his father, part of whose job was to watch for forest fires. "I wish *I* was big like him and could do that. It makes me *mad* to be just a little boy."

Interest in the dramatic-play possibilities of toys like trucks, trains, boats, and airplanes is shared by most small children. These toys seem to represent strength and power; probably the young child, who experiences smallness and weakness, expresses his wish to do "big" things when he uses them. A car can go at great speed, a truck can carry big loads with ease, and a fire engine can make a tremendously loud noise; he himself can do none of these things. He also likes to hitch things such as trains and trailers together, and he wants them longer and longer. A small child would like to be longer and longer himself, like his enormously tall parents.

Emotional meaning also attaches to doll-corner play. The adults at home are emulated in washing and ironing, cooking, and house cleaning. Both boys and girls dress the dolls, take them for rides in the stroller, to the store, to picnics, and to the doctor. They feed them, put them to bed, then leave them with sitters and "go out." They "go to work," too, carrying toy lunch boxes, and "repair" a family car made of chairs. In this way they act out their own experiences, but with themselves in the controlling position, and thus balance their lives. Playing the role of a baby in the doll corner is popular, too; this allows a child to express his envy of a new sibling or his wish to receive the kind of care he has outgrown in real life. Playing mother and father gives children a chance to create for themselves the closeness between their parents that makes them jealous. That doll-corner play has more than routine interest—is emotionally satisfying—is evidenced by the seemingly unreasonable violence with which children reject any child who threatens to disrupt it by wanting to come in when the cast has been chosen.

Dramatic-play materials, as well as being helpful to individuals, bring children together. While a child's painting, collage, or clay modeling has a good deal of meaning to him, it seldom has much for other children. On the other hand, a doll, a truck, a child's broom, a fireman's ladder, or a toy coffee pot are reacted to in similar ways by most children. If Angus puts the baby doll in the oven, someone else who has similar feelings about babies will respond by laughing appreciatively. Patrick starts his train circling through the tables and chairs, and this appeals to Tad, who so far hasn't been playing much with others, encouraging him to follow it with his own train. But Tad does more than just imitate; his personal involvement with the train idea then leads him to add details. On an overturned chair, he puts a toy man to watch and "ring the bell" as the trains go by. In ways like these, dramatic-play experiences are enriched by other children who share the same motivations. Fuller and freer expression is also invited; if supported by a playmate's participation in the use of dramatic-play materials, a child feels braver about venturing into new, untried areas. Most of all, perhaps, he gains a comfortable acceptance of the dreams and wishes he has been working out in his play. It is as though the others said to him, "You're not alone or different; we feel like that, too."

Dramatic play that expresses the emotions felt by a number of children often draws a group into a common activity. Sandy had come to school talking anxiously about whales after she had seen some on television. A creature of immense size and unpredictability frightens most young children; their usual feelings of being small and helpless are thus experienced in exaggerated form. A band of children, for several days, helped Sandy chase away an imaginary whale until it was "too scared to come back," and several children were, in this way, involved in group play for the first time. Similarly, a "mean doctor," called "Doctor Cement," was ground up in the toy cement mixer day after day following the usual fall immunization shots, and it was obvious that relationships in the group were being cemented, too, in the course of play.

A teacher's appreciation of dramatic play helps it start, keeps it going, and makes it a richer and more meaningful experience. In the midst of a group's deep involvement in the use of dramatic-play materials, a teacher may feel like an apprentice assistant to a group of artists working on a momentous project.

● One day block building for small-scale dramatic play took over the entire playroom floor. Beginning when Hal's and Babette's structure, a long, flat tunnel for a train, wound its way across the room, buildings grew everywhere. David and Chip worked together on a fortresslike castle, on top of which many toy people were lined up to defend it. Melanie made an extended series of connected rooms, containing furniture for a large family. Miles, aided by Alice, built towers, and Livy and Janie made roads for toy people to use en route from one to the other. Angus built a fenced enclosure for farm animals. And Patrick's truck driver took orders and made deliveries of blocks. Everything, that day, gave way to this burgeoning enterprise, and the teacher cleaned up around the artists' buildings, helped now and then to steady something, and hunted for extras suddenly needed, until finally the momentum slowed down near dismissal time. Parents were invited in to view the scene, and the children went home glowing.

VII

Materials for dramatic play in the large scale—that in which the child himself is the protagonist—include both basic necessities and often many other things that are added to help spark ideas and enrich and prolong play or to support a group's special interests. Much of this material can be handmade, contrived, or donated from household castoffs.

Among large-scale materials, a doll corner or other reserved space would certainly be basic, though with considerable flexibility possible in its furnishings. There would be beds for dolls (but of a size children could curl up in, too) with sheets, pillows, and blankets, and a child-sized table with chairs. Also needed would be a dresser in which to keep a variety of doll clothes (easy to put on and take off), a cupboard containing dishes, silverware, and cooking utensils, a child-sized stove (no heat), a toy iron and ironing board, and a sink with or without running water. The kinds of dolls that seem most desirable are babies (washable), and girls and boys of different races (anatomically correct, if possible). Enjoyable additions might be a picnic basket, toy razor, mirror, doll hairbrush, clock, small suitcase, telephone, baby bottles and rattles, and handbags. Some kind of pushcart or dolly with castors that could serve as a stroller for a child as well as a doll, along with a toy dog that could be taken for walks and perhaps another "pet" or two would be welcomed. Dress-up clothes such as long skirts, capes, vests, and hats seem to suggest many themes for play and are easily supplied, but they usually need some alterations to enable children to put them on and take them off independently. Whatever is in the doll area needs to have a special place; if a child is packing up for an overnight trip, for example, and must hunt everywhere for the items needed, interest may well flag before the idea can be worked out.

An outdoor playhouse might be furnished only with boxes of different sizes that could also serve as needed for store shelves, trains, boats, or cages for animals. Sandbox supplies, such as soft plastic dishes and utensils and rubber dolls and animals might be used there, too. Sand, invaluable for dramatic play, can be food, coal, water for swimming and doll showers, and many other things. Materials to use with it might include buckets, large and small shovels, scoops, rakes, brooms, sieves, funnels, and molds.

Much of the large-scale dramatic play in a nursery school will focus around a jungle gym or other climbing apparatus, a slide, swings, and boards and standards if these are provided. Basic equipment like this can be anything a child wants it to be in a play drama. A realistic boat, train, car, or store would limit children to those ideas only, leaving nothing to use for the other things he might need, such as "sailors' bunk beds," "batmobiles," "alligator tanks," "a diesel Caterpillar," or a "spaceship," to name only a few. Standards are most usable if they vary in width and height, and boards, cleated at both ends, if they are of different lengths. Attached to the jungle gym or used apart from it, the standards and boards can be arranged by the teacher as needed for tables, shelves, inclines, "horses" to bounce on, seesaws, wide and narrow slides, "up and overs," bridges, fences, and walking and balancing mazes, as well as for buses, trains, or planes, with small boxes as seats.

Other materials for large-scale dramatic play might be rubber tools, a ticket punch, a steering wheel, a short length of rubber hose for firemen, a bell on a cord, plastic keys, hobbyhorses, tarpaulins to make roofs, walls, or tents, a play doctor kit, hollow blocks for child-sized structures, small slates ready for sign-making and hanging, and a child-sized stuffed animal or doll.

VIII

Dramatic play in the small scale has its basic materials, too, most of them kept on open shelves beside the largest floor area. First in importance is a plentiful supply of floor blocks in multiple units and a variety of shapes. Block accessories such as family and community figures; farm and zoo animals; a barn; a house or two, with furniture to scale; and some rolling stock, such as a train, car, bus, fire engine, tow truck, moving van, bulldozer, dump truck, boat, and plane would be kept nearby. Other suggestions for the small-scale play might be wooden trees, road signs, a small motorcycle, ambulance, helicopter, camper truck, and houseboat. If at all possible, toy people should fit into all these. For outdoor play, another bulldozer and dump truck, along with a road roller and cement mixer, would be useful in the sand.

Small-scale dramatic materials are valuable for private play or twosome play in a separate room. For that purpose, there might be a dollhouse, model car set, small trains and tracks, or perhaps a village set to spread out on a painted cloth. Puppets are best used in such semiprivacy, since playing before an audience is not natural at this age, and since, in any case, a preschool audience always has a hard time passively watching and waiting for turns.

IX

Another category of dramatic-play materials includes those that are prescribed for individuals with special needs, things that might be offered to a child with an interest or a problem for which, at the moment, the regular equipment provided no answer. These extra materials would be stored in readiness for such situations, and, because needs like this are hard to predict, new ones would probably be added from time to time. A passive, inactive child who has never learned to play can often respond to a toy especially selected to help release him into the beginnings of self-affirmation.

● Cornelius had no brothers or sisters and had spent his time at home being read to, looking at television, being taken for walks, or being pushed in a swing at the park. With a child like this, it is often necessary to start way back, perhaps with feeding play. His teacher selected a small rubber dog and doll from a collection she had made of durable animal and human characters, and then put a full basin of sand on an outdoor table, near where he stood. "What is that for?" he asked. "For play." He sat down at the table passively waiting. "How do I play?" he asked her. "Well, here's a spoon." He began to stir the sand. "And here's a dog, if you need one," she told him casually. "Oh. Yes, I do." He began to feed the dog with the spoon. "And a boy?" suggested the teacher, bringing the rubber boy doll over to him. "Yes." Cornelius fed them both awhile, and then the boy doll suddenly jumped into the midst of the sand in the basin. "He's getting it all over him!" said Cornelius, delightedly splashing around. With the teacher responsive to each step, Cornelius moved on to water play and to more and more lively activity. Gradually he was loosening up enough to be able to jump in and play like his boy doll.

Some children, while not entirely inactive, have very constricted interests. With them, watching awhile is a teacher's first step. The child is usually doing something, holding something, or at least watching something, and a link can be found to move him or her into ongoing play. Paul, who carried his bear around everywhere in a backpack and did nothing else, was helped into play by being offered a special soft blanket for it. The teacher and he then made a bed of blocks for the bear, and she also offered it some crackers. Daniel, at first, only rode a tricycle; an old camera to "take pictures on his trips" helped him expand into more play with children who asked him to photograph them. If a child is already pretending to be something, the choice of special materials is made easy: for a policeman, a badge, stop sign, or whistle; for an engineer, a cap and some tickets; and so on. Noticing what a child watches gives a clue, too. If it is the doll-corner play, for example, perhaps some milk bottles to deliver to the group playing there can get him started.

Some children are unable to get involved in anything because they are preoccupied with worries. A boy who stands around and talks only of spiders needs a rubber spider; this symbol can then be brought into touch with the real world around the child, and his fantasies, acted out, can progress somewhere. Similarly, a little girl whose thoughts are all of witches seen on television needs some representation of a witch—a hat for herself, or a (harmless-looking) witch puppet. These dramatic-play materials offer a direct route to the inner worlds that are the present exclusive focus of such children's attention. At the moment, they cannot play, or paint, or project themselves anywhere, and everything else is ignored. They are emotionally invested only in spiders and witches, and these ideas are bottling up all the others they might have. As the spider or witch is played with, it becomes linked to other kinds of play. It is covered with sand or blocks, hidden in boxes or baskets, and used to attack other toy symbols, with variations daily becoming more free and creative. Eventually the feelings behind such blocking of activity are played out, and the child's enhanced sense of self makes him able to turn to new things.

Other children are immobilized for a different reason: emotionally, they are still at home. Such a child may just sit in his locker, wander about aimlessly, or stand on the sidelines watching with an expressionless face. He is not bored with his surroundings; he is scarcely aware of them, because his thoughts are elsewhere. It is the teacher's task to relate to him on the basis of those thoughts. A child like this can be given a special stuffed animal, hand-sized, to keep in his locker for his own private use. It has his name on it and stands for his own identity, individuality, and privacy. Also, when the teacher gives it to him personally and says, "It's just for you," the child then feels he is somebody special at school, as he is at home. He can treat his little animal as he wishes he were being treated right then at home—cuddle and care for it—and thus, as its parent and helper, feel his own needs vicariously satisfied. Since the toy animal engages the child's feelings, which have hitherto been attached to his home alone, it serves as a link to new experiences. When he is ready to try out a truck, the toy animal will ride in it first, and if he feels too shy to approach another child who attracts him, the toy animal can touch noses with the other child's animal or doll. Because a child will want to identify with the animal, the teacher selects it carefully. A timid but angry boy would probably like a lion. Another, almost ready to join in socially, might make the leap more easily after his toy frog did a lot of private jumping.

● Larry was given a toy cat to keep in his locker. He had been playing the role of a cat constantly at school. The teacher had shown she was friendly to Larry the cat with pats and offers of pretend food. Playing an animal role allows a child a mild disguise of what he really has on his mind. If the animal is babyish, the child may be identifying with the baby part of himself or with a baby at home. But sooner or later the animal reflects not only baby wishes but aggressive ones. While playing an animal role, a child can be primitive and uncontrolled; children who played with Larry soon found him alarmingly obstreperous, and his quick changes of mood from seeking petting and feeding to scratching and biting upset them. When Larry was given the toy cat, the change from large-scale to small-scale dramatic play in no way interrupted the working out of whatever had originally suggested the animal identification to him, and it protected his relationships with the other children. While Larry, as the cat, was wild and noisy, ate all the "food" in the doll corner, knocked things off the table, and was generally impossible to play with, the toy cat gobbled up sand, bit and jumped on the rubber animals, threw them off the jungle gym, and so on, and no one minded at all—in fact, they enjoyed its antics. Thus Larry received warm response and support, and, in letting this part of himself be seen and finding it accepted, he learned to live with the feelings he had formerly projected into the cat. He gradually stopped being wild with his toy animal and became more gentle and loving with it. At last the little cat, the load lifted off it, sat forgotten more and more in his locker. But even when Larry never played with it anymore, he would sometimes hold it to his face a moment, speak to it, or pet it as he passed by his locker on other business. In just such fashion do lucky adults think of the children they once were, fondly remembering.

X

Dramatic-play materials are particularly appropriate for the development of many kinds of learning experiences. Whenever a child is freely and fully engaged in the use of these materials, any learning that fits in with his or her own goals receives the full force of the child's powers without blocking or fragmentation of energy, and the evasions and resistance so often seen in formal teaching situations are unknown. In this state of readiness, there are many opportunities for development that encompass all aspects of a child.

- Observing Agatha in the doll corner, motivated to play the role of a housekeeper as realistically as possible, one could see her learning how to control the flow of hot and cold water to make the right temperature for washing the doll dishes, how to carry full cups of water to the table without spilling any, how to insert the dolls' arms and legs into pajamas, how to fold and fit clothes into the doll suitcase, and how to make up the doll beds so they would look like the real beds at home. She swept crumbs into her little dustpan with her broom, emptied the pan in a wastebasket, and hung the broom up afterward, tipping it so as to manipulate its screw eye onto a right-angle hook.

  Agatha learned some things about people, too. Livy, who was with her, would play a baby role in the house only as long as it was pleasant to do so; she refused to be picked up or spanked, for instance. When Agatha insisted on doing these things, Livy threatened to leave the play, but it was possible to convince her to stay by relenting and offering to take her for a ride in the stroller instead. And on the trip across the playroom, Agatha mastered some large-muscle skills, as she pushed the stroller around and between block buildings.

- The way in which information is sought out and eagerly evaluated and utilized in dramatic play, as well as the display of cooperative planning, will be seen in the following description of a group project that began when David decided to use a board laid across two standards as his horse. At once Miles, Chip, and Hal fell into the idea of riding board horses, too, and these were set up. "We'll need saddles," Chip told the others, and he cast around, coming up with some rubber mats which he threw across the boards. "But what can we use for reins?" Miles asked. They discussed this and asked the teacher for ropes, which she supplied. "What else do we need?" they asked each other, gathered around their horses. "Food!" Buckets of sand were brought over. Miles told the others that horses ate oats, so "Here's *my* horse's oats," was heard from each. They brought over buckets of water, too, and this led to the idea of washing the horses. Miles turned out to have an extensive horse vocabulary that the others lacked. "You wash them *down*," he said. "And you brush them; that's called 'curry'." They wandered around looking for the right kind of brushes, rejecting the workbench hand-broom, but accepting small scrub brushes produced by the teacher. Next they set to work washing their horses, and afterward, since the boards were rather wet for riding, put their heads together and decided to dry them off with paper towels. ("You rub them *down*," Miles told them.) Soon the words "curry," "saddle blanket," "graze," "hoof," "mane," "bridle," and "stirrups" were all in general use, learned both from Miles and from a horse book the teacher read them. The problem of how to fasten the clothesline reins, which kept slipping off, was solved by David's friend, Melanie, who was able to tie knots.

The children played with these horses for several days. Miles was often referred to as a consultant, after he convinced the others he had really seen and ridden horses ("*live* ones") on his uncle's ranch. The length of time the children remembered the new facts was impressive when this activity was revived several months later. Social learning was achieved, too, as the close-knit group found it helpful to use the resources of others—Patrick's good-humored filling of many buckets of sand for them, Livy's holding the reins for them when they left the horses, and Roddie's vigorous bouncing when taken up behind someone on a horse.

Other examples could be found everywhere of factual learning and the development of reasoning and ingenuity in dramatic play. Children review, too, the many experiences they have had in their homes, in stores, in parks and zoos, and on vacation trips. They share bits of information, correct each other's misconceptions, make use of the teacher to answer questions, and consult books as references, studying the pictures closely. They explore the environment for answers, too, and many problems they encounter are solved in that way.

XI

Materials that involve a child in active physical play encourage total investment. For example, in the use of equipment such as slides, wheel toys, bars, walking and balancing boards, climbing ropes, and ladders, strength and energy are summoned and large-muscle skills are developed, side by side with the solving of intellectual problems concerning space, size, and gravity, and many social and emotional ones.

● In David's boat play, which finally included most of the children, a simple inclined board used as a gangplank to the boat (the top level of the jungle gym with a "sail" attached) led to many experiments. While going up and down, children estimated and tested the gravitational effect of the slant of the board when it was adjusted at different angles. They tried different hand grips and body positions in crawling, sliding, or walking upright on it. They noticed the effect of slippery soles as against sneakers or bare feet. Their bodies, as they played, were learning their own balances, flexibilities, strengths, endurance limits, and vulnerabilities to pain, and each child grew to a new understanding of his capabilities. David discovered how his own motor skills compared to those of Miles and Roddie, for instance, as he asked for help from the one and assisted the other. On his first successful climb up the steep eight-foot board, he communicated his triumph to Chip and, as he started confidently up again, bid for notice from Babette and Melanie. He tried sliding in tandem with Chip, then in a line of children. He waited for those ahead of him and watched out for others at the foot of the board, and also protected himself from being crowded or pushed, all with the social grace that was his special gift.

Two children who like to swing together are often motivated by their wish to do something in a twosome, apart from others, in a kind of symbolic harmony; here, too, the child as a whole is involved. And similarly, two children often support each other in their wishes to show strength and speed; in the search for companions in tricycling, they choose those who share these power motivations, and in this they are acute judges. A child can be emotionally involved, too, in wagon pulling, ball throwing, hoop rolling, knocking down tenpins, running fast, and in sliding, jumping, balancing, and bouncing. In using the materials that encourage these activities, he finds he can let out his strength safely, and experiences the power in himself fully. He enjoys sensual satisfaction, too, in using his muscles strongly, with no guilt cluttering up the good feeling, as it does when he hits someone as hard as he can. In letting out freely with full muscular exertion, a child may also be releasing the tensions of violent feelings for which he has no satisfactory outlet. As he learns to enjoy and be comfortable with this all-out expression in play, he can become comfortable, too, with open expressions of anger in words that clarify relationship problems. He can let his tears go when very unhappy—his laughter and joyous dancing, too, and his warm hugs for friends.

8 Self-Directed Learning Experiences

This is an "on your own" school—
If you want to paint,
You see if anyone is using it, on your own.
You don't have to ask the teacher.

If you want to play in the playhouse,
You can, if no one is there.
And if someone is there,
You ask them if you can use it, too.

If you want to play inside, you can.
If you want to play outside, you can.

When you want to play with just anything,
You can do it on your own,
By seeing if someone's using it or not.

You don't all the time ask grown-ups.

—Jennifer

I

The wide range of interests and curiosities in any nursery school is reflected in as wide a range of self-directed learning experiences.

● Within a group, special interests find expression in learning combined with play. Zeb and Anthony, for example, became absorbed in projects involving spaceships. With the teacher's support, their spaceship in the jungle gym became elaborated with additions such as a large nose cone made of corrugated paper, and they examined pictures of launchings in search of more detailed information. Simplified versions of reported voyages into space were read to them, and the teacher brought two leather pouches on belts, which they wore, along with the helmets they devised from paper bags, to gather "moon rocks" from the sand. As interest in the pebbles themselves increased, they cleaned and waxed them, and the teacher brought in a rock collection and a picture book about different kinds of rocks.

If information is not pressed upon him, but, instead, is offered in response to a child's seeking of information, he soon learns to use the teacher as a resource whenever he is unable to find out something by himself.

- On her arrival one day, Gabrielle came directly to the teacher. "I have something to ask you," she said. "A cow has been in my backyard every night." "Was it a dream, maybe? Dreams can seem very real." "No, not a dream. I sat up, and I heard it mooing and mooing; that's how I knew it was there. Why does it come?" The teacher answered, "I think you could ask your daddy when he comes for you if you can hear the foghorns from your house. They sound like this—Hoo-oo-oo—and they blow every foggy night out on the bay." Gabrielle and the teacher then looked at a book showing different kinds of boats and discussed why foghorns were needed. Afterward they tried making some foghorn sounds, with a short rubber hose and mouthpiece and with a megaphone. Gabrielle's father, when he came, said he thought they could go down to the harbor some evening and listen to the foghorns as the boats came in.

Two examples follow in which the teacher helped a child think through a problem and discover the answer.

- Maggie, always very positive in her opinions, was telling Sandy about God, having acquired some ideas from Sunday school. "He comes in the night," she told Sandy. "Isn't he scared?" Sandy asked her. "No," said Maggie, firmly. "He's not a bit scared. He's some kind of fairy. He lives in the sky. I know all about God, because I go to Sunday school now." Sandy said, "I know all about him, too. I saw him on TV," but she felt uneasy and sought the teacher out. "I don't want God to come in the night," she told her. "You think that might happen, Sandy?" "Yes, Maggie said he would." "And what do you think?" "I'm afraid he might come and hide in my house." "Where in your house?" "Maybe in the closet. Or in the cedar chest. Or the refrigerator." "Where in the refrigerator?" "On the shelf." "On the shelf?" "Behind the milk. But there's not much room there." "You're thinking about him being pretty small?" "Yes—but if he was little, he couldn't reach the doorknob." "He'd have to be bigger?" "Well, if he was as big as a giant, he couldn't get in our door." "So he'd have to be not too little and not too big?" "Yes, like people—like a man." "And would that make you afraid?" "No. He'd knock, and my mommy would say, 'Come in,' if he was nice, but if he wasn't nice, my mommy and daddy would say, 'Go away,' and call the police." "So they would take care of it?" "Yes, they always do. I think Maggie doesn't know everything. She thinks she does, but I don't think she does. She told me her brother would tell Santa Claus not to bring me any presents, and I cried. But I got lots of presents." "You've decided about that for yourself. It sounds as though you've decided about God, too." "Yes. I don't think he comes in the night at all," Sandy said, and she went off, giving a little carefree hop as she headed toward the playground.

- Ralph, whose mother was soon to have a baby, spent a good deal of time playing out what looked like a birth scene with small family dolls. He would place the baby between the mother doll's legs and then make it drop out again. The teacher finally ventured a guess. "It looks like that baby is getting born," she said. "He is," Ralph told her. "He's coming out of her vagina." "You know about that, I see." "Yes. Her vagina is her special place for babies, not for B.M.'s and wetting." "You've heard about it?" "Yes, but one thing—I wonder, how did the baby get in there?" "Do you have any guesses?" "It grows from a seed. But where does the seed come from?" "Any guesses about that?" The father entered the scene, now, in Ralph's mind, as he went on, "The daddy went to the seed store and bought some." "You think he bought the seed there." "Yes," he answered. "And he gave it to my mommy, and she ate it, and it grew into a baby in her stomach." "Your guess is that she ate it." As Ralph went on playing and talking, he seemed to be thinking with his fingers, too. He picked up the father doll, looked closely at it, put it down, and picked it up again. Then he said, "No, the seed is inside of *him*. It was there all the time." "Then you don't think he bought it at the store and gave it to her to eat?" "No, it didn't go in her mouth." "Where, then, do you think?" He picked up the father and mother dolls, touched them lightly together face to face, and said casually, "In her vagina." Most preschool children are interested in where the baby grows, and they may ask how it will get out, but they rarely ask how it got in. Ralph, whose parents had a tendency to treat him as though he were older, had given him all the facts, but, as is common with children, his fantasies about how it happened had interfered with his really hearing and assimilating all he was told. When he had worked his way through these fantasies with his first answers, the half-heard or perhaps rejected information occurred to him, probably as though it were his own idea.

II

Self-initiated experiments and inventions are prominent among self-directed learning experiences. Here are examples.

● Patrick slammed his blocks against the floor whenever his building fell down. "I wonder why you're doing that?" the teacher asked him. "I'm spanking it; then it will stay. It makes it stay," he said earnestly. "The block feels the spanking?" "Yes." "It cries?" "Yes, it does." "Has it a mouth?" "Yes" (but with a little smile). "Then it's alive?" "Oh, yes." But he put the block down and looked at it a moment. Then he picked it up and walked it with his hand. "*Now* it moves," he said. Later in the day he put down another block, picked it up and walked it, and put it down and watched it again, repeating the process several times. Young children half believe that inanimate objects are alive and only gradually give up this idea. He was finding out for himself.

● Penny's was joint research. "Come and see!" she said, tugging the teacher's hand. There was a long rubber snake lying in one of the lockers. "That's a toy snake; it's Candace's," the teacher told her. "Will it move?" Penny asked, holding the teacher's hand tightly. The teacher put the snake on the floor, and Penny watched it. Then, "Make it move," she directed the teacher, and as the snake was pulled along, she watched closely. "Again," she said, and "Again," once more. Then she said, "Now me," and timidly touched it, then moved it a fraction of an inch, snatching her hand away quickly. As the teacher stood by quietly, she tried again, pulling it a little way, then watching it some more, then pulling it again. Finally she laughed and said, "Yes, it's a toy snake." A thinking person tests things out if possible, rather than blindly accepting what anyone says, teacher or no.

- During a long rainy season, a temper tantrum seemed imminent when Bobby was told he would need to put on his rain clothes at dismissal time. The teacher thought he was probably tired of the rain, but when he was encouraged to explain, that wasn't all. "If I put on my rain clothes, it will *never* stop raining!" he said. "Oh," she said, "You think it rains because you keep wearing your rain clothes. Try and see." So he made the experiment of running outside as he was, stood a moment, held out his hands, shivered, and ran back in. "It didn't stop," he said, as the teacher toweled off his head, and he went to put on his gear.

- Independent learning can lead to what are really child inventions. Susan noticed the teacher cutting off pieces of cord to be used for stringing Styrofoam rings and asked for the ball. She pulled out a section of cord that reached the length of the playroom and asked to have this piece cut off for her. Then she explored its length in many ways, rolling it up and stretching it out again, walking along it, folding it in half and then once again, wrapping it around herself, and so on. Finally, beginning at the back door leading to the playground, she stretched it down the steps and outward, then came running back inside, saying, "I need a bigger piece." Given the ball of cord again, she unrolled it to the back fence of the playground, and that piece was cut off for her too. Hurrying back in, she spread out the two pieces side by side, with one running out the back door; then, telling everyone that the playground was much bigger than the playroom, she said, "But the bathroom is much littler," and followed the same procedure there. Thus did Susan invent the tape measure.

- Daniel invented the process of the stencil one day. Making a random cut from the middle of a sheet of paper by poking it with his scissors, he ended up with an irregular hole. There were water colors nearby, and he painted over his hole, finding on lifting up the paper that the shape, in paint, was there on the table. Excitement hit him, and after a long period of cutting and painting, laying one paper over another, with the floor a snowstorm of false starts and experimental failures all around his chair, he produced a true stencil and used it to make designs in different colors. Then he taught some of the other children how to do it.

The creative excitement of inventing something makes it different from other learning situations. If the teacher were to tell Susan that to make marks along her cord would enable her to compare the lengths of the different areas she was measuring without having to cut new pieces of cord, Susan would have learned about tape measures, but would have been robbed of the experience of inventing a primitive method all by herself. Similarly, to have explained to Daniel, "What you're making is a stencil; you paint over them, and they leave a shape in paint like the cut one," would have made him feel that what he was doing wasn't anything special; it had been done before. Most important, through endeavors like these, children are learning something more valuable than facts and skills and achieving something more worthwhile than a product. They are learning how to think.

● Bo's many inventions from paper and cardboard were worked out with crayons, scissors, and paste, in the use of which he was very skillful. One day he said he wanted to make a "six-foot mechanical mouse." Often children like Bo have quite grandiose schemes; the child's problem then is either to approximate his vision, adapting it to the limits of reality and of his own skills, or else give it up and develop a new idea. With inventions like Bo's mechanical mouse, the temptation of a teacher might be to reduce his aim to something more manageable by saying, "Well, you couldn't very well make that, but you might draw a mouse here on the easel," or to enter into the project with him to such an extent that she became the one doing the inventing, rather than he, in order that he shouldn't be disappointed at the outcome. But being disappointed, discovering the problems and devising solutions, and trying again, are all part of the experience of invention. The teacher's role is to provide what the child thinks he will need in the way of materials, perhaps to hold something if an extra hand is required, and to offer information as to technique or skill, such as "Glue might work better there; it's stronger than paste," or "If that cardboard is too hard to cut, you might try sawing it with the serrated plastic knife," or "We don't have any longer pieces of wire; you could twist two pieces together, or would you like some string or tape?"

For his six-foot mechanical mouse, Bo asked for some "very big cardboard." There was nothing on hand that day with six-foot dimensions, and the teacher offered him the biggest thing she had; a four-foot cardboard tube. Bo made his first adjustment to reality limits comfortably; he stood the tube up beside himself and was pleased to find it considerably taller than he was. From then on he worked independently at the table, cutting and pasting. When the mouse was finished, he was delighted with it and brought it to show the teachers and children. A large face with ears and whiskers had been drawn on heavy paper and cut out. With great effort, he had made two slots at one end of the tube and inserted the face into them. He had also drawn and cut out four slender legs with toes at the ends, and these dangled from the sides of the tube where they had been taped. A long thin strip at the bottom, in back, served as a tail, and waved with the four legs as he carried his mouse around the room. And, as he went triumphantly past her, the teacher saw, taped near the bottom of the tube, a windup key—sign and seal of a Mechanical Mouse.

III

The everyday practical experiences in the nursery school are important sources of learning. They include such problems as how to find what one wants or needs, how to identify one's locker, how to open the gate on coming in and going home, how to turn on the water faucets and take out paper towels and cups, how to flush the toilet, and how to keep track of one's possessions.

How to take off and put on wraps is a useful part of what is learned. This includes finding one's things, doing what one can to manage them, and taking the responsibility of asking for help with the rest. In a program that permits free indoor and outdoor access throughout the day, the child is motivated to do more for himself, since he is dressing or undressing according to his own self-chosen schedule rather than that of someone else. In helping children learn to handle their clothing, teachers' demonstrations, as well as words, communicate explanation. Many three-year-olds like to learn how to lay their jackets or sweaters on floor or table with the inside up and the collars toward them ("This little tag is just under your nose when you bend over," says the teacher) and, putting their arms straight down into the armholes, flip the garment over their heads. This means it is never upside down, and the usual problems of getting the first arm in the proper sleeve and then getting the second arm in are avoided.

- Miles, who was four, wanted to put his jacket on the way he saw grownups do it. He then had an experience of following verbal instructions, accompanied by demonstration. "You can hold your jacket up this way in front of you," he was told, "so you can see both holes. See them? Now you can let go one hand—just one—and let that side drop down." Both hands let go, but Miles started over, and this time he heard "just one," and held on tight with one hand. "Here's a free hand, ready to go," the teacher said, swinging it, "so that hand can go in, right under the other hand, in that hole." Started off right, he managed to squirm the jacket over his shoulder and get the other arm in. Later he was seen to hold up his jacket and gaze intently at the two armholes, release one hand—jumping back as though he thought the jacket were going to get away of its own accord—then triumphantly finish the process. (This is a typical instance of difficulties with inside and outside, front and back, and right and left.)

  Angus was not able to use either Miles's method or the flip-over one. His teacher held his jacket for him and waited, without words, while he tried the wrong arms in the holes, found the back across his front, puzzled, tried again and found the same result, then reversed his arms and smiled with satisfaction to see the familiar zipper-opening where it should be. When jackets or sweaters need to be held up, a child can do this for a friend, and he can also hold the friend's cuff so he can pull out his arm to start the taking-off process.

- In their readiness to learn the same thing, children vary for individual as well as developmental reasons. Livy fussed and lost her temper when she couldn't get a doll's shoes on, during the period when she was setting herself too high standards of perfection. The teacher told her then, "Sometimes, you know, people need to ask other people to help them. So you could say, 'Will you help me?'" Miles, who was trying many new things at that time, brought the doll shoes to the teacher and asked how to put them on. "This is the way I do it, but you might find other ways," said the teacher, and she slowly demonstrated putting the shoe over the doll's toes and then pressing the heel down. But Rosie came over and over again with the same request—"Put her shoes on"—and the teacher just did it, feeling that Rosie didn't want to learn how, but, instead, sought proof that her teacher liked her and would give her help she needed. Rosie usually brought mismatched socks, too, but they were put on without comment. Suddenly Rosie began matching the socks and putting on the shoes by herself, showing, at the same time, other more outgoing, mature behavior. Part of a good relationship means accepting a child as he is, if he indicates a growing, learning impulse that is responded to, but so is a feeling of wanting care and help.

Many practical learning experiences are provided by the need for the school to be kept in reasonable order. When children are able to find what they want quickly and easily, not only does their play proceed more smoothly and with a longer attention span, but they also feel secure and independent in a setting they understand.

Teachers often "spotlight" an activity not currently arousing much interest by moving it to an area where children are unaccustomed to seeing it. A painting easel on the grass or books on a mat in a corner of the playground would be immediately noticed by a child. In the same way, but less usefully, objects out of place in a disorderly playroom impinge on his consciousness and distract and overstimulate him. A young child cannot blot out irrelevant stimuli and select relevant ones, as an adult can. The result is that, in a chaotic environment, he becomes chaotic himself. A jumble of blocks and toys on the floor leads him to kick or plough into them, or fall on them. Disorder suggests more disorder, and he seems irresistibly impelled to mess things up more, much as he is tempted to put his hands into his spilled milk or step in it. Fortunately one of the strongest desires of the small child is to be important, necessary, and useful, like the rest of the world—a desire there are few ways to satisfy at this age. "Helping the teacher" often turns into slowing her down considerably, and tactful though she may be, children are aware of this. But a teacher does really need children's help in keeping the many appurtenances of a school in order, and they themselves can see the usefulness of that order as they play. (However, as a learning experience picking up is successful only in proportion as it is self-motivated. For example, right after a child has thoroughly expressed his interest in something and has become satiated, he seldom wants to stay with it and put it away. He either needs a discharge of tension through a different kind of activity, or has a new interest to be explored in a burst of enthusiasm.)

Throughout the day the teacher will be putting away things no one is using that are cluttering up spaces, and this activity of hers will be noticed and imitated, as will her readiness to take responsibility for the school's orderliness, no matter who was playing with what. Whenever the teacher is tidying up the room, "I'll help you" is almost always heard from one or more children. At pick-up time children's small capacity for selective awareness of stimuli shows clearly; they cannot sort, and, if clutter has accumulated, they have no idea how to proceed, short of dumping everything into one box. Feelings of inadequacy from past experiences with picking up have also left some of them resistant. Knowing their vulnerabilities, the teacher will have preorganized a lot, pushing together blocks of the same kind near the shelf where they belong, and eliminating some categories of objects to make sorting easier, and she will also perhaps give them a start by saying, "Would you like to look for animals? Here's their basket," or "You might pick out something you know how to put away—that truck you like?" There is no general announcement of picking-up time, but individuals using toys are warned to finish as soon as they can, and the teacher may ask children who are between occupations to help, probably suggesting things they have taken out and therefore will know how to put away. But she accepts "No, I don't want to." (Rarely she might say, "I can't do it alone by story time; I need you," and some will always come running.) Occasionally a group wants to pick up "all by ourselves," perhaps devising a cooperative system. Every day is different, and if, on some occasion, everyone looks very occupied, the teacher would rather do it herself than interrupt them. The children seem to accept one reason for cleaning up the playroom well—a need to get it ready for a morning (or afternoon) group to follow them. ("Do you think they'll like me putting the dolls' clothes all on for them?") They are interested in these unknown children; sometimes one will ask the name of the child who will be using his locker. As time goes on, they help more at picking-up time, and also help to keep clutter down during the day by spontaneously putting things away when finished with them, picking up spilled objects, hunting for lost parts, and so on.

Other housekeeping experiences will involve sweeping, dusting, and washing. A short-handled push broom can be used for sweeping sand off sidewalk areas, and doing this beside the teacher with her big broom is the way a child learns how it's done. Children are hard on feather dusters, but they can use hand-brushes to dust outdoor shelves, boxes, and other surfaces. Sponges are their delight, and a bucket of wet ones will last them quite a while for the washing of their outside play equipment. ("But don't wash where people sit," they remind each other.) Unless it's an all-out water-play day, the teacher will need to wet the sponges beforehand. The children's hands are too small to squeeze out excess water well, and water runs down their sleeves.

Taking care of their possessions is only gradually learned by children. Many leave trails of jackets, toys from home, papers, shoes, and other belongings. It seems best if things never disappear by magic from where they were last used, so a teacher needs to draw attention to them, not just pick them up herself. "Your picture is still on the table, did you know?" But she can also draw attention to them by offering to put them away for the child, and this leads to many instances of children putting things away for her and for each other. "Whose lunch box is that on the table?" "It's Roddie's." (They always know, apparently.) "I know where his locker is; I'll do it. Hey, Roddie!"

Food and the sharing of it with others is another practical experience that can be very meaningful to children as an expression of love dating from the infancy period when a baby first received love in that form from his mother and his relationship with her began to grow. When lunch is eaten at school, teachers try to make it an occasion at a child's own level by allowing as much freedom as possible for a choice of time, place, and companions. Four-year-olds, under supervision, can eat in small groups without an adult at the table. They learn new tastes, serve themselves, pour milk from small thermal pitchers as desired, decide when they've had enough, and clean up after themselves, meanwhile experiencing much social warmth from peers.

At school, cooking with heat requires a good deal of teacher direction and supervision, but there are other ways children can work independently with food and then serve it as snacks or special treats. They can prepare raw vegetables by scraping carrots, shelling peas, or breaking string beans and asparagus. They can pick seedless green grapes off bunches, cut up ripe bananas with round-tipped serrated plastic knives, shell peanuts, squeeze orange juice, and peel hard-boiled eggs. They can also decorate whole-wheat crackers of different shapes with cheese spread squeezed from a tube, and press walnut halves into dried prunes, apricots, and figs. For children who enjoy getting their hands right in, "cookies" can be made by combining peanut butter with raisins, nuts, and crushed cracker crumbs and then rolling the mixture into small balls. Especially enjoyed is the making of original "mixes" in dishes, using dry cereal as a base and vigorously stirring in almost anything else on hand. The children who are interested can work alone or in pairs; when they emerge from the place reserved for their use bearing a tray of food, there is always much appreciation. A child may also bring a treat from home, and if he is allowed to share this as he wishes, perhaps with a special friend or two at a little table in an adjoining room, relationships prosper.

IV

An occasional excursion away from school can be a learning experience if it involves only a few children in response to their particular interests, rather than an entire group. No planned trip will be appropriate to the developmental level of every child in a group, and those who feel overwhelmed by too many strange, confusing sights and sounds will learn very little, if anything. Nor does time spent in passive observation while following adults into a world too big for one help in developing a sense of self. In addition, some have worrying thoughts, such as "What if mother comes, and I'm not there at school?" That would be a real separation. The child would be gone, and the mother would not know where to find him. The teacher's explanation that they will all be back before dismissal time doesn't help; as the child sees it, if neither knows where the other is, both are lost. For reasons like these, and others, a planned excursion often ends in children's being more impressed by some minor event on the way with which they felt comfortable—leaves floating down the gutter or a fly crawling all the way up the car window—than with the excursion itself. On the whole it seems better for young children to have simpler experiences that they can really grasp and in which there is also a chance for active participation. In some groups the children may already be spending too much time driving here and there with their parents. And it might be even more important to postpone trips for very inexperienced, naive children until they are a little more mature.

Using the resources in the immediate neighborhood is one way to avoid the problems and keep the gains of excursions. If a few children at a time can go on foot, the overexcitement that arises in cars and makes additional escorts necessary is not a factor. Also, children can have a free choice about whether to go or not; no child needs to go along unhappily. No one must stay longer than he is interested, or leave sooner than he is ready. Fatigue and emotional stress are precluded, too. If there is a walk around the block, for instance, children get away from school into different scenes, but under their own power and with the feeling that it's all under their own control. They will soon return (usually running the last part of the distance), and seeing them safely and cheerfully back, timid ones are often ready to go next. They may carry musical instruments and wear dress-up clothes, or bring favorite animals or dolls, or take a snack to eat on the way. Perhaps a wagon might go, too, to pull a child or chosen provisions. On the way the teachers can help by example to open up the children's eyes and ears; there may be a cat in the window of one house, a motorcycle by the curb to be closely examined, fallen leaves and cones to be gathered, pigeons in a row on a telephone wire, different kinds of trucks and cars passing by, a man using a power mower on his lawn, a baby in a stroller—always something new.

Quite often there are sewer repair operations, telephone linesmen, or tree-trimming trucks, either near the front door or close by, and a pair at a time can go out with a teacher to watch for a few minutes, those most interested probably making several trips. David and Chip appeared so regularly in the school's yellow hard hats to watch the similarly garbed workmen engaged in street repair that one of the men invited them to sit in the high seat of his rig with him on his lunch break. This led to one of the chief gains of excursions, the enrichment of dramatic play. The two boys initiated extended projects using working trucks in the sand that many others joined, with increased vocabulary and information for all.

For Hoddie, who had always been very much afraid of fire engines, a visit with two others to the fire station helped greatly. He had been a little skeptical when the teacher told him that water, not fire, came from the hoses of the firemen. At the fire station he asked the man who greeted the children, "What comes out of your hoses?" Told "Water," he still looked unsure, and the man left to put on his large black fire hat. Then, more impressive, he said, "It's water," again, and answered the other questions the teacher had helped the children plan to ask. At the end of the visit, these children, too, were invited to climb up into a strange-looking machine and examine it more closely. Opportunities like this are much more likely to occur when the group is very small; then informality, rather than a tour and a lecture, is usual. Other special-interest excursions for a few children at a time might include a visit by animal lovers to a Baby Zoo, a facility many parks have which allows children to feed and pet live animals and thus to be active, rather than passive.

Many advantages of excursions can be better gained from inviting visitors to the school or looking at materials brought in from outside. A cellist, a trumpeter, or a drummer would interest both musical and machine-oriented children, for example. When musicians come to the school, it's well to explain to them that the children will not be required to sit still and listen, but that things will be just as they always are; the children will be free to choose what they want to do and to come and go as they like, though they will be asked to play somewhere else if what they are doing is disturbing. Sometimes a musician might play for children who like to dance; this is one way to provide for active participation.

Other visitors that children enjoy are those who come to work at the school. When a teacher has become acquainted with a community, she begins to know which plumber, which carpenter, which roof-repair man, and which gardener offer children the kind of relationship, as well as demonstration of skills and equipment, that she wants for them. Those most desired will be comfortable enough being watched in a circle of intent faces to go on quietly doing their work, answering questions, no matter how naively phrased, with the same respect they would give to adults, never teasing the children so that they become self-conscious or begin to show off. A school custom already established of allowing others their privacy and space will pay off here; the group will accept the idea of remaining beyond a psychological barrier, such as the bathroom door (for a plumber), a line of chairs, or a rope to mark limits if the work is outside. When adults of the kind described can be found, arrangements can be made for many jobs to be done when children are in school, particularly the four-year-olds (most three-year-olds would rather things stayed the same). Furnace servicing, painting in an area not too near the watchers, resetting of floor tiles, window washing, garbage collection, resurfacing of cracks in pavement—all these interest children. When new grass is seeded or pruning is done, children can participate by weaving streamers into a chicken-wire fence to keep birds from eating the seeds, or by carrying armloads of prunings to the gardener's trailer. And when new sand is delivered, they can be in on that, too, watching it being dumped and then helping by running loads up boards into the sandbox in their dump trucks and small wheelbarrows.

People with special interests can also be invited to share these with the children, if they understand the philosophy of self-directed learning. Many adults tend to talk too much, take over too much, and flood children with stimuli. From a wish to give them everything possible, they thus end by taking the ball away from them. But it isn't the quantity they offer that is important; it is the quality of the experience. Children needn't be shown everything that might conceivably interest them; they have their whole lives before them for that. But whatever is selected should be shown under the best conditions, in a setting in which each child feels secure and relaxed, and in which there is freedom to explore and investigate independently, ask questions, think about the experience and relate it to previous ones, and have feelings about it and express them.

In addition to visits from outsiders, a teacher can bring many interesting things into the school. Rather than a trip to an art museum, for instance, pictures can be secured on loan for short periods. One of these, kept for a while and really examined, is better than rooms and rooms of them half seen. In addition, the teacher can choose something appropriate to her group's interests and maturity, and accidental exposure to frightening or bewildering pictures will be avoided. Seeing how things work is a special interest of this age, but excursions are not the only way for them to have that kind of experience, either. Machines can be brought in that they can not only watch but try themselves. Examples might be a coffee grinder, a butter churn, an ice cream maker, a bicycle pump, a typewriter, a metronome, a rock tumbler, a pencil sharpener, a heavy-duty stapler, a tape recorder, a dictaphone, or an intercom set. For safety's sake and also to prevent the tension of watching and waiting for turns, the machine would be shown in a separate area, to only one or two children at a time.

V

Many kinds of nature experiences can be provided by a nursery school. The fall, winter, and spring seasons all add color and beauty to the playroom. In autumn there is the brown, russet, orange, and yellow of displayed leaves, Indian corn, gourds, or chestnuts, with these colors seen, too, in collage materials and paints, so that children become more aware of them. A "nature box" can be kept near the door for other contributions, such as leaves, shells, cones, driftwood, moss, wheat stalks, seeds and pods, bark, and perhaps some feathers. In winter, the natural decorations would have the deep, rich colors of evergreen branches and the bright red of pyrocantha and holly, and these colors, too, along with snow-white, would be among those in the room and in the art supplies. And in spring, children and teachers bring flowers, pussy willows, and budding branches. Pulled-off flower heads can always float in a bowl of water, and dandelions and plucked weeds can dangle from bud vases. Some children like to make arrangements with flowers and leaf sprays. Then white paint is often mixed with the other kinds, so that the clear, light colors and pastels of spring, with their delicate, more subtle effects, offer a new experience. As well as these seasonal room decorations that help to bring the outdoors inside, there can be a familiar spot in the room for examining changing exhibits such as a rock collection, a shell collection, polished samples of different kinds of wood, a budding plant, or a miniature cactus garden. One group found interestingly shaped bare branches in their nature place and set about making things to hang on them. Whatever the exhibit, it needs to be left for children to explore at their leisure with a minimum of direction, demonstration, and explanation, except in response to questions; in this way, there is independent learning.

One focus of children's absorbed interest is their outdoor play space. Sand, earth, and water inspire enthusiasm that never flags. If there is a large sand area deep enough for digging, this provides endless opportunities for experimenting with hills, tunnels, ditches, and, in warm weather when a hose can be used, with canals and dams. Gathering pebbles is another favorite occupation. Some children like to try to root cuttings from plants like ivy and fuchsia, using paper or plastic cups filled with wet sand, or may plant things like peach pits, apple seeds, beans, or carrot tops to take home. Flower seeds or bulbs may be planted in a small, specially reserved area by an interested child or two. Real gardening, however, needs so much supervision that it is hard for a teacher to make it the experience of independent functioning so gratifying to the growing sense of self. In addition, young children seem better adapted to more immediate results.

Coming upon ladybugs, beetles, worms, snails, caterpillars, or even, with luck, perhaps a tree frog, are important parts of the outdoor adventure. A terrarium can hold backyard finds of this kind. Sometimes it will be possible to keep the caterpillars children find in the fall until they have completed their cycle. A nylon net over a terrarium will stop them from escaping until they have spun their cocoons. When they emerge as moths or butterflies, they can be released to fly away, a fascinating sight, especially if they first open up their wings and make trial flights. Sometimes a moth will lay eggs in the terrarium. If that happens, children may be able to see the tiny, voracious worms eat and grow into fuzzy caterpillars, starting the cycle all over again. The rapid growth of these, and of the baby snails that sometimes appear in the terrarium along with the adult ones is especially interesting to small children, who, though they have often been told they themselves are growing, have some trouble believing it. Snails, when placed in trays with a little water, put out their horns and walk, climb overturned glasses, or crawl on top of each other. Children enjoy protecting them from falling off things and crawling away too far, learning to handle them confidently. Part of the experience with the backyard creatures is their fairly early release and return to the places where they were found.

An increased awareness of what is all around in the real world comes from active explorations in an outdoor area. Curiosity has an outlet, and learning results; attitudes of distaste or fear change, too, and self-confidence increases.

● The intimate relationship of learning and emotions is seen in Kiki's experience with an odd-shaped leaf that she discovered in the playground. She saw it, partly hidden in some ivy, and came running, frightened, to the teacher. "It a bad thing on the fence, it going to get me!" she said, drawing the teacher by the hand to see. The teacher pulled out the leaf and showed it to her, telling her that though it was curled, and dry, and brown now, when it had been growing on the tree it was a green leaf like those she had often seen. But Kiki didn't listen; she shrank away, saying, "No, no! Don't touch it!" So the teacher put the leaf on the ground and sprinkled some dirt on it, saying, "Would you like to cover it up?" Kiki did a thorough job of burying the leaf, and stamped on it for good measure. Then she dug it up again and looked it over carefully. She kept it in her locker until dismissal time and took it out then to show her mother, saying importantly, "Don't be afraid, mama. This a leaf. It just a old crunkled leaf." Afraid, Kiki had been unable to hear the facts first offered; relieved of her fear by her own action, she was ready to learn.

It is important, when offering information about nature, to keep in mind the vulnerability of a preschool child. While he may on occasion need a mild warning about a bee, there is probably no need for him to learn about poisonous snakes, black widow spiders, or tarantulas, and certainly none for him to hear at this age about the dangerous aspects of wildlife remote from his world. Nothing would be gained, because not only would his sense of security be shaken, but a child who learns too many frightening facts about nature may turn away from learning anything at all about it afterwards.

All children are fascinated by live animals. Pets from home can be brought to school to visit by children or teachers. Other sources are pet stores and pet lending libraries. If there is a farm that might be persuaded to lend something, a goose or perhaps a lamb might spend a day or two. In this way children can become acquainted with a wide variety of creatures, such as birds, guinea pigs, fish, turtles, puppies, kittens, rabbits, chicks, hamsters, rats, and mice. Norman, whose home companions aside from his parents were his pets, often brought a horned toad to school, and it rode everywhere upon his shoulder. Norman had a special way with animals. However, many a preschool child treats animals with smothering attention or rough domination. When he uses his toy animals this way, adults can accept both his behavior and the feelings he is showing, but when the animal is alive, adults react differently, and sometimes this is hard for him to understand. Sometimes, too, he feels jealous when he is interfered with in his play, as though the animal were a kind of sibling whose part the adults were taking against him; then he resents the animal and feels like treating it even more roughly. For reasons like this, play with animals that visit needs close supervision, or, if that is not practicable, cages with screened sides that keep fingers out will be required. There is always the danger that a child may be bitten or that he may himself hurt an animal, either accidentally or intentionally, and feel painful guilt afterwards.

Short visits seem to work better than long ones, because after a time the animal begins to seem like a member of the group. But animals that become pets at school may die, or accidents may happen to them, and then the loss is felt as though a loved friend had disappeared from their lives, as all parents know when a family pet has died or run away. It is better if first encounters with death do not involve personal loss and grief. Also, because children readily identify with animals, there is always the thought in their minds that if, for example, a rabbit kills its young or baby chicks are pecked, perhaps the teacher cannot take care of them, either. A pet that can be expected to live a long time and is relatively immune to injury, such as a tortoise, might be an exception, but substitutes for live food would need to be found for it. Though a child sometimes steps on snails or bugs out of fear ("Let's watch" helps overcome the fear), he identifies with the live flies and mealy worms that reptiles eat as small creatures needing protection. Nor could he comfortably accept the fact that the teacher whom he trusted to keep everyone safe in the school was feeding one small creature to another. Similarly, since the difference between animate and inanimate is still unclear to children in the nursery school, it is too early for them to see dissections of any kind. No matter what might be accomplished in the name of science teaching, it would be far outweighed by seeing one's own teacher, one's model, apparently inflict harm. The goals of achieving relationships of trust and of acquiring the sense of security that leads to self-affirmation would both have been set aside. If a group is exposed to the idea of death through coming upon a dead bird, or in some other unavoidable way, the experience would be met with honest discussion, but to intentionally expose a child may result in too much, too soon.

The visit of an animal will have different meanings to different children; one may ask questions, a second may have fantasies about it, a third may be alarmed, and yet another may see it as a challenge to show his superior strength. Each child thus has his own needs. A simple, direct relation of child to animal, motivated by the child's personal interest, can take place if he is able to look and explore to his heart's content, with time and quiet for his thoughts to develop and be expressed and for his questions to be answered. So, for example, if a rabbit is brought to school, the first experience might be its examination in a safe cage by one or two children at a time in a separate room. Other children might be invited to see it, again one or two at a time, when between occupations. Children could stay as long as they wished; several days might be needed for all to see it. The teacher would sometimes participate, perhaps by helping them to hold the rabbit or feed it, but much of the rabbit research could be independent.

VI

Parties at school can have special benefits, if they are really the children's parties, rather than ones planned and directed by adults. The latter can actually diminish the sense of self; a child loses control of proceedings, wonders what will happen and what will be expected of him, and is often prey to too much anticipation and excitement. He is not a doer; something is being done for him instead. As only a passive recipient, he characteristically both looks and feels smaller than usual. If he is to sit at a table, play games, wear a hat, or open favors, as one of a group all doing the same thing, this makes for some loss of his individual identity and sense of self, as well as perhaps requiring behavior beyond his level of social maturity. But certain kinds of parties do enhance the sense of self.

Usually on a child's birthday he has a new feeling about himself, and he seems to be better able to pin this feeling down and grow on it when his birthday receives special notice. So a child might bring cookies to school that he helped to make or shop for, or perhaps another kind of treat of his own choice. And he decides where, when, and how to have his school party.

- For her birthday party, Maggie decorated place mats and napkins for the largest table, helped by Sandy and Candace; then she put a cookie that she had frosted at school on each mat. Glasses of the "pink juice" she requested were on a self-help tray in the middle of the table. She started by summoning the children who were inside, and later she set another table outside for the rest. Maggie handled the serving entirely by herself. She kept the plate of cookies in front of her and responded to requests for more by passing them until they were all gone. Following their usual snack custom, children left the table when they had finished eating, and those who drifted in from other areas took their places.

Some, as always, preferred not to sit down, and Maggie let them have cookies and depart.

Bill, a younger child, arrived on his birthday with cookies, but he seemed uneasy about the party idea. He was encouraged to put his cookies in his locker and play. The teacher told him, "You could take some for yourself, and if you feel like it later, you can give one to somebody you like." He brought Alex to see them after a while, and they sat munching together in adjacent lockers. Two or three others, passing by, asked, "Can I have one?" and it apparently struck him then that he was in the important position of being able to confer favors on people. As the word got around, others came to him, and he doled out cookies directly from his hand into theirs. At length he decided that was all, and he put the rest in his locker to take home for his family.

Some children may prefer just to sit down, when ready, with the box of cookies in front of them, and as others notice and ask for some, either let them help themselves or select cookies for them. Soon there is a tablefull, and "Happy Birthday" might be sung. (Many a child, when consulted, would rather not have a song sung about him, however.) A host child who finds sitting at a table too formal or uninteresting may decide, instead, to go through the room and playground bearing a basket containing his treat. The teacher needs to help him keep control of his party by reminding the children to ask first, to take only one at a time, and so on. After once or twice around, often the leftovers are left on a table for children to help themselves; the child has had all he wanted of the experience and has gone on to something else. And there are always other birthday children like Al, for instance, who treasured all his cookies for himself, and like Angus, who had a private party for Patrick and himself in the top of the jungle gym. The teacher makes it clear to the other children, as well as to the child himself, that he is the one who decides how his party will be. To have to share when there is no sharing feeling is not a sharing experience, no matter what outward gestures are made. The teacher's aim is not to overwhelm the child, but to let him proceed at his own pace, so that, however small and simple, the party for his birthday remains his.

At Halloween, the teacher might carve a pumpkin, letting the children see the procedure and participate, too, by helping to scrape out the seeds and saving some to take home for roasting and by testing how the finished jack-o'-lantern looks through a window and in a darkened room. A big part of any Halloween party can be dressing up in clothes added to the usual supply. It seems best if these are not designed for specific roles but, with the aid of imagination, can fit any role the child wants to assume. Thus he is not directed by the material toward any fantasy other than the one he has in his mind. For this reason, masks would not be included, leaving the child free to imagine his face as he wants it to look. The roles selected by children are usually either those of power figures or reflect "fairest of them all" ideas; often, however, a child wants to be something by which he has been frightened, perhaps in a story or on television, thus turning the tables. Another addition for the party might be a basket of Halloween noisemakers; some may want to parade through the school, or perhaps around the block.

● Halloween is a time when fears may be aroused. Rory asked, "What's a ghost?" "You've heard something about a ghost?" the teacher asked him. "Yes, my brother says there are ghosts that come out on Halloween." "And you've never seen one?" "No, but I think they are all white and scary." "Any more you've heard?" she asked. "They're people, some kind—not animals, I know that. Did you ever see a ghost?" The teacher replied, "The only ghosts I've ever seen are little boys and girls all covered up with sheets that have holes cut to look through. When you see them dressed that way on Halloween, they might look strange and scary. But under each sheet is—" Rory burst out, relieved, "A boy—, a girl—, a child!"

Halloween masks, skeletons, and so on, can be threatening to the nursery school child if he gets from them the idea of a person with something wrong, missing, or hurt in his body. Commercial masks often play frankly on such fears by showing distorted and mutilated faces. Formerly, when the child saw things come apart, crack, or tear, or noticed the difference between boys and girls, the thought had come that parts of people might break off, too. A teacher can sometimes help a child toward a better hold on reality, if an incident has aroused fears about his body's soundness, by saying, "Here you are, all of you—your eyes—one, two; your nose, mouth, ears, neck, chest, arms, hands, stomach, penis [or vulva], knees, feet—it's all you, and you're just the way you should be." The child usually wants this repeated. (When a teacher reassures a child this way it is not done solemnly and heavily, but more as though it were a kind of gentle joke between them—as though they both knew, *really*, but just liked to say it.) Masks that are fierce-looking, or weird and grotesque like a child's own fantasied creatures, can upset his equilibrium, too, and make him feel, again, small, helpless, and unable to cope. If some children arrive at the party in costumes from home, a sign for parents to read saying "Please carry masks in hands" is useful. An unfrightening mask can be made available for examination; children handle it, peek through both sides, and discuss what it is made of. Some are reluctant to put a mask on, partly because it is hard to see with it on, but also because they sometimes think, in primitive fashion, that to have a different face is to change into a different person. Some four-year-olds like to wear masks, however, and even try to make them in the hope of mystifying or scaring somebody, but the ones they achieve by their own efforts cause no trouble.

For many children the best part of the Halloween party (or any other) is the enjoyment of special party food. If there is no particular time for eating, there will be no building up of tension and excitement, but, rather, a gradually developing, continuous party that lasts until the food is gone, with munching and trips to the apple-juice table as different children change their occupations. Several solitary snack times might recur more than once, a few small groups might eat together, or perhaps a party for two might take place in a corner. There would be food on the tables, both indoors and out, and a child or two might also carry around a basket of treats. Plastic glasses of juice, and basins ready for the used ones, along with napkins, can make self-help possible both indoors and out. The consequence of a more natural and informal party like this is that teachers are free to help individual children use all the day's experiences for learning and growing, as they do on any other day. Highest praise from teachers after such a party would be "It was their own party all the way through," meaning that the party was yet another self-directed activity.

If there is to be a winter recess for the school, a party serves to mark the occasion and help the children understand that it's good-bye for a while. At the party, there is sometimes an orgy of wrapping "presents," ranging from pictures and clay and wood products to half-eaten crackers or imaginary things. If materials are plentiful—foil precut, tape in strips, paper bags, boxes, rubber bands—the children can usually cover their presents to their own satisfaction. If help is needed by some, they can be referred to those more expert. To have another child, rather than the teacher, do what is too hard sometimes seems more helpful. There is no concern about not living up to someone else's expectations; the other child is not apt to have any. There is also more confidence that if one watches it may be possible to learn, since the gap between another child and oneself seems smaller. This kind of situation often encourages a child to try new things, and it increases the helping child's self-esteem, too. (For the same reason, a teacher often asks a child to help another find a toy, open a door, put on shoes, and so on.) Because the creative process is primarily an expressive one, for the teacher to suggest that a present be made for someone is not very appropriate; in any case, giving feelings arise from loving feelings, and not on suggestion, or because it is the time of year for gifts. A painting made to order, for example, might be rather slapdash, and, if the child really got involved in it, he would probably want to keep it. (A child not uncommonly wraps a present and then says, "This is for me.") At the party, as at any other time, the teacher avoids setting goals for children that are not their own. Sometimes there is little or no interest in holiday gift-giving; sometimes, too, all the interest arises afterward, stimulated by the presents the children have received at home.

One of the most meaningful of school parties is the last-day or good-bye party at the end of the year. For this, the children who are not returning in the fall might bring treats or favors for everyone, if they wish. These might be peanuts, gum, cookies or cupcakes, tiny apples, pretzels, raisins and dates. (Materials for making treats would be ready at school, too, for anyone who got an idea later.) Favors might be things like paper hats, crowns, or balloons. At intervals during the day, one or another child decides to pass out his treat or "surprise." Everyone is aware that this is a good-bye party and last-day children feel warmly appreciated. The party helps the children to leave feeling that they have done something especially friendly, rather than that they have deserted or rejected their old playmates. And it also helps those left behind. When a friend is missed, they can be reminded, "Remember? She gave you a good-bye treat."

VII

In groups of four-year-old children, spontaneous interest in number concepts, writing, and reading can be observed in some individuals. Number concepts will have appeared earlier, and usually by the time a group is ready to graduate, evidences of interest in printing are appearing in one form or another in several children. In any group, however, most are not mature enough for reading (and some will not be until they are five or six years old, or even older). In a few, one might see signs of interest in reading that come and go, and one or two may develop that interest further and for longer periods as time goes on, though with phases in which it still drops out completely in favor of other involvements.

In any nursery school, when one watches children using materials and interacting with one another, many examples of the beginnings of number concepts can be seen. Often this appears when they are dividing objects to be shared. Treats may be counted out ("Everybody gets four"). Paper-doll dresses may be placed in piles to be used by a group of friends; then the piles are counted and recounted to make sure they are equal. Even the youngest children might spill out a basket of small toys on a table and divide them into piles that appear to be fairly equal; apparently, though most cannot count with any accuracy, they have a pretty good idea of "more" and "less" as they look at these piles, seeing which children have too many and which too few without counting. In building with blocks, too, one sees children take out the number of blocks from the shelf that will be needed to make one half of a building equal to the other, or use two units that, together, will equal the size of another block. Older children comprehend still more complicated problems of halves, quarters, and eighths in the use of the block units, and in building with them, they match dimensions as they work on their structures. This familiarity with the ways blocks can be used comes before the learning of words such as "triangle," "rectangle," "square," "cube," "pyramid," "cone," or "cylinder"; the teacher mentions the names casually, and these then enter the children's speech naturally, as other words do when useful. "I need one of those." "A cube?" "Yes, a cube."

● Paul had a special ability and interest in the use of number concepts. The contrast between his chubby, babyish appearance and immature speech patterns and the evidence of his mathematical awareness was startling. On one occasion, when the teacher was cutting large blocks of Styrofoam into halves, he looked at the sections on the table, glanced into the basket of uncut rectangles, and said, in his almost incomprehensible speech, "Oo'll have 'ixteen." It took the teacher several moments to realize that she would indeed have sixteen halves. Another time, he and his friend wanted some elastic ropes with hooks to stretch across the jungle-gym bars; as the teacher approached with seven in her hand, he glanced at them and said, "No, we want 'ix, we not want 'even." "Why, Paul?" "We want both have the 'ame." And he explained patiently, as though, like older mathematical geniuses, he was used to not being understood, "Th'ee for me, and th'ee for him." It was obvious that Paul never counted, as the others did; he just knew, somehow, with a glance, how many of any objects there were. When a group of the four-year-olds was sorting picture tiles into a sectioned box according to the number of objects on each tile, the difference between his way of working and theirs was striking. Each tile showed from one to ten objects, divided into either two or three groups. Sometimes, when there were two groups on a tile, each having the same number of objects, the other children would count all the objects to find the total, pointing to each. But Paul would notice that the groups were identical and say that there were eight objects, explaining to the others, with a slight look of surprise that it wasn't obvious, "There *two* four; that make eight." When he couldn't multiply by two because the number of objects in one group was different from the number in the other, and even when there were three groups of objects on a tile, Paul still made no use of his fingers to count, but would look at each group, add them in his head, then pop the tile into the right compartment for seven, nine, or whatever it might be. Paul's dealings with numbers always involved real materials. Being able to recite "two and two are four" has little or nothing to do with being able to understand and use number concepts in life, any more than being able to say the ABC's indicates reading readiness, or even an understanding of what reading is.

Interest in numbers is often seen, as well, in children's desire to have their friends' telephone numbers pinned on their shirts so they can invite them to visit when they get home. After these numbers are printed out for them, sometimes they practice dialing them on a toy telephone. At the time of his fourth birthday, the number four suddenly became important to Alex, and he wanted a four printed for him on one of the cards the teacher gave to anyone who expressed an interest in seeing how a number or word looked. He copied his four carefully, then laid it to his cheek, saying, "O what a fine little four!"

Like interest in numbers, interest in printing words also arises out of everyday situations. Each child's locker has a label with his name printed on it. Children learn their own and their friends' lockers at first by location, by the color of the labels, and by the shape and appearance of the names, without regard to individual letters. It appears to be a mark of friendship to know where one's friend's locker is, and a very social child may even try to learn all the locker names, asking several times to have the teacher read the whole row. Learning to make names, starting with one's own, and then adding that of one's special friend, leads children to copying letters, and sometimes a few of the older four-year-olds might be seen sitting in chairs they have brought over in front of the lockers, copying favorite names. In the early period of Steve's friendship with Jay, he printed Jay's name over and over, taking the papers home with him at the end of each day, and there was no doubt that to him a word was a symbol, as he thus took his friend home with him and seemed comforted thereby in those difficult partings. Children may also ask the teacher for cards with their friends' names on them and, after copying these, give the products away in large gestures of generosity—"Here's your Name!"

The teacher is also often asked to make signs for play, such as "Bus Station," "Grocery Store," "Doctor's Office," "Please Wait," and "Come In" to hang at the doll-corner door, or "Please Save" for sand castles or block buildings, and some observe the writing process closely. Though less interested in individual letters, one may say, "That's in my name!" and hear, "It's a *B*." Some children even like to copy whole phrases, such as "To My Valentine," "Happy Birthday," and "To Dorothy from Tammy," from cards given to them by the teacher on their request. All these experiences with printed words (usually employing both lower case and upper case letters, since both will be found in the books they will read later) help children see that they really represent something meaningful.

Children also learn about the process of writing and its meaningfulness when they dictate stories, poems, or messages for people to their teacher and these are later read by their parents and others. As they say a word, seated at the teacher's side, they watch her hand moving from left to right across the page, see her stop for the next word, and learn to slow their speech to enable her to keep pace with the dictation. To see the images in their minds take shape on the paper seems to interest some especially, and they may ask, "Where is 'dog'?" "What says 'I cried'?" A few may "read" these dictations to themselves or others later, relying mostly on memory and making many changes, but sometimes recognizing a word as they do when pretending to read aloud at the story table. Most impressive of all to children as evidence of the value of written communication are dictated letters—an invitation, a note to an absent teacher who sends an answer, a greeting to one's father away on a trip, or a letter to one's mother to explain something that had been hard to say.

Just as with numbers and printing, the teacher responds to an interest in reading without taking the initiative away from the child, supporting it when it contributes to his own present purpose. Concern about a child's future academic success unless he reads early seems to be unwarranted. In fact, stress on early reading can cause feelings of inadequacy and tension about learning in general. Eyes, too, are not physiologically ready. The young child tends to be far-sighted, and even though he begins with large print, he cannot be prevented from reading print of any size once he is under way, with consequent strain. In an environment that provides plenty of other things to do, young children's interest in reading and writing develops only gradually, as they grow in other ways. And this is a protection, since otherwise they would be exposed too soon to anything and everything found in newspapers, on magazine stands, and in adult books, and a window to the world would be opened to them at a time of life when they were not mature enough to handle emotionally what they saw there.

That it is possible, during a period of interest in reading, for a child to learn on his own in a school where self-direction is the modus operandi is seen in the examples of Martin and Nigel.

● Martin, who was almost five, made "books," taping or stapling them together himself. He was an expert in drawing, and his books were collections of his pictures, with stories about them dictated to the teacher and printed by her on the opposite pages. He had been interested in this printing for some time and recently had been dictating one word at a time, then watching carefully to see how it was made. He also asked the teacher to label some of his paintings, and after this had been done for a while, he began to copy these single-word titles—"Boat," "Tree," "Dog," "Whale," "Me,"—finally laboriously copying "Caterpillar."

At length, one day, Martin's self-imposed task was to copy a longer title, "All these people live in same house." (Martin was bilingual, and, like many Japanese-American children, commonly left out "a" or "the.") The teacher gave him each of the words on a separate card, one at a time, and he copied them, putting the cards in a pile in order as he finished. Then he wrote his words on a sheet of paper which he decorated with figures of people and his usual pointed-roofed house. His printing was accurate enough to be legible; his only problem was that he needed to paste an extension on the sheet to finish it. After he was through, Martin took the pile of cards and mixed them up, as his group often did Lotto cards; then, using his printing as a guide, he arranged them in order on the table. Pointing to each word in turn, he slowly pronounced the words in order. He made only one mistake, which he corrected himself, the placement of the word "in." Shortly after this period of interest in printing and reading, Martin became involved in making canals and dams in the playground, spending his time, instead, in vigorous outdoor activity.

● Nigel, at four and a half, had shown no previous interest in printing or reading. He had none of Martin's skill in drawing and had not even attempted to print his own name yet. One day he came into the school after a clash with his father at the gate and asked the teacher to give him his father's name, *Bob,* on a card. He kept this in his pocket and took it out to study several times in the course of the morning. A few days later he put a small stop sign on top of the easel and tried to copy the word "STOP" in huge letters, with a felt pen. (Most of the children could read this sign, having used it on the floor in block play, and Nigel could, too.) On his first attempt, the *S* was reversed. Noticing the difference between his *S* and the one on the sign, he asked the teacher for help. She suggested he start with his right hand straight out, rather than across his body, and then move it toward the other shoulder as he made the top stroke. He stood back a little from the easel and practiced this right-to-left gesture several times. Finally he achieved "STOP," and he took the paper outside, telling the children they must do as it said. After playing with his big sign in the playground, he met his dad with the gleeful words, "You'll have to stop, now, when you do what I don't like."

The next day, and for many days afterward, Nigel made "STOP" on the easel over and over, taking home a bagful of papers. In the first few days he continued to make mistakes, usually in the *S.* Finally these dropped out. Then he began to vary the look of some of the letters by making them tall, very small, slanted, and so on. Following this success in varying elements without mixing himself up, he began to stress the basic shape of the letters by making them with double lines, again at this point reverting to many mistakes with the *S* and sometimes with the *P,* and occasionally he started with *P* and ended with *S.* He continued to refer to the small stop sign on the easel when he got confused, and to take his starting stance and preliminary arm gesture as needed. When he was again making fewer mistakes, he started to decorate the letters with cross-hatching, to fill in the *O* and *P,* and to use several colors. During this phase mistakes increased, and then decreased again. Sometimes he played his "STOP" game with the children and reviewed the meaning of the word this way, too.

One day Nigel asked for "GO," and this was printed on a block of wood to keep on the easel in the same way as the stop sign. In a much shorter time, he then learned to print that. "GO" was then interspersed with "STOP," and it, too, was worked over with decorations and variations. Both signs were used in play, and new ones were added every day. Finally Nigel said, "I'm going to read now. Put these in a book," and he handed the teacher his large stack of papers, which she stapled together for him. Starting at the beginning, he went through them without a single mistake—"Stop, stop, stop, go, stop, go, go, stop, stop, go, stop, go, go, go"—without being in the slightest confused by elaborate changes in the size of words or letters, by elongated or squatty shapes, or by extraneous ornamentation. Following this tour de force, Nigel took his book home and dropped the subject. It would be hard for any teacher of reading and writing to think up the many drills and reviews that Nigel set himself, to say nothing of holding a child to the performance of them.

The variations among children in regard to their readiness for prereading experiences can be seen in a description of some four-year-olds who wanted to send greetings to a housebound teacher. One drew her a picture; it was not of anything recognizable, but had bright colors and vigorous lines. Another drew a picture of her on skis, and put his name on it. A third dictated a letter: "I did the new puzzle. Why did you break your leg?" And a fourth child's letter was printed by herself from word cards she requested one at a time. She began, "How do you make 'Dear'?" and was told, "I'll give you a 'Dear' card, and you can see for yourself." "And now make her name." "And now I need 'I miss you.'" A fifth child printed his name all over a sheet of paper, and still another, a little girl, covered page after page with scribble writing. All were equally satisfied with their productions, including a child who said, comfortably, "This is for her," and wrapped up a piece of his lunch apple with paper and much tape. If children's learning is really self-initiated and self-directed, they feel no pressure to perform according to an outside standard, and there is no tension in their projects.

9 Books and Language Expression

I can't go to school today,
Because I have to take
My Chinese Yo-Yo,
And go,
Surrounded,
Into the mountains,
                    —Richard

I

Adventures with books and language expression have an important part to play in helping children toward self-affirmation. From books they acquire the beginnings of an appreciation of literature, information that orients them and makes them more secure in their world, and a familiarity with vocabulary, sentence structure, and form in both prose and poetry that aids them in communicating their own ideas and feelings.

When considering the provision of materials for children's use in nursery school, discrimination is nowhere more needed than in the selection of books. A great variety is available. Probably some can be eliminated at once—for example, those that project a condescending attitude toward children by emphasizing their smallness and cuteness, or by indicating that their misconceptions are amusing to the adults in the stories. ("'Oh no,' laughed father.") Another kind of book might be rejected because it is poorly written for reading aloud. Many writers use "do not," "are not," and so on, avoiding contractions studiously even in dialogue, and some books for children still have artificialities like "'Oh, see the clown,' cried John." ("What was he crying about?" the audience always wants to know.) If a teacher is to read simply, as she would talk to children, it is impossible to make "do not," "Oh, see," and similar literary conventions sound

185

natural. Also, since at this age a child needs to gain fluency in his own speech, one might avoid a book too loaded with inversions, such as "said mother," "replied John," and other patterns not heard in speech. Books whose style is too formal have a bad effect on children's own dictated stories, making them stiff and self-conscious. Most teachers would want to consider variety, too, in subject and in complexity, and also to make sure there are not too many showing sex stereotyping—mothers cooking, fathers working, boys playing with trucks, and girls playing with dolls— since these would give too limited an idea of the range of possible activities for both sexes. Similarly, books that show only middle-class families and their way of life, or only black or white people, or that otherwise present too narrow a view of society need to be balanced with books of other kinds.

Some books for young children stress realistic, factual information. The pictures are usually clear and detailed; some are beautiful. Most contain a picture opposite each page of prose; this helps keep children's attention, and provides an art experience, too, in some cases. Texts are often carefully worked out so as to be brief and clear. When well chosen, books like these help a child to separate fantasy from reality. The stories are about home and family, about nature, about "things that go," and, as he grows through the preschool years, about a wider range of interests that includes the neighborhood, the stores, the laundry, the post office, the library, the airport, construction sites, or the zoo. One of the purposes of reading books of that kind is to help a child feel secure in what he already knows—to give him a kind of review experience. This is why a child will want a book like Lois Lenski's *The Little Auto* (1942) read over and over. It has clear, simple drawings and tells how Mr. Small drives his car and takes care of it. The child knows what to expect, and each time it is read he can say to himself, "Yes, I know about that; it's just as I thought. Some things don't change." Books like this also prepare him for new experiences closely linked to familiar ones. He can learn about a farmer and the barn and animals, for instance, even though he has never been to a farm. Farmers are people, just wearing different clothes and doing different things. The animals look different from the dogs and cats he has seen, but not so very different, and they, too, are fed and have places to sleep. Similarly, he can learn about different kinds of boats. "The freighter is a very big ship," the story tells him, and he sees its picture on the opposite page. When he sees the real things some day, he will be prepared. By means of pictures and stories that skillfully link the new to the familiar, a child becomes acquainted with much more than he could learn about firsthand. And most of the information is useful—not just facts for facts' sake. He may ride in a plane or bus himself before long, or someone he cares about may do so. He will have realistic mental pictures of these things, and when he sees them, will half recognize them and quickly fit them into previous concepts. For benefits like these, it helps if the child can examine the books by himself or with friends, and if, when she reads them, the teacher sometimes just lets him talk about what he sees in the pictures and answers his questions. Factual books also need the enrichment and humanization of children's own observations and experiences, because feelings and personalities have little emphasis in them.

In stories, animal disguises, usually introduced with the idea of making a book more interesting, at best tend to confuse young children with regard to both animals and people. Anyone of any age identifies with the hero or protagonist of a book; the art of the storyteller purposefully brings this about. Preschoolers only hazily differentiate animals from people in any case, and writers often make the distinction even harder by having the animals dress, speak, and behave like human beings. An older child can keep more distance, but a small child, with his less firm sense of self, is swept helplessly into identification with animals as with people. This means that what the animal characters do needs to be something with which the child is comfortable in identifying, as in Elsa Minarek's *Little Bear* (1957). Unfortunately this is not usually the case. For example, if the animal characters in "The Three Little Pigs" are translated in the child's mind into human figures, then the story tells how three little boys' angry daddy-person (the big bad wolf) threatens to catch and hurt them. They hide in their home, but even there they are not safe, and finally they unite to kill him and succeed in doing so. All stories like this are too strong medicine for children of nursery school age.

In realistic stories of animals, a threat is often introduced to provide plot and action. The one experiencing the danger is usually a smaller animal, and again the listening child identifies with it. A little duck, for instance, lags behind its mother, is lost, and almost caught and eaten by a hawk. Some realistic nature books go even farther; in the interest of providing factual information, they show a small animal actually being caught. There is no way that a naive preschool child can know his own security is not similarly threatened. Putting disturbing ideas into heads already full enough of private worries is unwise.

Another common device in children's books is the animation of a machine—a tugboat or bulldozer, perhaps. Like the animal disguise, the machine invites the child to identify with it, since it has a face and talks.

But here, as well, things often happen to the machine that the writer would never think of describing as happening to a child or to the members of his family. Old machines are thrown away or threatened with being chopped up for scrap, for instance. As in the other children's books containing threatening ideas, everything turns out well in the end, and the theory is that the threat only adds harmlessly to the suspense. But suspense is not really essential in young children's books, and the building up of tension to sustain interest has a reverse effect; the sensitive small child attends better and certainly understands more when he or she is at ease and relaxed.

Many of the books with machines as heroes have a competitive theme. The competition is between a smaller machine—a train, perhaps—and a larger, stronger one, and the small one always wins the race or somehow turns out to be better. An older child can enjoy that, knowing it to be a fantasy, but a young child is in conflict. He wants to win out over his parents, but at the same time he wants his parents to care for and protect him. Competitive books, as well as competitive games, are ill-suited to his needs. He gains more from playing out his own competitive feelings with his toy trains or cars. As he does this, he gradually comes to see that ideas of being bigger and stronger than adults are only wishes he needn't fear will come true while he still needs their care. But in play, he can have it both ways. "What is the engine going to do now?" asked Hoddie. "You will decide," the teacher told him.

Some writers for children introduce fantastic elements in the form of extravagantly unreal happenings and bizarre creatures. These are often taken seriously and literally by three-year-olds, and even four-year-olds feel confused and bewildered because they have no point of reference from which to judge the events, whereas in the realistic story the unfamiliar is linked to the familiar by means of common elements. Even children close to five years old who realize (albeit vaguely) that the books are supposed to be about "pretend things" feel uneasy because they are never quite sure which part is real and which is some kind of joke. Humor, in any case, is difficult to write for young children. It must be based on something about which a child is perfectly sure, so he can recognize the humor as a departure from the usual. The story *The Backward Day,* by Ruth Krauss (1950), is an example of that kind; a child can thoroughly enjoy it, knowing he is not for a minute fooled. If a story is too outlandish, some children's sense of reality will be shaken, and they will feel frightened.

There are also books that purposely frighten children by presenting grotesque creatures that shock by too great a departure from the familiar but afterwards turn out to be harmless. The aim is to deal with fears by describing a victory over them in fantasy form. But a child's own monster would never look just like the book one; it might look like a fireman or even a vacuum cleaner. In addition, if read to a group, the book would suggest to those who had not had such an idea before that there might well be scary things just around the next corner. Small children often pretend to kill scary monsters, and they find this very helpful in ridding themselves of fears. But it is not necessary to read about such things to give children a subject for dramatic play. There is always a monster within— their own aggressive impulses—waiting to take some form with which they can wrestle in play of that kind. To offer alarming figures from outside just adds others to the inner monsters they carry around with them.

The argument that reading such books helps children be more imaginative is probably not too sound. Imagination is a special gift of the very young, and in the rare case of a child who is too inhibited to let himself use this faculty, the answer would be to help him express his own fantasies, rather than overwhelming him with full-blown adult ones. If he is unable to use dramatic play in this way, it might be because his inner monster seems too frightening to look at. Such a child's monster (his angry feelings) will become less terrifying when he sees anger being accepted as natural by the teacher in many real-life situations. As he learns to recognize and express his own anger in unfrightening ways, his monster becomes a familiar acquaintance. Then, when it is reduced to manageable proportions, he can let it emerge in dramatic play in whatever form it takes, and deal with it.

Some of the newer mental health-oriented books for preschoolers, however sound in themselves, discuss problems that individual members of a listening group might not be ready to look at yet. In general, it is better not to go into a child's hidden emotional problems, but rather to wait until he brings them up himself in talk or play and then respond. Reading books about sibling rivalry and similar common concerns takes the initiative away from a child who has not indicated such concerns himself, even though he may have them. Nor can a teacher know whether or not the time is ripe for an individual child to tackle such concerns and come to terms with them.

Another kind of book that creates difficulties is one that points a moral. Old-fashioned books (the McGuffey Readers are examples) showed "good" children being rewarded and "naughty" ones being punished. The modern version is the comic book based on television superheroes, with its good guys and bad guys. Young children already have a tendency to think in polarized ways—someone is always big or little, friend or enemy, boss or slave, right or wrong, and books that support this kind of thinking reinforce their worries about where they fit into the scheme. "Are you a good boy or a bad boy?" Chip asked David soon after entering school. "I don't know; I'm just a boy, a rather nice boy—yes," was David's answer. Reassured, Chip's next question led to the deeper concern. "Am *I* a good boy or a bad boy?" But David had never learned to label people, so his reply was: "I know you're not a *bad* boy. I just like you."

Books that point morals accentuate many problems. Children wonder if they are "bad" enough to have hurtful things done to them; sometimes they feel they are, especially when they feel like hurting someone themselves. Is it a good thing, though, to hurt bad people? Is it necessary, maybe? If a child's inner conflict between his "good" and "bad" selves is reinforced by the stories that are read to him, he may be led to punish himself, provoke punishment from others, or project his "badness" onto others and punish them. And if he becomes too impressed with his wrongdoing (or wrong-thinking, which to him may be the same thing), fears of rejection or desertion may follow.

Folk and fairy tales also present difficulties. Older children, no longer confused about what is real and what is not, may gain comfort from these fantasy worlds in which wishes come true. But the preschool child cannot use them that way. When he hears a story about someone who overpowered an enemy, he is unable to feel wholehearted relief; with his extraordinary capacity for empathy, he winces with the victim. Neither does the traditional happy ending help, because it is the story's high point he will remember, not the ending. And in any case, his sense of time is too shaky for him to be sure what came after what.

There is another reason, too, why reading folk and fairy tales to a child of nursery school age is disturbing. A teacher stands for reality in the school; it is she who helped him orient himself there. Yet he is full of his own fantasies, which, at base, are much like those in the tales. If he hears them confirmed and even expanded in a story read by his teacher, what is he to think? The young child does not understand very well what reading is—how it differs from what his teacher tells him when she is not looking down at a book. He accepts what she tells him as true (and should be able to). "These things happened, and therefore they could happen to me, too" is a child's thought as he listens. Saying, "It's just pretend" does not help him, either; he knows from intimate experience that what one pretends is what one wants to do and may actually do in a moment of shaky control. Now evidence comes from outside to indicate that those fantasied events he was just beginning to recognize as only his own wishes and fears might actually take place in the real world the teacher seems to be describing as she reads.

It is valuable for every child to learn that other people often feel as he does. But in the stories, the people do more than have feelings; they act on them. The young child depends on adults to stop him from carrying violent feelings into violent action, but in the stories, such actions are stopped only by still more violence. It is the preschool child, caught at the very moment when he is struggling to achieve control over his destructive impulses, who is most harmed by the example of hostile behavior of adults. His sense of self is far from being strong enough to resist identifying with them. What he needs help in learning at this stage of his life is that feelings are not the same as actions and can be accepted both in himself and others.

A better antidote to the dryness of a diet of wholly factual material in children's books is poetry and poetic prose of a quality that will increase a child's sensitivity to imagery and impressions, create a mood or an atmosphere, and communicate on a feeling level. Reading of this kind also helps a child see that words can be a creative outlet like art, music, or dance, and often leads him to use words this way himself. Pauses for children's responses after reading a poem are thus especially important. Poems need to be read many times to be appreciated; they are like songs, in that the better they are known, the more they are liked. At first a child only looks for meaning in the words, but after many repetitions he responds to the poem's rhythms and to other aspects of its form. Like songs, too, poems should be short enough to be recognized and remembered when they are repeated later, and when the same short poem is heard often at story time, children begin to say it along with the teacher, just as they begin to sing along when they know a song well. Not all are equally responsive to poetry, just as not all care in the same way about songs. However, it's well to remember that interest is not always expressed by joining a group. Bits of songs and poems will often come back from a child as he plays, if a teacher also sings songs or recites poems informally so that children who choose to stay away from the story table can hear them, too. (But she is careful not to interrupt what they are doing; she makes her contributions responsive to the themes of their play or special interests.)

Choosing poems for children presents some problems. No distinction is made in most anthologies between poems for preschoolers and those for older children, so a teacher will probably need to make her own collection. Scrapbooks, with an illustration on each page if possible, seem most satis-factory. She will want to hunt through several anthologies to find enough selections right for the age that also have quality as real poems. Poems that are suitable for young children are those that are related to their own experiences and express feelings with which they can easily identify; this rules out, for instance, poems about elves and fairies, the man in the moon, and so on. A good measure of a poem is whether a child might conceivably write one on the same subject himself. And, as well as subject matter, the form needs to be easily recognized; this is one of the virtues of Mother Goose rhymes. Repetition of a theme, if there are several verses, helps. Rhyme and rhythm also make the form clear. In free verse, mood and imagery need simple and vivid expression, as in Japanese haiku, which are so brief that the question "What does that make *you* think of?" will sometimes lead to a child's own poem of two or three lines.

Storytelling can provide a more individualized language experience than reading, for a small group or just one child. Many books must be made appropriate by crossing out words or removing pages; a teacher has to play it safe by ruling out anything that might conceivably make a child feel inadequate, foolish, confused, anxious, or frightened, because when reading to a group, it is seldom possible to notice every child's reactions and make sure that anyone whose response seems to be unfortunate can at once ask questions and work out his difficulty. But in storytelling, some-times enriched by pictures, the teacher can have more range, as well as more flexibility. Subjects, vocabulary, and the length of the story can be adapted to meet the needs of mature or immature children. One child might hear about the hospital he will enter shortly, and another might be told a little about the language in Mexico that he will hear on a coming visit. Special interests of some of the children might well be too complex and developed for the group as a whole to hear about, and stories could be told about those subjects. However, although storytelling can be respon-sive to many individual needs within her group, a teacher must keep in mind that children are remarkably alike in emotional needs. Even very bright, articulate, and emotionally stable children are as vulnerable to disturbing concepts as the others; there is no way to hurry the emotional maturation that occurs before five. Every child must live through similar stresses in those years. And this is always the case, no matter how preco-cious a child is in other ways, and no matter how many demands he makes to be treated as though he were older.

II

Because it differs in important ways from the rest of the nursery school day, the story time needs special consideration. Most materials—toys, puzzles, dolls, blocks, art supplies, and the like—are out and ready so that children can use them independently and whenever they choose, either alone or with their friends. But though they may look at the pictures in books and discuss them with friends, to know the stories inside those books, children need the aid of an adult. Most schools have a special time for stories, because a teacher cannot stop what she is doing to read to individuals whenever the interest arises. Nor can a child always have his choice of book. Unlike any other time in the day, story time requires that a child come on schedule, that he share the experience with all who want to come, whether or not he knows or likes them, and that he be entirely dependent on the adult and allow her to have the center of attention.

For these reasons, problems arise at the story table that arise at no other time and would not arise there if a teacher could read to only one or two children whenever they were interested in a book's contents. A child in such a private reading session could interrupt with his questions or thoughts and also sometimes add to a story, change it, or improvise an entirely new story of his own in response to it. Confusions would be cleared up at once, and past experiences could be compared with what was read, so that a child would always be able to keep his facts straight. Instead of being passive most of the time, he could be active and creative with words himself. For a young child, it seems unnatural for an adult to continue to keep the floor and talk more or less steadily, as the teacher does when she reads. He wants to talk, too; speech to him is a give-and-take affair. But at story time, if he wants to say something, he feels he is interrupting, nor has he the time to collect his wits to speak. He is flooded, swamped, and buried with a flow of continuous words, a flow far above the level of his own verbal fluency. However, even if it were possible to have enough adults around all day to make individualized reading available on request, such a large group would, in itself, present problems, and to have volunteers or even paid professionals present only at story time would make it difficult to integrate them into the school's general approach and goals. (One solution for schools that are teacher-training laboratories is to use students in this role.)

There are ways to mitigate the problems, however. If the story time can be extended to half an hour or forty-five minutes and children are able to come and go as they wish, groups at the table will be smaller. Children can also be independent at least in selecting the books they want to hear and bringing them to the table as they come, although the teacher will still need to decide on the order in which she reads them and may choose some herself, depending on the group gathered before her. If a circular table with an attached continuous bench is provided, children can slip in and out of places without disturbing the reading. Then, provided that arrangements can be made for children not at the table to play somewhere else, listening to stories can be more like the self-initiated, free-choice activities during the rest of the day.

While the story reading is under way, however, other problems arise. A child may not be listening to the story chosen because it is unsuited to his developmental level; because it is too familiar; because it is too unrelated to his own life to be meaningful; or perhaps because it arouses some uncomfortable thoughts and feelings that he wants to shut out or escape. Sometimes a child is uneasy and restless because he is being ignored by the group focusing on the teacher's words; perhaps he feels strangely shadowy and anonymous, a nobody. He may feel angry, too, that everyone, even the teacher, seems to have forgotten him, and antagonistic, therefore, toward the book in which everyone seems so unreasonably interested. "Look at *me!*" he wants to shout. "*I* have interesting things to say, too!" A small child has no capacity for sitting still and doing nothing, so lack of involvement, for whatever reason, leads to sabotage of the reading. There may be complaints of not being able to see or of being crowded, getting up and down, giggling, tickling, pushing, making noises, asking persistent questions, or starting conversation or play with a neighbor. In these ways a child handles his lack of occupation and also, by drawing the teacher's or the children's attention away from the book, proves he is still important to them.

Whether the child is uninterested in the story or the convention of the reading situation is rubbing him the wrong way in the sensitive area of sharing attention, he needs relief. An attempt might be made first to see whether the trouble is just that he is unable to pick up the thread of the story, by saying something like "Here's the boy; see him riding on his tricycle? He's going to look for the cat, remember?" Or perhaps the child's need for notice will be satisfied by moving him nearer to the teacher or even onto her lap, using his name often, or by saying something like "Did you ever do that, John?" to give him the floor legitimately. But if nothing that is tried draws him into involvement with the story, or if involvement is achieved only momentarily, he probably needs to have other choices pointed out. The teacher would not want him to tune out and learn to be bored by books or to enjoy being a disturbance, so she suggests, "Maybe there is something else you'd rather do? There are things outside and in the other rooms to play with, and other people to talk to, you know?" He might jump up with relief. Or, if he is unwilling to leave a friend, she can suggest he ask his friend to go too. The teacher is not disturbed if there is an exodus of listeners. They will be back, if not that day, the next. And she knows if she starts a new story later, perhaps in a corner of the playground, another group will gather around her. Young children have more need for active than passive experiences, and if John needed that, or wanted one-to-one attention, he could find them better away from the table.

Competitiveness is a special problem at the story table. All kinds of jealous feelings may arise. Some children will be very insistent on sitting beside the teacher, for instance, and she must handle these feelings by reminding them, if they cannot sit by her, that there are other times, too, for closeness, and also that another teacher is available to them. When the teacher is ready to choose a book from the pile in front of her, another situation arises. Cries of "Read my book first" and "No, read mine!" are bound to arouse the competitive feelings of other children, so the teacher makes it clear that, now they have made their choices from the shelves, she will make her own from the pile, adding that she likes to do this by herself. She will explain, too, that she might not be able to read all the books. If a child says, "Read mine," after this, she will probably need to talk to him about it privately before the next story time; small children often have trouble taking in things said to a group, and need a more personal approach.

A sense of inadequacy also arouses competitive feelings. If something in the story confuses a child, he has a special need for his teacher; he cannot feel on top of things without her explanations. But since he will seldom get this help at the very moment he needs it, he resents the children with whom he must share the teacher. The more competent and independent children feel at the table, the less their relations are disturbed by competitiveness. Reading a little below their level of comprehension, rather than above it, is better, therefore, when a group is large, and it can also serve as a useful review of known facts and vocabulary. More difficult material can be offered when the group is smaller, and the teacher may even talk the story through the first time, with plenty of eye contact to be sure everyone is with her all the way.

When stories are being read, children's own ideas sometimes begin to develop, and often a pause for discussion brings a new language experience. A talkative child usually has a lot that he wants to say. But if he goes on talking too long, the others become restive, either because the speaker's lack of fluency makes it hard for him to hold their interest or because they want to talk themselves. Clamor for the floor can then arise. A teacher can develop a good deal of skill, however, in picking up and repeating, thus emphasizing, the essential parts of what a child is saying; this serves two purposes. It helps hold the group's attention, and, for the child himself, it is a reflection of his thoughts that convinces him the teacher is really listening to him and interested in what he says. It would be hard for him to feel that way if he got the idea he must hurry to finish because she wanted to go on reading. So, for a limited time, she keeps the group with him by making comments something like the following: Earl—"*I* went to the zoo, too." Teacher—"*You* went to the zoo, once, too. Earl is saying that once *he* went to the zoo, and—" Earl—"And we saw—we did—all the ones—and a effalent." Teacher—"You really saw an elephant, a real live one?" As the teacher listens intently, children are apt to follow suit, and it is striking to see how a child's fluency improves under those conditions. An attentive listener makes it worthwhile to speak as clearly as possible and keep one's ideas from wandering vaguely and subjectively. Then a tactful linking in to the story, by the teacher, starts the reading going again before the group becomes restless.

Active expression of children's own ideas contributes more to the sense of self than passive listening, so the teacher sometimes sets the book aside altogether and lets discussion take over, concentrating on helping the children communicate in a natural and unregulated way without tension or competitiveness. Book experiences then become chances for self-expression. But she must also keep the needs of the whole group in mind. If there are a number of children at the table, she might suggest that those who are particularly anxious to speak share their offerings with another teacher or friends in another area; when a group is changing from listening to independent expressive activity, its size is of special importance. Sometimes this change has started when a spontaneous phrase is picked up by one or more children and the teacher can underline this by joining in, with the result that a chant develops: "No—books—here, No—books—here" (while hiding books on laps), and so on. When there is a joking addition to a story she is reading, such as "He ate his *hat*," she can encourage more nonsense contributions by responding with, "He did?" and laughing, and group word play might go on to "He ate a house," "He ate a shoe," and other ideas. Drumming feet also indicate a change from passive to active participation, and these sounds could be commented on with "Bump, bump go the feet, feet," or perhaps it would be "Hands going pat—pat, pat, pat." When actions are commented on in this way by a teacher, they move from the fringe area of chaos into the foreground of order and purpose. But even more important is the teacher's acceptance and appreciation. She communicates this often by joining in herself: for example, by drumming her own feet or patting her hands on the table. Rhythm helps children organize their impulsive actions, and is another aid in the transition from passivity to activity.

Responding to children's spontaneous impulses to speak at the story table seems preferable to suppressing speech at one time and trying to draw it out at another. Remarks in the middle of a story may add to its significance for everyone, and if a discussion then developed, that would be the time to give language expression preference. Offerings by children that arise from their own communicative urges are what the teacher wants, and she uses questions sparingly, since a shy child then feels pressure and becomes self-conscious, a less verbal child lacks time to get his words out before others have answered, and an eager one will try to talk everybody else down. Rhetorical questions to which the teacher already knows the answers would be avoided in any case, since they turn a natural give-and-take situation into an artificial one. If the teacher keeps herself in the background, reflecting and clarifying remarks and entering as a participant, rather than a leader, the children's speech will be easy and informal.

III

A child's language develops form just as his art products and music and dance improvisations do, in the years before five, and, like them, it can become a medium for creative expression. When children discover this possibility in language through their own word play, through what is read to them, or through teachers who involve their interest in finding just the right word for a thought, they begin to use this medium more and more.

Adults may tend to think of a poem as something that is only found in books, but the young child spontaneously and naturally makes them himself. He would not be asked to make a poem in nursery school (poems are not produced on order), but sometimes one is either offered directly to a teacher or overheard by her in the midst of play. Then she can write it down, perhaps to read to the child afterward, perhaps to give to him to take home, or perhaps just to preserve it.

The organization of words into some kind of form distinguishes these special productions from ordinary speech. In talking, a child organizes what he has to say in order to communicate better—to make his meaning clear—but when he is engaged in creative organization of his words, he makes use of the elements of language in very much the same way that he works with color, line, and shape in painting. No matter what materials any artist uses, the principle is the same; through partly conscious and partly unconscious awareness of relationships between parts, he is able to draw these together into a unified whole that has its own individual quality and identity. Sometimes the recognition of relationships comes before the artist begins. At other times the relationships are recognized later, and the product takes its shape from them as it develops.

It seems somewhat easier for teachers to notice form in children's art—in repetition of one color here and there, in a single wavy line across the bottom that ties the whole picture together, in clumps of sandy texture as the element common to a lot of differently colored areas, and in a myriad of other ways by which "painting" becomes "a painting." But to see that a child's spontaneous words have formed a poem is harder. Writing down these fragments of language as often as possible helps one learn to recognize them when heard. If the teacher is careful to record exactly what she hears, representing pauses by spaces, the form often becomes clear to her when she rereads what she has written. Then, while she can still recall how the child said the words, her next task is to divide the poem into lines to make it read the way it sounded. In the following poems, form will be seen progressing from the very simple to the more subtle and complex.

Repetition, as seen in these early poems, is a frequently used way children discover to give form to their words.

> Poor Marc
> Fell off his trike,
> And his face was sad,
> And his ears were all red—
> Poor Marc.

> High birds!
> High birds!
>
> Flying in the sky.
>
> All singing!
> All singing!

The following two poems on similar themes make comparisons; the first one contrasts two things, and the second one clearly and concretely differentiates three.

> You know something?
> In the daytime
> I have a big bed to sleep in—

As big as you are.
But in the nighttime
I sleep in my little crib,
And dream about Santa Claus.

When Teddy Bear was a little boy,
He lay down in a basket.

Now he's a big boy and he plays with toys,
And rides on an engine.

And when he grows up, he'll work downstairs,
And go to daddy's school.

Some children's poems have a motif as a unifying element; in the following poem, it is the words *once more*, which are repeated like a refrain.

I went swimming
Once more,
And big Katie fell down the stairs
Once more,
And pouring water on my head and Jennifer's head
Once more.
And I ate dinner at seven o'clock,
And went to bed at ten o'clock,
And we dumped water on our heads,
Once more.

A later poem by the same child shows form in its total structure and musical quality. The first two lines have the same cadence and are followed by a shorter line; the next two lines are like the first two; and the final line stands alone like the third line, but the fact that it is as long as the paired lines completes the poem satisfyingly. This is an example of the need for careful attention to pauses in recording, so that each section will stand out as it should. The form, with its flowing rhythms and its spaces, gives this poem as much of its evening quietness as the words do.

I went to the playground with Jennifer,
And Robbie and Katie and Ann,

And daddy and mommy.

And it was raining outside,
Last night when I went to bed,

And the two cats were outside.

Sometimes children's poems are derivative; this is to be expected of poets of any age now and then, although the child of nursery school age is more free of influences and thus usually produces fresher material. The little girl who dictated the next poem had been to Sunday school, where she had heard of angels, and her "dancing in the moonlight" also came from some place other than her own experience. But "presents for everyone" is pure child, and the next to the last line is pure gold. The reappearance of one line of the first verse in the second one, the ending that each verse has in common, and the dance rhythm give this poem its unusually clearcut form.

> Angels are dancing
> In the moonlight,
> Having a party
> At three past one.
>
> Having a party,
> Presents for everyone,
> *Gold on my shoulder*
> At three past one.

The young child often plays with words instead of using them to achieve a purpose. This kind of language expression is often not recognized as a creative activity because we associate meaning with words and tend to ignore children's "meaningless" talk. One child enjoyed the sounds words make. Told the name of a new boy at school, Peter, she at once made this poem, apparently entirely suggested by the half rhyme of "Peter" with "eat it."

> Once I had a doggie,
> And his name was Peter.
> I took a cherry—
> Awful tender,
> Awful ripe—
> And I put it in his mouth,
> And he *eat it*.

In a later poem by the same child, the flowing, mellifluous sound of her title was perhaps more important to her than its meaning, and throughout the poem she used words to express both feeling and a sense of design and form, as others might use paints, clay, sounds in music-making, or movements in dance. She also enjoyed their manipulation as sensually. One could see how she relished the word "cows," as she shaped her mouth around it, and the way she savored the two *s* sounds in "horses" and the alliteration of "passing" and "pasture." Repetition of the word "never" also patterned her haunting little poem.

The Many Years of the Cow

There's cows and cows
And horses in the meadow,
But the horses never
Say a word,
While the Man is passing
By, in the Never
Pasture.

Pleasure in the sounds of words is also seen in the poems of two children who used rhyming, the first child pairing "stars" with "flowers" and "sky" with "high," and the second child using a triple rhyme that expressed his fantasy as he slowly and ponderously worked his way up and down the jungle gym.

The sun's out!
Hi, sun!
You're not having any stars,
And I can reach the flowers,
And I'm pumping up the sky
In my high
Swing!

Here I go—
Dash! Smash! Crash!
Down to the ground!
Up the chimney,
Then Dash! Smash! Crash!
Down!

Related to the pleasure in words and their sounds is the use of private language and nonsense. Clowning and being silly with words are very releasing. If a teacher can keep behavior from going too far overboard at the same time, speech standards that weigh a child down fall off his shoulders, and anything goes. Tara's mother was pregnant, and what lay behind Tara's constant use of an invented word became clear one day when an incantation came out.

Co-co-co,
Co-co-co,
Don't you come,
Little one!

Don't you come,
Little one,
In my house.
Co-co-co.

Two boys produced a nonsense poem together, repeating it several times, after hearing some Mother Goose rhymes.

"Gregory, what's your last name?"

"I don't know, goodbye!"

"What's your last name again?
What's your last name again?"

"I don't know, goodbye!"

Clowning, whether in words or actions is part of being four years old.

I'm going to eat the busses,
Busses, busses,
I'm going to eat the busses,
All around the town.

I'm going to eat the towns,
Towns, towns,
I'm going to eat the towns,
'Cause they are so tasty.

Rhythm, an outstanding feature of many children's poems, was combined by Hilary with movement play. To accompany her dances, she used her own chants. As she spoke the one that follows, she advanced, retreated, and turned, with both her voice and her foot-stamps emphasizing the two accents in each line except the last one. Her big cowboy hat fell off once, and almost fell off a second time, but she worked that into her chant without missing a beat.

Òne, fòr (your
Hàt falls dòwn—
Tùrn a-roùnd and
Tàke a bòw)

One, two (oh
Oh) for the cowboy,
One, two,
Gunflash!

The next chant followed the same rhythmic pattern. "This is the cowboy's nighttime dance song. One cowboy is dancing in the street," she
said, and she began, her small cowboy boots hitting the floor hard.

Là, là,
Là, la, là,
Call "Neigh"
For the horse.
One, two, the
Ring-a-round,
Ring-a-round the
Manger.

One-two-three,
Four-five-six,
One-two-three for the
Cas-ta-nets.
One cowboy hat,
One cas-ta-nèt— the
Cowboy castanet
Costume!

A teacher who is interested in words herself often involves children in that
interest by example. "The trees don't seem to really be *waving* in the
wind, today—it's more like *quivering,* isn't it?" "Yes, quivering and shivering." "Do you think that bird is frightened of us, sitting over there and
watching?" "No, not frightened, more like *shy.*" Two children showed
their delight when, on sharing an experience, each thought of just the right
word.

When I went outside one night,
I saw the moon and stars,
Over this way,
And over this way,
Going *Twink! Twink! Twink!*

When Betsy tried to slide,
She cried,
And so I went

> To help her come,
> And she came down—
> She *smiled* down.

A poem can be an outlet for troubled feelings. Listening attentively and recording a child's words, to be either taken home or left with the teacher for safekeeping, seems to help him externalize the feelings and makes them more manageable. Here is one little girl's poem of that kind.

> I don't like him.
> He's not very nice.
> I don't like him at all,
> And he does everything bad.
> He keeps saying, "That's mine! That's mine!"
> And then I keep saying, "That's mine! That's mine!"
> And I push him,
> And then I hide.
>
> He finds me, and then he runs and runs and runs all
>   over until he falls down;
> Then he cries, and my mommy thinks I pushed him
>   again, but I didn't.
>
> He is still very naughty.
> He does everything I don't want him to.
> I took his train,
> And then I put it down and he grabbed it.
> I was very mad, but I didn't push him.
> He was out in the hall and I didn't push him because
>   the hall is slippery and he might fall down the
>   stairs and I knew my mom would get mad.
> But I felt very mad.
>
> He is so naughty.
> I'm going to make a mad face at him when I get home,
> And make a funny sound—a bad sound.
>
> I want to make my brother go away.
> And I don't want him to have my daddy, either,
> But my daddy likes him.
> *He* is mad at my *daddy* sometimes, and *I* am mad at *him*.
>
> He is not so nice at all.

IV

Prose that is dictated by young children ranges from lists and enumerations, through short descriptive phrases, to stories with complete sentences and an occasional little essay on a subject of interest to a child. The booklets kept on hand for dictation may be colored in afterward, if a child wishes, and sometimes two or more can be stapled together to make more pages. Children rarely start with a title; though they may have a beginning idea, the rest of their thoughts often take other directions. To ask, "What is this story going to be about?" is thus as inappropriate as to ask, "What are you going to paint?" The words just come as they come.

A three-year-old, who expressed an interest in "making a book" after watching others do it, used what he saw nearby as his subject, as often happens.

> Graham crackers—they're shaped like this, and you eat them. I have my own basket at school.

Two examples of enumeration follow, one limited to listing, though of things not seen at the moment, and the other in sentence form and elaborated by naming the purposes of objects.

> Maybe guitars, maybe violins, maybe banjos, maybe bells. And that's all.

> There was a house for some people. There were toys, too. And books, too. And there was a swimming pool to swim in, too. And there was a telephone to call on.
> In the house there was a mother and daddy. There was a little boy named Tommy and a little girl named Kelly. They had two swings to swing on and a seesaw to play on and tables to eat on and chairs to sit on when they had carrots. They ate potatoes, too. They had a car to drive. They had a train to go to school in. And clothes to wear to school. And pictures all over the house to make it pretty.

Sarah's style of enumeration first listed the things at home that she liked, then moved on to less concrete things, and then to things she did not like.

> I like my Barbie doll. I like my Pooh Bear. I like my green dress.
> I like to go swimming. I like to have company.
> I hate peanut butter. I hate when my brother uses my Magic Markers.

Jim's enumerations expanded to include some fantasies of the things he would like to do. Though many children begin by enumerating, expansion in one direction or another soon follows.

> I'm thinking about playing the drums. And climbing out the window and dinging a bell. I'm thinking about playing the piano. And telling somebody

something on a real phone. And putting a pirate hat on. I'm thinking about having a real airplane, and driving it and blowing the horn. And putting ear muffins on.

Descriptive prose often accompanies pictures children make, such as Drew's drawing of what he called a "Car-Carrier Van Boat." He dictated a creative story full of images.

It can carry a sail, but it can't carry big heavy trucks. It can't carry you. It carries airplanes with a little, teensy window. It carries campers, like blue ones. It has a giant smokestack.

It is very, very big—bigger than a dinosaur. It's bigger than the whole world. It has *two* smokestacks, with a night-light. It also has a motorcycle light. The End.

Reed dictated an essay, entitled in advance "About Skating," presenting his thoughts on the subject in an orderly way.

When you're skating, you can only go *half* fast, because when you go *so* fast you fall down. When I was fifteen, I could skate *so* fast. (That was a dream.)

When I had my birthday and I was four years old, I put my skates on my feet and I went fast, and I didn't fall down, either.

When Jonas skates, he always walks. But when I skate, I put one knee up—and then the other knee up—and then my feet close together—and I *slide*.

Young children's dictated prose is often in the present tense, without progress in time. In reporting what happened in real life, a child may start at the end or in the middle, then work backward, then forward again, so that mental reassembling by a listener is needed. (The story that ends this chapter is an example.) But in the next two stories by Brad, action moves steadily forward. Brad's unusual maturity in language development is also seen in the long sentences with subordinate clauses. Dictating was this child's special interest.

The Lion and the Jungle

He was just walking along, and he saw a palm tree. He didn't mind if he saw a palm tree, but he saw a little black thing behind it. He ignored the little black thing; that lion was so silly he ignored everything. (You should always look back of you in the jungle, because there might be something dangerous.)

Then he saw what it was—a gorilla that was banging its tummy. He kept banging and banging his tummy, and he roared, 'till the lion got up with his excitement, and *he* roared *back!*

The Elephant and the Lion and the Big Fight

Elephant was walking along 'till he met something asleep on the ground. The elephant didn't know what it was. So he went over to it and moved it. Then the thing woke up. It was a lion that woke up in the daytime.

He ignored the lion for a minute to think what he could do. So he decided to go over to his big cave where his father was. He stopped at the door of his big cave. So he opened the door, and there was his big father standing there, but he didn't know what he came for. So he told his father all about it, until he went in. Then he was finally in. And that was the end of the elephant and the lion and the big fight.

A teacher frequently offers to write down a child's thoughts if she thinks he is angry or sad. Several unburdenings of this kind follow.

It's a silly day, and I'm mad. I'm mad about the yellow shovel. The children didn't want me to have the shovel. I just *wanted* it. But I couldn't have it, because he didn't tell me he was through. So I feel mad. Just mad. The day would be fine, but I couldn't help my day.

The Sad and Happy Book

I'm sad about my daddy that brought me. I don't want him to go home again. I wanted to get candy or something at the store, first. Sad-oh, sad-oh.

I'm happy about toys. And feeding the birds outside and the fish, at school. I have a cat at home, too. And when I get bigger, I'm going to Katie's and Ann's and Robbie's house.

I'm mad at Sam. If she came to my house, I was going to buy her bubble gum. But she didn't. I wanted to play with Sam, but she was playing with Lisa. Then my mom got mad at me because I didn't get my library books.

And then we went to school, and I hit Sam. Then Sam told Lisa that I hit her, and then I hit her again.

It was raining, and I went out in the rain without my raincoat on, *or* my boots or my rain hat, and I was barefooted. And I got wet.

I was mad at my baby-sitter, and I cried. I messed up my room because I was playing bus. And I had a table turned upside down, and a chair. The bus driver was me, and also I was all of the school-bus children, with my little brother Michael, who is two and a half.

Anna made me mad, because she yelled at me and made me cry.

I also splattered all my clothes out because I wanted to put lunch things in the suitcase—it was too full of things. My Jennifer doll was in there, and her hair was sticking out.

Then my mom came home and put her sweater on me, which looked like a dress.

My baby-sitter speaks Spanish. Sometimes I can understand her, and she can understand me. *Bonita* means pretty.

To feel that somehow everything is going wrong and that nobody understands, and then, through the magic of words, to find oneself understood after all, must deeply impress a child with the power of language.

10   Art, Dance, and Music

Play that same music
We were dancing on—
I love that music,
And when I dance on it
And my head goes,
The light is dancing, too.
    —John

I

The expressive outlets found in art, dance, and music activities help a child in many ways, but probably the most important one is the deepening and enhancing of the sense of self. Creative activities and young children have a special affinity. Broadly speaking, the word "creative" can apply to anything that comes from within a child as an outward expression of thoughts and feelings that are uniquely his own. Because small children are not apt to compare what they do with what others do, they tend to permit such projections to happen without interfering with them or inhibiting them, and in this way they are different from the rest of us. In order that a child may move toward creative self-expression, teachers want him to begin to develop the kind of feeling that permits, and even urges, a clear, straightforward statement everywhere, whether in the form of a painting, a block building, a dance, an ingenious solution to a problem, or an approach to another person. With all such statements a child becomes more aware of his own powers and their influence on the people and things around him.

A creative activity is one in which a child sets his own goal and decides himself whether he has met it or not. Activities that require teacher assistance and supervision have in common the problem that a child cannot invest enough of himself into them independently so that they become creative. There is too much subordination of the child's own ideas and feelings to those of the adult. The activity is thus not apt to become symbolic and deeply meaningful to a child; he cannot shape and pattern it in accordance with an inner image, because its form is already set. In many a teacher-guided "activity" there is, paradoxically, too much passivity. There is not enough exploring, and too much watching and waiting. In order to project himself into an experience so that it becomes a creative one for him, a child must be continuously and actively involved and make things happen himself.

II

Materials particularly appropriate for art experiences are unstructured ones, such as paper, paints, and clay. They are made ready and set out so children can select whatever attracts them and handle the entire process independently and as successfully as possible, according to their limits. For example, soft wood with the grain running the long way of the pieces makes for hammering in nails without splitting. Clay and dough need to be soft but not sticky and made ready in balls about the size of a child's hand. (Sometimes, instead, a large mass can be offered on a turntable with tools, ready to be excavated and modeled from all sides.) Cloth needs to be cut into sizes that are easy to use. Each color of tempera paint, mixed with liquid starch or the like to both extend it and give it body, will have its own long-handled brush standing ready in it, and the jars or cups of paint will be in a box or holder where they cannot tip over. For this age, materials to be used should be laid out ready, with aprons (self-help ones) hanging near and chairs in place. Thought is also given to how a child is to reach all he needs without getting up or stretching across someone else's work, and where he will put his product when he has finished (laying it flat, for instance, if wet, since hanging will be hard for him). A young child has neither the skill nor the patience to scrape clay out of a crock, hunt for paper, or clear a working space. He needs to get rapidly involved when the impulse strikes him, and if he cannot, he will find something else to do.

Basic unstructured materials, most of which would be ready on any day, should probably be paints, white glue, paper (18 by 24 inches for painting, and 12 by 18 inches for drawing), dough or clay, wood for gluing or hammering, colored paper both in sheets and cut up into small pieces, soft crayons, fat pencils, felt pens, scissors, and paste.

Each day children should see changes, however. So one day paints might all be bright primary or secondary colors, or perhaps include black or white or both, and another they might be pastels or greyed tones, or new colors might be put out, such as magenta, yellow-green, blue-violet, wine, brown, flesh, or gold and silver. Six colors could be offered at one time, either on an easel or in a container on a table; they would be selected so a child could have a choice among cool and warm colors, and so that light and dark contrasts would also be possible. Brushes might be changed sometimes, too; the usual long-handled ones might be replaced by short, wide ones, thin-tipped ones, sponges, rollers, rubber scrapers, or strings. Instead of the usual sizes of paper, too, there might be small cards, half-sheets, or double or even triple-sized sheets. (Used computer paper tears into a variety of sizes and is of good quality.) The paper could be black or colored, or it might be corrugated. Or there might be things of different shapes to paint on, such as egg cartons, tubes, boxes, or paper plates. Other surfaces besides paper might be painted, too—for example, cloth, rug samples, pieces of wood in all shapes and sizes, and Styrofoam. Clay might be used with hands only one day and with wooden tools on another, or there might be dough along with rolling pins, blunt plastic knives, bowls, and small plates. Wood offered might be large pieces to use as bases and smaller pieces to glue on them, scraps to nail together, or large squares into which a child could hammer nails and then stretch rubber bands, wires, or yarn across them or use them to support spools and other things with holes. Materials for glued collages might be found, too, on some days—shells, pebbles, beans, cloth scraps, seeds and cones, tiles, leather, scrap hardware, pegs, buttons, and lids, together with a variety of materials to serve as background. For collages made with paste and colored paper, there might be things like feathers, ribbon scraps, nut cups, confetti, or cotton balls to add.

Other art materials could be offered, too, on occasion: objects to thread on strings—maybe Styrofoam rings, cut-up straws, macaroni, or paper scraps with holes punched by the children. For the threading, a clothespin clipped to one end of the string can keep the objects from sliding off during the process, and the other end of the string can be stiffened ahead of time by fingers dipped in paste. When the string is filled, the teacher can tie the ends together to make a necklace, if the child wishes. (When she makes a knot, she stands behind him, facing the same way, and, holding the string in front of him, does the tying with her hands in the same position his own would be in; she says nothing about his trying until he demands to do it himself.) Another offering might be simple sewing. A square of mesh or burlap is clipped onto an upright frame or into a large embroidery hoop, and the child stitches on it with a blunt upholstery needle threaded with yarn. The clothespin needed at the end of the string can be managed by the child, but he may want help to thread the needle. The teacher does this, too, in front of him, pushing the yarn through the large eye doubled over so strands will not get caught, and she also demonstrates how the needle can be held so it remains threaded while in use. Some children like to sew patches in other colors on their squares, too.

Mobiles can be made with any objects that have holes by fastening them together with pipe-cleaner pieces or electricians' wire. Builders' wire, which is thicker but still pliable, can be used as a base to hang things from, as can coat hangers, but many children prefer just to link a lot of objects together. As with the tying and needle-threading, the teacher demonstrates the basic technique needed; she puts the two ends of the pipe-cleaner piece or wire together, then twists or "screws" them, rotating her wrist. Stabiles can also be made by sticking things into bases of clay or Styrofoam, and these can then be painted, if desired.

A teacher's first decision about a day's materials depends on what the group has been interested in and what she has on hand. Then she watches to see if more or different materials are needed. She could have guessed wrong; few children might be drawn by the ones she has ready. By observing their choices of activities, she sees what they are drawn by instead, and then supports that. Perhaps there is a lot of socializing, and they will go later on in groups to use what she has set out. Perhaps there will be building with blocks, or music-making, or dancing. Or it might be one of those days for drawings, which flood the tables and spread out on the floor as the teacher provides more and more extra-large sheets to catch the mounting enthusiasm at its height. Perhaps there are a lot of children in the sand, making marks with shovels and fingers. How about a board covered with sand on which to do that better? And perhaps, if sand is the interest of the moment, there might be an area where damp sand could be molded into free shapes. It is a matter of a delicate matching of what is within a child with what she can offer in the environment, and it is the latter that she changes if need be.

III

The teacher's role is important in helping children receive the many possible values from art activities. New skills, vocabulary, information, and an ability to plan and organize can be developed. A teacher can help best with this learning if she understands some of the limitations of very young children and allows for them. There is a time when balls appear in clay, for example, and a later time for snakes. And there is also a time for flattening clay down and a later time for building it up. In sequences common to all, but at his own rate, a child becomes aware of flat shapes, of insides and outsides, and of depth. Experiences with boxes show some of these stages. Many children, for example, decorate the inside bottom of the open box.

Not until the top is replaced do they see that the picture is hidden inside and there is now another surface. As they work with boxes, fill them with objects, open and close them, and take things out and replace them, they come to new understandings. From all appearances the child, who as a baby experienced everything he saw as though it were flat, on a screen, only gradually learned about depth as he reached for and touched things and is still learning about it in the nursery school. Small squares of thin linoleum might be glued one on top of the other, each carefully covering the previous one, as though the child were trying to make a tower as he does with his blocks, unaware that the linoleum, though not so different in size, has no depth. And it is quite startling to see a four-year-old boy, quite sophisticated about cars and trucks, glue round discs for wheels on edge underneath a block of wood, as though they were legs supporting a person, rather than to the sides of the block as we would. When a teacher turns the piece of linoleum and shows its thin dimension, or rotates the block so the car-maker can see that it has sides, a look of bewilderment may be seen.

Realizing that children have much to learn about the properties of materials and ways to work with them, the teacher is responsive to their needs along these lines. For instance, if a child is gluing an object in such a way that it is bound to fall off, she helps him see the problem, and they discuss other ways for him to achieve his purpose. She provides information in the situation where it is needed. "When you paint on wood or Masonite, you can use a lot of paint. Paper is thinner and can't hold so much; it tears." "That round spot in the wood is called a knot. Nails won't go into it very well." "Do you want your long stick to stand straight up like that? You might turn the whole job upside down, like this, and nail the flat piece on top of *it*; then you could turn it right side up, like this, and there it would be." "The pipe cleaners need to be twisted together so things won't fall off your mobile; they sort of open up, otherwise." "If you dip your needle down in the cloth and right back up again, making a little pinch, like this, then the yarn won't get wrapped around the frame, and you can get your cloth off when you're done." As the teacher gives these verbal explanations, she demonstrates and uses many gestures, pointing when she says "that round spot," "your long stick," and so on. The teacher makes suggestions and offers ideas only in regard to materials or techniques, and these will always be based on a child's own aims. But he may reject the information, too. Evident in this kind of help is the same attitude the child is learning to expect in her everywhere: respect for his own decisions and choices.

Juxtaposition of materials—paint and paper, for instance—leads most children to try combining them, but some may not be so adventurous. The teacher can help by picking up, handling, and naming the materials herself; as she does this, a child's deep-seated impulse to use his hands may be aroused, and he may follow suit. Then, because interest is fleeting at this age, she helps him with his apron, finds him a seat, and stays nearby awhile to see that he gets a smooth start. Time is needed for a child to realize that he may touch and act upon everything within his reach at school and to discover that unstructured materials, as well as structured ones, have something to offer him. The example of other children will help, too.

IV

To meet the needs of individuals in an area as closely linked to emotional development as art, a watchful waiting must help the teacher once materials are ready and in evidence. Over a period of time, she will learn which children go to them as though impelled by a strong drive, which seek them only occasionally, though with pleasure, which go along primarily to be with their friends, and which ones very rarely or never go. For the first group, her role is to see that interest is sustained and involves all parts of the personality, including the intellect, by offering special materials now and then for them. She studies the others to discover whether they are using another creative medium instead, such as dramatic play, music, or dance. If they are free and imaginative in their chosen outlets, they may have little need for art. But some paint or color without real involvement, and others apparently take no part in any creative activity. She must be guided by clues they give.

● Arturo often watched others paint, though he hastily said no if any child said, "Let's paint." It seemed to the teacher that his watching meant that painting could have special value to him. Using the principle of linking the familiar and trusted with the unknown and feared, she began to help him approach the new experience. While studying him, she had noticed that Arturo seemed to be spending much of his time in the sand near the painting table. Though he usually had a truck in his hand, it began to appear that the truck was only incidental to the use of the sand itself. He was not loading or dumping his truck; instead, he was running the truck around in the sand to make lines in it. First, then, the teacher dampened his sand, with his approval, so that his lines would be more visible. Then (these steps extending over several days) she brought him a large piece of Masonite which she laid on the sand near where he was playing. He spread sand over that, then, still using his truck. She next gave him a squeeze bottle of glue, and, since he had been keeping his hands away and using an intermediary (the truck), he could use the bottle in the same way, squeezing lines of glue on the board. When she showed him how, by pouring sand over his lines and then shaking it off, he could bring out clearly what he had made, he was delighted. Several days later, after many sand paintings on papers laid on his board, she put a wire basket holding paints and brushes down on the sand beside him. Holding the brush by the very tip (and thus keeping his distance), he began to add color to his pictures.

One could now see the difference between Arturo and children who are primarily in a manipulative phase. While Arturo was drawn by the same material, he never mixed sand and paint in gluey gobs. He refused to wear an apron, yet he rarely got paint on his hands or clothes. Also revealing at this time was the fact that, though Arturo wanted his pictures saved, he never wanted to take them home. This suggested that, as the youngest in his family, he was unsure how his pictures stood up in comparison with the accomplishments of his older siblings—or perhaps how he himself did.

So far, Arturo had been painting on the ground. One day the teacher suggested he might be more comfortable standing up at the table. He was willing to move there, but so delicate are the links a child uses to preserve his sense of security unbroken that he stood at the end of the table where his feet were actually only a few inches from the sand where he had been before. Also, he still wore no apron, though the others did; perhaps he felt he could escape more quickly if need be, or deny that he was really painting, either to himself or others. After several days of using glue, sand from a box, and paint on his familiar board laid on the table, he was offered a tray containing some dabs of paint into which he could run his old truck around to make lines. Soon in went his hand as well, and he was finger painting without the truck, though with a lot of hand-washing along the way. As he grew freer, the finger painting began to show form and design, as had his lines in the sand, and he did the same thing on paper. He then branched out in other directions. He decided to put on an apron, definitely committing himself, and next, as his ego expanded, he made larger and larger paintings, until at last he was ready to take one home, the biggest of all. His progress was orderly throughout: from the use of lines only to the use of color, then to the incorporation of depth by means of objects glued to his paintings, and finally to three-dimensional wood constructions, clay products, mobiles, and stabiles. Through using his own linking process, art activities became a central part of his day.

● Jem was involved in art activities only when his friend of the moment was using them. When they painted side by side, Jem's eye was so seldom on what he was doing that the result was chaotic and the table around his paper was streaked with paint. Whenever his companion finished, "I'm through, too," he would say immediately, throwing his paper and apron down and rushing off to follow. He drew, or rather, scribbled, again without looking and only as long as the other child's pencil kept going, and his wood products fell apart almost at once since he couldn't stay to finish driving his nails in if he were left. And when he glued wood structures, he was so focused on keeping the other child at his side that his pieces wouldn't balance and his glue ran all over.

Distrustful of adults, Jem used them only as tools to his purposes and otherwise ignored them. With children, he pleaded, coaxed, tried to be charming and interesting, manipulated, demanded, and, if all else failed, used force, to get them to play with him, but his ever-echoing "Play with *me!*" "Let *me!*" "Come with *me!*" and his possessiveness were more than they could long endure. He was in a constant state of fidgets, his voice always loud and his movements plunging and heedless of his own and others' safety. To reach another child, he stepped on and fell over intervening toys. He pushed his trucks toward anyone near him, and if this failed to keep the focus of attention on him, he touched and pulled at the other child. It looked at though he couldn't bear to be left alone a moment. Was he afraid to be left alone with his thoughts? As yet there was no clue to what those thoughts might be and no outlet for their expression.

One of the things Jem did in his usual hasty, companion-oriented way was to play with dough and clay. The outside teacher came to the door one day, calling to the inside one, "Come quickly and see what has come out of Jem's clay!" He had used great quantities, piling it end to end, and he said he had made a "monster." It was about two feet long and five or six inches thick, lumpy and scaly-looking, like an iguana or mythical dragon. The teacher responded to this emergence of an idea of Jem's own by moving it to a long board so it could be carried home and by listening to him tell her about it. When she examined it unfearfully and with interest and acceptance, he could examine the scary fantasy it represented. Next followed a phase in which Jem would work with clay as long as his teacher stayed near. While she sat by him, he talked a good deal about monsters. Once he told of a dream in which he himself turned into a monster, supporting her theory that monsters might personify his own angry feelings from which he had been trying to escape. It seemed most important to keep this outlet open for him, and to that end the teacher devised a table for two in the corner of the playground with its own crock of fresh, soft clay balls, calling it "Rachel and Jem's table." Rachel's mother was a sculptress, and Rachel had long ago chosen clay as her favorite medium. Her attention span was exceedingly long; she never left before Jem did and was always ready to go to the table when he asked her.

The use of the art medium was not the only cause of the improvement in Jem that followed, but it played an important part. He could, at will, produce terrifying inner images, then, with a quick smash, destroy them. He began to calm down, ceased disrupting his relationships with others by being too demanding, and became strikingly more trustful of adults, often leaning against them or taking their hands. Finally, one day, he actually chose to play alone in the enclosed side area of the school, and so diminished was his anxiety that he was able to remain there for almost an hour in quiet, uninterrupted digging and excavating with trucks and tools. Here, as so often, there was a link from the old to the new; dirt, with its claylike plasticity, was now combined with a new, more reality-oriented interest in bulldozers, tractors, and so on, and this interest then began to be reflected in his products at the workbench, glue table, and easel, where he could now remain long enough to finish them.

On his last day at school, Jem was taken for a private ride by his teacher, and an intimate talk began with his "Remember when I used to—" showed his awareness of the change in him. Never before having mentioned his father, he said then, "I get along with my dad better, now." Having shown his teacher his fierce monsters, he felt that he had told her about his feelings, and of course he had, using his own symbols in the emotional language of children.

V

In her interest in widening possibilities for expression in art, a teacher also needs to remember that some young children already have, or will soon discover, one art medium with which they will stay, finding there the same satisfaction that an adult artist has when he has found what is right for him.

• Building with blocks was Kirk's choice of medium from the first. Use of blocks follows the same sequences as the use of other unstructured material. First the blocks are manipulated; they are piled into trucks and dumped, stacked and tumbled down, balanced, and clapped together. Next they are formed into nonrepresentational patterns and designs. Many children move away quickly from this kind of block play into a representational phase, particularly if buildings are needed for small scale dramatic play. Kirk, however, continued to use blocks as an art medium; often his elaborate arrangements held his attention for a long time. His material, to begin with, was a basic hardwood set of unit building blocks, together with Montessori geometric forms and cubes of clear Plexiglas. He used only three-dimensional shapes, ignoring colored cardboard squares and rug samples, for instance, and, since his buildings were not representational, he also saw no use for the wooden trees, people, and furniture that others added to their constructions.

The need to preserve products for Kirk began to be seen when he asked to have his block buildings saved. The teacher then brought him bases of plywood on which to build, and to these he enjoyed gluing structures of scrap wood to take home. Though this involved working in a somewhat smaller scale, he was unconcerned. (Size is important to some children. Some like to paint on a playhouse wall or a fence, or work with chalk on a long stretch of sidewalk. But a first painting may be on a very small paper, rather than on a tall easel, and children who have organized earlier paintings with confidence may respond to a very large paper or board by painting only in a corner, scribbling wildly to cover it all, or stiffly printing A B C. The projections of a young child on unstructured material often break down when the product threatens to be larger than the child.)

Kirk's materials could now include new things. Color was offered for the first time in the form of different kinds of wood scraps and samples of finishes: teak, walnut, rosewood, mahogany, oak, and birch. Less angular shapes could be provided, too, such as curved and weathered pieces of driftwood. As Kirk arranged his wood pieces on the bases, he began to learn how to balance them or prop them up, and problem-solving kept pace with creative ideas. His products now began to look like sculptures. Though Kirk was exposed to other three-dimensional media, like clay, wire to bend, or paper to fold, he never showed an interest in these; he stayed with his preferred medium. Shortly before leaving nursery school, in the manner of five-year-olds, Kirk began to link his art with outside cultural influences. He had learned the word "architect" and started making what he called houses. These had strange, swooping roofs and slanting sides, and showed their link to his powerful wood sculptures clearly. Kirk was unconcerned with the insides of these buildings; he never made enclosures, but constructed all his houses in solid pieces. They were, in fact, sculptures of houses, to which he sometimes added pieces of tile, brick, tanbark, pebbles, or waving bamboo leaves.

● Mathilde was a child with an absorbing interest in art, and as she explored many media, she began to develop a definite individual style that was instantly recognizable. She began with painting, on pieces of paper, cardboard, cloth, wood, tiles, and mats of various sizes. She used brushes, rollers, wooden forks and spoons, scrapers, her hands, and once or twice her bare feet. She worked on tables, on floors, on the grass, and on upright surfaces such as an easel or sheets of heavy paper fastened to the jungle gym. She sometimes imprinted shapes in her paintings with blocks of wood and other objects, drew in them with sticks while they were wet, sprinkled sand over them, or spattered them with water.

Mathilde's special concern with line was evident early. She used squeeze bottles filled with paint to make curves and swirls, and she flattened clay and drew lines in it, too. When she became interested in texture, she added cloth, tissue scraps, leather, cotton, and other things to her paintings, but her absorption with line continued throughout; long strands of yarn wound their way through the collages, glued in place. She also tucked yarn strands into rug samples and pegboards, and wove and sewed them into wire screens, mesh, and burlap. In making two-dimensional collages, she used small pegs laid end to end, beads, buttons, and the like, glued to backgrounds of Masonite, plywood, veneer, or linoleum, and in the placement of these one could see again the same evidence of her sense of line, as well as her sense of space as something either to be filled or used as part of the composition.

Awareness of line continued to be evident when Mathilde explored three-dimensional materials. For wood-gluing she chose pieces with curves, and, with great economy, stopped when she had achieved one rhythmic sweep of upward line. Even when she made a mobile, using wire to fasten together some spools and parts of an old clock, she added several long strips of paper with curving lines drawn on both sides. At that time, drawing was becoming very important to her. Her drawings were not representational at this stage; her special interest seemed to be the use of space so that drawings and background were a unified whole.

Some were very large, others minute. When she worked on a circular surface such as a paper plate, one could see her awareness of the round shape as she swung her lines in harmony with it, and when there were odd-shaped surfaces to draw on, such as a triangular leather scrap and the back of a long linen wall calendar, her drawings took into account the angles of the one and the length of the other in relation to its width.

In due course a face began to appear in Mathilde's pictures. She moved very rapidly, then, to whole figures, birds, and animals, being much less interested, apparently, in representing inanimate objects. One could see the link with previous art experiences. Her lines flowed; a nose line curved into an eyebrow, and, with very rapid, sure strokes, she would make the lines of the upper part of a figure flow downward into arms that were not merely added sticks but seemed to grow out of the body design. Her people and animals all moved; they ran or jumped or danced, and her birds flew, tipped in the direction they were going. Wide skirts on girls filled out the bottom of pages, and long sweeps of hair followed the same curves. When Mathilde included other things in her drawings a little later on, these too fell into the same rhythmic lines, each becoming part of the whole composition. In one drawing, branches of a huge tree filled the entire upper area, and from the tree hung a swing in which a little girl sat leaning back, just beginning the forward swoop, with her long hair streaming out behind her. Nor was Mathilde always literal in her representative phase; she played with ideas, as well as with line. A hat on one person held a flower whose stem extended to the very top of the sheet; the tiny figure and the blossom were thus seen at the ends of one long wavy line. A picture of a mother rabbit holding a baby one was made up only of swirling lines; long ears, long arms, and concentric circles formed the mother's body, with the baby's face and ears curved into the very middle. Another picture, of a man walking, consisted entirely of lines built up by rapid, short strokes back and forth until the man's shape was achieved. Color was less important to Mathilde as her drawing developed, but when she did use it, as in a mural of a girl and a dog that she made, it served not to fill out what she had drawn but, instead, placed both within and without the lines, to emphasize those. As a result the total composition was a unified combination of the representational and the nonobjective.

VI

Movement play, probably a universal outlet for self-expression in young children, is at the same time a form not readily recognized as creative. A teacher may have the impression that her children seldom dance because she tends to think of dance as only occurring in conventional ways. But small children dance in their own way, in movement play throughout the school day, and this can be appreciated and supported by teachers once they begin to see it for what it is.

● Chuck and Dennis were running back and forth from one end of the playroom to the other. Since running indoors can sometimes be disruptive or hazardous, it needed to be evaluated. Was Chuck chasing Dennis? That might have to be stopped with, "Better let him go, if he wants to run away. He'll come back when he's ready." Or is it a big-muscle, space-covering kind of interest? "The outdoors might be better for that," the teacher could say. But in this case, their feet were beginning to hit the floor at the same time, and a rhythm was being established of which they were delightedly aware. The teacher cleared their path, picked up their rhythm on a tom-tom, others joined in, and dance was under way.

Molly was going round and round a post in the patio with a rhythmic movement. As the teacher sang, "Round and round she goes," making up a song to fit what was happening, Molly began to extend the experience, leaning her body inward on the turns, catching the post with one hand and swinging the other arm in a wide arc, and reversing direction. Soon a group was circling the other patio posts, weaving in and out, and some began to turn themselves in space. It was a short dance—often these experiences are very fleeting—but nonetheless enjoyable and creative.

Movement play which developed into a variety of patterns was enjoyed by two boys for several days. It began when they threw feather dusters into the air and tried to catch them. Noticing the interesting flights these took, the boys began moving with them; as the dusters flew high in the air, the boys jumped high, too, and as the dusters fell lightly to the ground, so did the boys. Two boys and two dusters waved from side to side and rolled across the floor.

The pattern of the circle is a simple, primitive one that children often make when a group is dancing. They may trot round and round for a long time, apparently enjoying making this shape on the floor and being in that arrangement with others. There is almost a hypnotic fascination about it, and they rarely change from this trotting movement until the circle breaks up into singles, pairs, or shifting groups. On the other hand, processional dance, another form natural to children, includes many different movements. If it is possible to go out of the playroom by one door and come back in by another, part of the group is invisible to the rest, and so the circle is not evident and each child moves in his own individual pattern. Drums are often played en route. Many wear hats or dress-up clothes. Some stamp their feet and raise their knees, some skip or hop, some wave their arms and turn in place here or there. There are always children, too, who invent a special way of going; perhaps two little steps and a gallop, repeated, or something similar. The only limit that needs to be set is on running, since this leads to trying to get ahead around corners and to a feeling of being pursued; also, those who are crawling, as some do, are unable to keep up. Processional dance may be accompanied by piano or phonograph music, and the procession may involve carrying such things as Japanese lanterns, flowers, balloons, stuffed animals, and dolls. Art is sometimes incorporated, too, in the form of long cardboard tubes to which paper or cloth flags or crepe-paper streamers are taped. Some processional banners become quite elaborate; they look rather like kites, take a long time to make, and are borne with great pride.

Movement play which includes the environment is play that is especially natural to children, but it may not be seen for what it is by adults. Toys in rows on the floor are jumped, tables and chairs are circled, and dolls are swung in arms. Boards may be ascended and descended, not for the purpose of getting somewhere, but for the joy in patterned movement for its own sake. Movement designs are often seen on the jungle gym and slide, and there it is the child's apparent awareness of the form in what he is doing, either rhythmic or spatial, that tells the teacher he is engaged in pure movement play. His prompt expression of delight when the teacher sings or drums to reflect and underline the play also tells her she is on the right track. Movement play can be quiet and solitary, too. A child fits himself onto the shape of a long, narrow board, curls up in a box, or lies within the circle of a track made in sand. In the swing he may hang over backward, his body supported by the swing strap, arms and head touching the ground at one side and feet at the other, and in this position he may move gently to and fro or from side to side. When a teacher's eyes are open to them, she can learn to recognize many subtle and fleeting bits of movement play that are really dance elements and respond to them. It is this kind of help that supports and promotes creativity.

VII

● Bee was a little girl whose special interest became dance. She began by dressing up. The intensity of her involvement in this activity indicated to the teachers that something very important to her was going on. Her dressing up seldom led to a dramatic-play role, with Bee then going off to play mother in the doll corner, for example. Instead, the way she used this material was to create designs with it, using her own body as the base or background for them. The available materials in the bin and hat basket were lengths of chiffon and lace, plain and printed full cotton skirts of different lengths, sleeveless bolero jackets, ponchos, capes, scarves, tunics, and also hats with large brims, high pointed peaks, plumes, feathers, dangling ribbons, or ball fringes. There was a wide range of colors to combine, some vivid and some soft. For use with these things, another basket contained leis, a long bamboo chain, beads and bracelets, wrist and ankle bells, necklaces that jingled, belts, and some elastic waistbands and headbands. There were some accessories, too, such as bright-colored feather dusters, sticks with streamers or woolen balls on strings tied to them, straw flowers, and a peacock feather.

In dressing up, Bee used the material with freedom and creativity. She put on many things from the bin, one over the other, with layers so arranged that all of them showed. She poked long scarves into her waistband so they would hang down her back. She wrapped long bead strings and leis around her waist and dangled them from her wrists, wore skirts over her shoulders, and sometimes completely covered her head. In her next period, she began to expand the possibilities by using art materials at the nearby table. (A child's ideas often spread within a certain spatial area.) She cut paper and fastened it to herself, tried pasting it on her forehead, and inked her fingernails in different colors. At this time, to help her independence keep pace with her burgeoning ideas, she was given a basket of clip clothespins, and these, together with elastic waist- and headbands, enabled her to secure things where she wanted them. Her individual way of using material was especially evident one day when the children had a pile of egg cartons and squares of tissue paper in all colors on their work table. Some were crushing the tissues into the holes of the cartons, calling them Easter eggs. Others were wrapping "presents," or cutting the tissue into small snips and pasting it here and there on the cartons. But Bee wrapped pipe cleaners around pieces of tissue paper to make bows of many colors that she fastened all over herself. On the ends of the longest pipe cleaners she then pasted squares of tissue, and she carried these in her hands as additional ornaments.

The next step for Bee was movement in space. The link between dressing up and moving was very easy to see and is the way many children begin to dance. The feathers and flowers nodded, streamers flowed from the ends of the sticks, skirts whirled and widened as she turned, leis and bead chains swung from side to side, and scarves of chiffon trailed behind on the floor as she walked forward and wrapped around her feet in circles as she turned in one place. She began to make designs in space now, by body movements. As is natural for nursery school children, Bee's first dances were all nonrepresentational, like the first paintings and drawings. Later on, corresponding to the representational stage in art, Bee introduced some dramatic elements. (But many dancers continue to prefer pure dance—body movement for its own sake or as part of the enjoyment of music—just as many children and adults continue to prefer abstract art.) Like the use of unstructured art materials, dance can provide an outlet for unfocused feelings, and suggestions by teachers of subjects for either art or dance interfere with that function. They also engender dependence on the teacher, and chances for self-affirmation are correspondingly diminished. Bee's dance was always motivated from within, the teacher's role being to recognize, respond, and support.

Movement with Bee developed at its own pace and in its own way. She began by emphasizing movements of the head and eyes. (A baby starts this way, too.) These head movements—tipping her head far back, turning it from side to side, and dropping it forward as she watched her leis and skirts swing in space—always gave her dance an expressive, flowing quality. Her spine came more and more into play, and then her arms moved, too. As Bee dropped her head forward, curving her upper back, her arms came forward and down; they stretched out when she turned, and reached up and moved from side to side. When she waved streamers, these extended and emphasized her arm movements. At first Bee only moved her feet in place or walked slowly around. Sometimes she sat or lay on the floor, using very small movements in a limited area. Later she expanded her body movements into space, running, whirling, and jumping; then she began streamlining her costumes and accessories, leaving behind the more encumbering ones. She moved as though to encompass the entire room, or, in the grass area of the playground, circled it or crossed it diagonally from corner to corner, as though drawing designs there with herself. All her movements seemed to start from the center of her body; no part moved separately from the movement of the whole spine. The teacher was careful not to comment on, or in any way draw attention to one part of her body—feet, arms, head, shoulders, or hands—so that this natural ability of a young child to move all in one piece might be preserved. (Often when young children start dance classes, they do lose this; when being taught technique, they focus on first one part of the body and then another. Free dance then occurs less and less often, finally being lost as an emotional outlet because of too much body awareness. For this reason, formal lessons are more appropriate after age five.) Visitors who watched Bee dance tried to express what they saw by such comments as "She has no self-conscious muscles anywhere" and "She's all purpose—like Zen."

The next link was to sound. Because the dress-up materials were in the music corner, Bee would often hear music going on there, either record-playing or children's improvisations with piano or instruments. She at first shut all this out, attending to her body rhythms only. But some of the things she chose to wear had bells sewed to them, and she often wore chains of bells around her neck or on her wrists and ankles. A basket containing rattles, castanets, clappers, and larger bells was nearby, too, and she sometimes carried these or tucked them into her waistband. As a result, she frequently made her own sounds as she moved, and since these were exactly coordinated with her movements, they were reinforcing, rather than distracting. Later the teacher improvised on the piano while Bee danced, watching and following her very closely, with the aim of enriching the experience. For many children, dance is closely related to music awareness. Some children always move when they hear music, as though the movement helps them both to take it in and to express the feelings it arouses. Alicia, another dancer who was also a music-maker, always did this, unless she herself was producing the music. But Bee appeared to be more visually and kinesthetically oriented, so, instead of playing music, the teacher next began to move with her, carrying out the lines of Bee's arm movements in space, curving her body over or beside Bee's as she bent down, or perhaps contrasting a movement with Bee's in a way that would support and emphasize it. In this way they improvised together, with Bee taking the lead. Bee never made any attempt to imitate the teacher; apparently she quickly realized that the focus was on her own choreography. Because of her larger size and her adult prestige, a teacher needs to vary her movements frequently or remove herself if she is becoming too strong an influence on children while dancing with them. Seeing her dance with enjoyment does seem to increase interest on occasion, however, especially if the teacher moves simply and naturally. For children especially involved in dance, like Bee, a teacher's responding in the same medium seems to have more meaning than just watching and making verbal comments. The teacher also improvised on the piano or another instrument with Perry, whose medium was music, and both Perry and Bee seemed to continue longer when this happened, sometimes asking for it. They were not dependent on the teacher's improvising with them, however, apparently feeling they could work alone perfectly well—as indeed they could.

As she moved into her second year in nursery school, Bee's intellect began to be more at her service in her dance. She learned to cut and paste well enough to decorate large pieces of crepe paper, which she then wrapped around herself for surrealistic-looking costumes, and she also made paper headbands and painted or pasted on these. (Her friends were pressed into service daily to help her try on her headbands and paste them together in the back.) She was not able to cut cloth, but she could decorate strips of it with paint or felt pens, and, if it was porous enough, sew designs or patches on it or gather it up into bunches with yarn; these products she used for sashes, scarves, head veils, or pompoms. She twisted soft copper wire and electricians' wire into necklaces and bracelets, and she made leis of macaroni or Styrofoam rings. Her skills with materials made great strides, as did her problem-solving and ingenuity. Bee's social development kept pace, too; by now she was interested in dressing up the other children as well, and she first learned to tie a bow when she wanted to help someone fasten a ribbon under his chin to hold a paper plate on top of his head.

At almost the end of her last year, Bee, now interested in kings, queens, princes, and princesses, owing to some outside experiences, began to make crowns for the others, and these were worn at school every day by many of the children. From this more culturally motivated interest a dance drama developed, with a shifting cast and a continuously evolving plot. It included dance, costume design, singing, dramatic action, and a drum accompaniment. With Bee as director, it was performed for a number of days. As may happen at about age five, Bee was crossing the line between the kind of dance which is just self-expression, unconcerned with anyone else, to that which is performed with an audience also in mind. Bee would say, "It's my turn to dance, now; you sit in the chairs." The audience, mostly other members of the cast, would sit in a row to watch. However, as soon as Bee began, she was usually carried away and lost herself in her dance; she would then continue until the audience grew impatient and demanded their turns. Often, if they drifted off, she just went on dancing by herself until she was ready to call them all back again. She still wanted to be the center of everything related to her dance ideas, as she had been when she danced alone, but she was not disturbed if the children left her or failed to follow her lead; her rich inner resources made her able to continue the dance drama by herself.

At some level, Bee seemed to understand that her favorite form of expression could help her handle uncomfortable feelings. There was a witch in the princess dance drama, and some episodes she wanted to include were scary for her—for example, the drum scene in which the toy bear in a witch hat was overpowered. Some of these ideas came from the movies of *The Wizard of Oz* and *Snow White,* which she had seen at home on television. The dance drama did help her work through these disturbing experiences, and other themes then emerged, such as the wedding of the prince and princess (repeated many times) and coronation ceremonies. Bee had a powerful ally in her creative medium, a means by which she could handle and work out many problems she might encounter in the future.

VIII

Children's own music is not always readily noticed among the various other sounds arising from activities in the playroom. It is sometimes hard, at first, for a teacher to think "music" unless a child is using an instrument or singing a recognizable song. Very many things make sounds that are interesting to children for their own sake. There are the sounds that feet make on the floor, the swish of sliding ones, the fast pattering of running, and the thudding of jumps, and there are the different sounds that feet make when they are bare and when they are in shoes. There is the clattering sound of puzzle pieces being dumped on the wooden table, and the sound that the parts of the village set make when they are stirred round and round in their big tub. There is the sound of pebbles going into a box, of water running into the doll sink, and of sand being poured down the slide. Children experiment with many mouth noises, too, like blowing into water with a straw, making clucking and sucking sounds, and using their voices in all kinds of unclassifiable ways. But continuing to make one sound and forming patterns with it, or combining several sounds purposefully, is different from other kinds of interest in sounds such as curiosity or enjoyment. These activities are creative projections upon the material, a rearrangement and ordering of it, rather than exploration alone.

Simple sound repetitions that a child produces on a drum may be tried out experimentally on a different instrument, or perhaps the pattern will next be enriched by variations within the main structure of the repetition. Many of these sound improvisations, like children's movement play, are very brief; often nothing more then occurs than a nod and smile of recognition passing between teacher and child. The teacher does not consider the length of the time involved when something like this happens, however; she notices the quality, rather than the quantity, of the experience. She knows, too, that flashes like these can be lengthened and will be firmer and clearer, and that a child can learn to extend evanescent expressions in the medium of sound so that he can really savor and appreciate them fully before they are lost and forgotten. A simple arrangement of sounds, such as a single tap on a drum which alternates with a hit of the stick on the wooden side of it, can change and grow in length and variety just as paintings change and grow with development and experience. In fact, change is inevitable, with the result that no music or dance improvisation and no art product will ever be repeated in just the same form. The essence of creativity is the making of something new. Unlike older composers, choreographers, and artists, a young child rarely polishes something he has produced; he just goes on to make something else.

Since there is almost always someone engaged in sound play in the nursery school room or playground, there will be many opportunities for a teacher to enrich it by some kind of participation, provision of materials, or interest and responsiveness. On days when the teacher does focus on these opportunities, sound play blooms especially; because there is no tangible product to keep, there is a special pleasure for children in sharing music-making activities with an interested person. As satisfying as the experience may be to a child, sound play that one does all by oneself is like talking to oneself, and communication adds another dimension to the enjoyment.

With each period of close observation, a teacher sees again the pervasiveness of this kind of play. In one group of nursery school children, for example, the following expressions of music interest were seen.

● Roddie slowly and rhythmically turned a jointed wooden figure over and over, as in a somersault, hopped it up and down in a livelier tempo, then ended with the slow roll again, repeating the sequence several times. Livy walked quickly around the room, turning the handle of the music box hanging around her neck that played "The Farmer in the Dell." Several children explored the sounds of the bells in the basket on the table; noticing the different pitches, they played them one at a time and then, vigorously, all together. Playing with blocks, Angus placed them in a pile, deliberately clapping each one hard on the previously placed one. When his pile fell down, he took one in each hand and clapped them together, paused, then did it twice more.

Intensity of interest began to build. Quincy sat down at the big drum, beginning a rhythmic pattern which he repeated over and over. On her way outdoors, Agatha did a galloping step to his pattern. Hal quickly chose another drum and sat by Quincy, coming in on his strong accents. The teacher picked up Quincy's pattern on the piano, then she began to improvise along with him, seeing that he was steady and sure. Alice tried the phonograph, but it was not very audible against the piano, so she took a tambourine and did a kind of stamping dance as she waved it about. Roddie next began to play the piano too, with a single, repeated note in the treble, and the teacher's improvisation adapted to that note, picking it up in the bass and emphasizing it. As David twanged on the koto strings, the music in the room began to take on the sound of all children's free music. It was like the voices and play of the children, an impression of progress and continuity with little themes emerging here and there from the overall blending and then falling back into it again. Chip began to dance, playing the ukelele he called his guitar, and to sing his own made-up song, and the piano adapted to that, too. Dressed-up Lucia turned slowly round and round, watching her skirts turn with her and ending each turn with a tap of her foot on the floor. Mary Ann, making big circular sweeps with her felt pen on the easel, was part of the pattern, too, responding to Quincy's rhythm.

Now the intensity subsides. Quincy's playing breaks and slows, and his drum beats become sporadic, mingled with talk with Hal. The children leave the bells. Chip's guitar song and dance is over (it was short), and the koto and tambourine are also deserted. Livy has taken her music box to the doll corner, where it is a television set for the dolls that are arranged in a group around it. Alice has drawn a chair to the phonograph, ready for one of her listening sessions. Roddie's one note on the piano continues softly a little longer; then, as if to round out the completed experience, he picks up the little wooden man again and slowly and solemnly turns it head over heels once more before going outdoors to play. This use of a theme in play to unify a period of sound and movement expression is often seen; children tend not to think in terms of "music" and "dance," but rather of a whole experience composed of many elements, all of which are brought together by the organizing mind. (This is one reason why a music room, separate from a playroom, is not as appropriate for this age.)

A teacher helps in sound play in various ways. Sometimes the piano might be her choice to support many diverse elements, because of its volume and range of possibilities. But she needs an unconventional, free and easy approach to its use, so as not to interfere with children's fresh and original concepts of the structure of music. Nor does she want dependence; when she leaves the group (as when the ukelele had to be rescued from underfoot after Chip abandoned it), the music goes on without her. And there are many other ways in which a teacher can participate. She might join a group using instruments, or she might carry a hand-drum or harmonica with her to another area or outdoors. Perhaps she may offer a wordless hum that seems to express the mood of a child or a small group. On one such occasion, a teacher played the old carol "Tomorrow Will Be My Dancing Day" on a recorder, while a child dipped and rocked near her. ("Again, again!" she cried, when the teacher finished.) Whatever form her involvement takes, however, the teacher keeps her part subordinate to the whole, just as does a good member of a group of musicians, dancers, or actors who improvise together. The participation of a teacher usually enriches the total experience in process, as evidenced by a further release of the children's ideas, but when it has the effect of interfering with the creativity of the group involved—when, for example, they stop to watch and listen passively, distracted from their own developing themes—she knows she is doing too much. Experience will help her find her place in each group, and as her sensitivity to what is going on increases, she will more and more easily be able to avoid a role that is either too passive or too active.

How can the teacher avoid being imitated at these times? If she does anything at all, don't the children feel overimpressed and try to do what she does, rather than following their own creative ideas? This kind of imitating would be more apt to occur early in the school year, and for that reason the teacher avoids participating very much in music and dance improvisations at first. As children go along in the school, however, they are learning day by day that the teacher is really interested in what they themselves feel and in what they have to say everywhere—in dramatic play, in art activities, in social interactions, in the making of stories and poems, and similarly in sound and movement play. Acquaintance with this new relationship gradually convinces them that the teacher wants a child to be him- or herself, and no one else. Here is where a consistent philosophy shows its worth. If this attitude is established in the school, there will be no need for a child to doubt it when the medium of expression changes, especially if music materials are available for use at any time, rather than being brought out at a special period, in a special place only, or with a special teacher who knows the children just in this situation. But since there are many other influences on children's music, from television and elsewhere, that encourage either passive listening or the use of conventional forms, the nursery school needs to stress less stereotyped kinds of music and encourage open, unconstricted sound play. The contributions a teacher provides to children's music-making come from whistling, humming, and improvised singing, from body sounds such as foot-stamps and hand-claps, from sound-making objects, from drums, wood blocks, bells, and rattles, from simple instruments like the zither, xylophone, and harmonica, and also, if she likes to use them, from an autoharp, guitar, recorder, or piano. But the key to the encouragement of freedom and creativity in sound play is a teacher's responsiveness to children's own music.

Some practical questions arise. This kind of teaching is highly individualized. Can it be done within the classroom by the regular teacher, who has other duties at the same time? In a school where there is free choice of indoor or outdoor activities, all the children are seldom in the room at the same time. In addition, since materials for music play are always available, and since children at this age play for the most part in twosomes or very small groups, only a few and frequently only one child would be using the materials at a time, off and on. Because independent play is stressed, they learn to use the record player and handle the various sound-makers and instruments with or without teacher participation, and the teacher is free to supervise the rest of the group's activities as needed.

What about the intrusiveness of sound play of this kind while other children are doing different things in the room? If anyone were bothered, either by the volume or the quality of the sound play, he might be encouraged to move his toys into an adjoining room, perhaps, or he might ask the player to take his instrument there or to a corner of the playground. Sometimes one child might decide to play records when another is at the piano, and complain, "I can't hear!" The piano player can then decide whether or not he is finished and respond accordingly. On another such occasion the child who wants to play records might well just go ahead, sitting on the floor by the machine and putting his ear close. (Children enjoy mixed sounds, too; they often wind up several music boxes, and the effect is interesting, as they all have the same tinkly quality.) Of course, with experiences of many different kinds available, there are long periods when children would choose other things, except, perhaps, for an especially interested child. In any case, sound play is rarely really chaotic unless a child himself is so. Both teachers and children become accustomed to the kinds of sounds and rhythms that children produce with instruments or with their voices; it may, in fact, be somewhat easier for children to accept them, since hearing conventional music has conditioned the ears of adults to certain expectations. The music in the playroom is at first a foreign language to teachers, while the children, not burdened by expectations, can be less critical. But in time a teacher can learn to hear and appreciate sound patterns that once sounded strange or even disagreeable to her; as her ear becomes sensitized, she will hear selectively and no longer react as though nothing but noise were going on. There is a kind of order and purpose in all that a child does, if one has eyes and ears for it.

Sound play may be upsetting to some children in a group during the period of their first adjustment to school. Loud, harsh, or sudden sounds may perhaps remind them of angry voices or their own anxious, angry, or pain-provoked crying. Many children also associate making noise with being "naughty," and if they hear someone doing this, they either shout (even louder than the noise), "Be quiet!" thus assuring themselves that they are not the scolded but the scolders this time, or else they anxiously identify with the child, with whom they expect the teacher to be cross. When the teacher, instead, participates or responds with interest and pleasure, they are reassured, and many such children for a time become the noisiest drummers of all. But because they hear so much of this kind of music—the children's own—soon everyone accepts it, and when it starts, others often run to get their own instruments or to get dressed up for dancing. If there is a loud segment of piano playing, they know it will in all likelihood be followed by a soft one or soon be finished, and they are not so bothered if, for a few minutes, their "babies can't sleep," or conversation becomes difficult. And even at first, they seldom leave the room to escape the sound if the teacher brings up that possibility. Soon sound play, through their own and others' participation, becomes just another form of self-affirmation. One will then often hear old children tell a new one, "That's his music—he likes it," taking it for granted as they do each other's style in painting or drawing. "He's just scribbling," a voice may be heard at the easel. "But that's his *way*," an old-timer may then answer in surprise.

IX

With this kind of program, the music in the air is mostly improvised by children, but there is the music of records and that of a teacher's playing and singing, too. A record library needs music of wide range, from very old to very new, and including many folk songs, perhaps Indian and African music, and so on. The record player and the records, occasionally changed, like the books, can soon be used independently by any child. It seems clear that in nursery school children are in no awe of music on records; they appear to regard these sounds much as they would those of a playing friend, and often go and sit down nearby to play an instrument or sing along, with no more idea of "following" the music than they would with that friend. At this age it seems more natural to most of them to participate in some way, rather than to listen passively. Songs are played over and over sometimes, apparently for the purpose of learning them, but once a child has learned a song, he often changes the words and tune freely and may add to it at length. Records can be marked with stickers to help children tell them apart, and a particular favorite one may often be chosen for dancing. Three four-year-old boys chose the folk song "Little Bitty Baby" for their dancing over a period of several days. (Groups of two, three, or four who play together often improvise together, too, in dance or music.) The boys structured the dance around the music. They took motionless poses until the record started, then would dance, each in his own way but aware of the others, and all responding to the music's changes of tempo; then at the end they would again make some kind of grouping and hold it. They took great pleasure in knowing just when the record was coming to an end and assuming their final position at exactly the time the music stopped.

Young children especially like to hear their teacher sing. When they have heard a song many times, they like knowing what to expect and often sing along. But the teacher watches for chances to encourage creative ideas here, too; the children may suggest different words or new verses, and sometimes a child sings an entirely new song of his own. Some folk songs lend themselves particularly well to this kind of adaptation—for example, those in which the refrain can be repeated to include what every child at the table is wearing, what his or her name is, what kind of ice cream each likes, and so on. Children add lines to songs like "What Shall We Do When We All Go Out?" ("Slide down the slide," "Swing in the swing," "Dig in the sand"), or "Hey Jim-a-long-long, Jim-a-long Josie" ("Laugh a-long-long," "Drive a-long-long," "Fly a-long-long"). Some songs get permanently changed (improved, from the group's point of view). In "Old

Joe Clark," the refrain after the verse ending "Every story in that house was filled with chicken pie" was changed by one group to "Eat along, Old Joe Clark, eat your chicken pie." "What Shall We Do with a Sleepy Baby?" was given a new verse by them, too: "Wake him up and give him his breakfast, early in the morning."

Some songs include gestures for teachers to demonstrate; they are usually called "finger plays." If used, these are best presented without any gestures to be imitated. Those who want to move then do so in their own way, and there will be self-directed, independent creative activity, rather than teacher direction and dependence. The teacher just sings the song, without indicating that anything is expected. Perhaps none of the children will think of acting out the words, but if someone does, quite original things might happen. When "Put Your Finger In The Air" was sung in one group, there was at first only interested listening, with some chuckles at the funny parts ("Ask it, 'How's the air up there?'" and so on). Then Molly reached across the table and beckoned the finger of one child after another to join hers in dancing in the air. This went on all through the other verses, apparently being more enjoyable than "Put your finger on your nose," "cheek," "chest," and so on, until, at the end, someone else had the idea, when "Put your finger on your finger on your finger" was sung, of everyone's fingers being entangled in the center of the table. Though sometimes the relation of gesture to song is not very recognizable, children's own ideas are often more interesting than suggested gestures, since they are less literal and not limited to hands. Also, they change whenever the song is sung, so its appeal continues. Finger plays, as usually presented, are like coloring books and other "busy work" in which a child fills in someone else's lines; they entertain and hold attention, but at cost to the growing sense of self that needs first consideration.

A teacher with an ear for chords often finds an autoharp easy to play to accompany her singing and increase interest in it. But the fact that the chords are all conventional ones makes it most useful for folk songs and nursery rhymes; it is not very satisfactory for accompanying children's own improvised songs, since they are ordinarily freer. Inevitably, however, children's music is conditioned in time by what they hear on the outside, just as children's art is influenced by the pictures they see in everyday life, most of which are representational. Some of the children who improvise often on the piano begin to move at the end of the nursery school period toward playing triads and other familiar harmonic and rhythmic forms. Any medium, starting out as unstructured, is first used by the child in highly individual ways; later he is more culturally influenced, as is to be expected. In the nursery school, some piano playing is mostly percussive, some shows a buoyantly free style, which nevertheless has its own form, and some may demonstrate a harmonious blending of creative expressiveness with the kind of music the children are hearing.

X

● Perry started school at three years of age, and it was apparent from the first that his special interest would be music. He had an affinity for sounds. He beat on overturned tubs and wastebaskets, and perilously upended the outside trash can to see what the sound would be like when he hit it on the bottom. He was drawn to any kind of drum, but especially to those with deep, resonant tones.

Music materials in the room included a number of Chinese and Indian bells, a Japanese koto, a zither, a ukelele, a steel drum, a bamboo two-toned drum, a kalimba, and wood blocks, rattles, xylophones, gongs, triangles, cymbals, tambourines, and other miscellaneous sound-makers, as well as a piano and record player. Among the drums and tom-toms there were large ones by which Perry could sit or stand, using his whole arm or both arms to beat them vigorously and freely, and smaller ones he could hang up and beat or carry around. He used his hands and also a variety of mallets and drumsticks, some with soft heads, others with hard heads, and wire brushes. Perry made frequent use of an adjoining room for especially loud or long drumming, and for playing on a cymbal (a professional instrument) about fifteen inches across. The cymbal's reverberations, perhaps more than anything else at this time, helped him to hear the subtle variations in the results of his muscular efforts.

Perry's drumming very soon took shape. He began to beat regularly, like breathing or rocking, then, as time went on, to break up these units into complicated inner patterns. At this time, because his patterns were so clear, his teacher began to play the piano or another drum with him, improvising to support his ideas, and there were sessions in which, as they played together, they experienced close rapport in sound. The teacher also reflected patterns of his on other instruments, thus underlining them and helping him to hear them. She used a xylophone, a wood block, her voice, or another percussive instrument with a different sound; to have parroted or echoed Perry exactly would have served less well to help him not only hear what he had been doing but grasp the idea behind it and move ahead.

By his second year, Perry was using several instruments at once. He and his teacher worked together to figure out how to make them all accessible at the same time; her job was to bring chairs, tables, or pegboards to hang things on and to tie cords, and his was to decide what he needed and test the results. It was evident, then, how his good intelligence was being brought into the service of his interest. He would sit with a large drum between his knees, other drums ranged around him, and, nearby, an easel hung fore and aft with gongs, bells, and wood blocks. This was his "drum set," which he used either alone in the office or in the playroom near the piano and other instruments. Now four years old, he began to work for longer and longer periods, always without any rise of tension that would necessitate a change of occupation, though he sometimes stopped and stretched like a cat. At this time the staff began to tape his music, both to preserve it and to study the changes in it. The emergence of more pitch awareness was seen in the use of the variously pitched instruments in his set. Often he sang or chanted along with his playing, varying the pitch of his voice according to that of the instruments. A series of songs involved "Jefferd the Cat," whose picture by Perry hung nearby—"Jefferd, the best drummer in the world."

Patterns became clearer and longer, and were enjoyed by the other children; the form in his music was now so recognizable that when he played in the big room no chaotic feelings were aroused in the hearers. It became a custom for children to dance when he played. He was particularly interested in having the teacher dance to his music, watching her closely as she reflected what she heard by moving in space and responding to note patterns and dynamics.

About this time, he played for long periods on the xylophone (tuned resonator blocks) using two sticks, as he had with drums. He named these selections; one he called "About a River," and another "About Me When I Was a Baby." His touch was light and skillful, and he could bring out a singing tone. The fluidly blending melodies and rhythms had a haunting beauty. While each improvisation had a complex inner design, there was always a clearcut beginning and ending; he seemed to know exactly what he was doing. He turned next to the piano, and the link with his earlier percussive playing was seen in his rhythmical kicks of the baseboard as he played. Another link was seen, too, when he used the piano with the front removed, so he could hit the strings with his two sticks.

Most interesting of all to him seemed to be an orchestration of sounds. With his teeth holding a Jew's harp, he hummed through it (without it, his voice was drowned out). His foot kicked something rhythmically, and his hands flashed about among a variety of instruments, including drums, cymbals, the xylophone, and various bells. Now and then a gong dominated, or a different kind of sound. He was very clear about the help he required. "I'll need the wood block pretty soon; would you hit it? Now!" he would say.

Later that year, the teacher asked a concert drummer to bring his set to the school and play for the children. Perry was out in the patio when the drums were arranged in a corner of the room and the drummer began to play. Some of the children drew near, and others brought chairs over. A face appeared at the first sound, peering through the glass. The door opened, and Perry walked with indescribably concentrated purpose to his own drum set beside the big one. For over an hour the two played together, and nonverbal communication and mutual support at the highest level were conveyed in this impressive scene. The visiting drummer, wiping his brow at the end, said, "I want to take him away in my pocket!" Perry himself seemed unaware of any difference in their respective sizes and abilities; he showed no fatigue at the end of the session and talked to the drummer as to a peer, examining the drum set, trying it out, and asking how rolls and other effects had been achieved.

By that time, Perry was nearing the end of his nursery school period. He was not quite five years old. It was felt that he needed a link between what he had been doing and what was in store for him in the future, and to that end the visiting drummer took him on as a pupil. His lessons consisted at first merely of visiting the studio and playing on the big drum set as he wished, and he was also supplied at home with a small set of good quality to use there on other days. He worked on a piano at home now, too, and he often played his drums along with tapes that had been made of his own music. He also played along with the music of the Beatles, whom he discovered at this time. (In identification with Ringo Starr of the Beatles, he now always wore a ring when he played the drums.) Just before he left nursery school, a film was made of him engaged in his music-making. The filming extended over several days. He was never at a loss; he had only to sit down at his familiar school instrumental setup or at the piano, and ideas began to flow. His poise and concentration were notable, as was his endurance. He seemed to take it quite for granted that the staff liked his music well enough to preserve it in this way—he liked it himself—and he never showed any self-consciousness while being filmed, always being entirely absorbed in what he was doing.

Perry's interest at this time was still in making his own music. His friend the drummer, in whose studio he played, made an abortive effort to teach him to read notes for the drum, but Perry, with the young child's clarity of purpose, rejected this. He needed to play the music in his own head. Perhaps he was unwilling to let his need for self-affirmation be subverted, as it would have been if he had had to experience feelings of inadequacy about his music then. His strong sense of self was of more value than any facts about music might be; those could all come later, and, given his interest and drive, they surely would. When the time did come that he was ready to learn to read music, a link with his previous creative experiences could be established by helping him write out and read his own improvisations, with the aim of preserving those he liked especially, or perhaps to enable others to play them with him.

The example of Perry shows that a motivated and gifted child can move as far along in developing his musical ability during the nursery school years as anyone could ask, or even dream, without the kind of formal teaching that is ordinarily considered an inevitable and necessary part of early music education. Perry was never taught songs, the names of composers, notes, keys, or time signatures, though he probably had the intelligence to learn those things. It was never suggested that he match notes, repeat note patterns, or learn singing games or rhythms like marches and gallops. Nor was any effort made to get him away from playing the drum during his first long period; later, he did move on to other instruments of his own accord, but earlier he had something to say that drums expressed for him. To have stressed facts about music with Perry, in nursery school, would have been as though, in the midst of play involving an intensely dramatic scene of a fireman doll's rescuing a family from a burning house, a teacher said, "This is a pumper truck. This kind of fire truck is not being used much any more in the bigger cities," or as though, while a painting was taking form, she said, "This is yellow; this is blue. Do you know what color they make together?" Creative expression involves feelings; to treat it as an intellectual exercise overlooks its source of energy. Facts needed for a child to achieve his purpose will play a part, and, as he grows older, their contribution will be greater. But in the nursery school, facts are second in importance to self-affirmation.

Perry was different from other children only in that he had unusual musical ability and could progress faster and farther. But otherwise one would expect the same kind of response in any child to similar recognition of his interests and creative impulses, and, if the learning process is not hurried but allowed to develop in its own way and at its own rate, the stamp of individuality on the music that results can be clearly seen and will probably never be lost. Now, at the age of twenty, Perry is gaining notice as a musician who is not only gifted as a performer on several instruments but also outstandingly creative as a composer and arranger for a group of his own.

XI

The development of Kirk's wood sculptures, Mathilde's art, Bee's dance, and Perry's music followed the same basic pattern seen in the creative productions of all young children: first, the exploration and manipulation of unstructured materials; next, the emergence of abstract form and organization; next, a greater role played by the intellect in problem-solving and learning closely related to expressive needs; next, the merging of the outer world of reality with the inner world, as shown by the use of representational images; and finally, the gradual incorporation of cultural influences. Throughout this process, the teacher's aim is that the core of individuality be maintained.

Nursery school mailboxes frequently contain advertisements for preschool "creative projects" in which every child's product is exactly the same. But in an activity that is really creative, no two children will ever use materials in just the same way or to the same end. Bee experimented with a pleated paper cup one day, pulling out its folds so it lay flat. It looked like a flower to her then, and she colored it, then cut it with scissors until it had petals. Her patience and persistence in searching for something to use as a stem were most impressive. She cut one from paper, and it wouldn't stand upright. She tried a thin wire, and it bent in an arc. Still keeping in mind a long, sticklike shape, she searched the workbench, but found no stick thin enough. Finally, directed to a storage place for miscellaneous collage materials, she came up with a drinking straw which she inserted through a hole she poked in the flower with her scissors. Then began Bee's flower dance, which seemed to say, *"No other flower in the world is like this one, and I, Bee Washburn, made it."*

Creativity is not limited to achievements in the arts. It is a quality belonging to a person that permeates all his activities and his ways of thinking. Sometimes children show creativity in ways we fail to recognize. Roddie and Miles discovered some lengths of builders' wire that the teacher had put on a table, ostensibly to be bent into different shapes and used with mobile materials ready there. But Roddie was holding a long, straight piece of wire upright in each hand. Standing opposite Miles, he made designs with them in the air, framing Miles's laughing face at the sides and then across top and bottom. Miles and he then engaged in a fascinating activity for which there was no name. (And why name it?) Each boy, holding a wire in each hand, made patterns with his own and the other's until all possibilities were exhausted. The wires were crossed, separately and together, tipped, touched end to end (hard to do), held forward as in dueling and upright like batons or wands. It was like a delicate symbolization of a relationship, and it was also an experiment in length and depth, a kind of measuring of space. To be sure the children remained well apart, the teacher moved closer. But she didn't say, "The wires are for making mobiles." Why one form of creativity rather than another? Every child is different, and through his creativity he celebrates that difference.

11 Children with Problems

DREAM

A man hit me down the road,
And the Gobblers hit me,
And I cried and cried—
They spanked me and I cried.

I wanted to go home.
Everybody doesn't know my favorite color,
And they don't know who I am.

—Mandy

I

Among the children whom a nursery school teacher sees, there are some who are not keeping their heads above water. Life at the moment is too much for them, and, if this is so, sometimes school is too much for them as well. There is a limit to the amount of help that can be given a child in the school setting. However responsive and perceptive the teaching approach is, and however highly mental health is valued as a goal, a child who has special problems must be able to get along without continuous help, since the nursery school teacher has other duties. Not the least of the demands on the child is that he be willing to share his teacher's attention with quite a large number of rivals for it; his need must not make him so jealous when he sees her comforting others and being affectionately interested in them that his relationship with her, and with them, too, is seriously disrupted. And it is especially necessary that, though some of his time in school is spent in working on his problems with the help of his teacher, he should not be so constantly absorbed in them that he is unable to turn his attention outward, at least part of the day, in order to avail himself of the growth opportunities the school provides. For the sake of the group, too, perhaps the child should not be in school. If he disturbs the other children too much, they may be learning, not what most people are like, but just

241

what one unusual person is like. The other children can only feel confused, angered, and inadequate if they must always have help from the teacher in coping with this child. And of course the child who creates hostility in others then begins to feel that people are in reality just what he feared they were—enemies—or else that he himself is an unlovable person. Such a child may need professional help in a one-to-one situation before he can use nursery school.

How does a teacher decide which emotional problems can be solved in a school situation and which cannot? There is a qualitative difference between those that can and those that a teacher probably should not try to tackle. One child may be in trouble all day. He may battle his way through every dilemma that he meets in school, but they are real-life dilemmas. Everyone knows what he is mad about, including himself. He is involved with the environment and the people in it, and thus it, and they, can teach him. Another child, even though less constantly in trouble, may be battling with ghosts and projecting these on other children, to their alarm and bewilderment. None of the ways of relating to people that the children are learning seem to work with this puzzling child, and when this is so, the self-confidence and security of some in the group can be deeply shaken.

On observing a child before he enters, when he visits the school, the teacher can get helpful clues. A very young-appearing child who still gets wet in the daytime and resists using the toilet, and whose speech is very limited, would probably not be ready, especially if he also clung to his mother. As to the clinging alone, however, a teacher is less concerned about how shy a child is at first than with how he makes use of the chance to overcome it that a school offers. Did the child change and progress on his own during the first, or at least a second visit? Did he take up toys put near him, get off his mother's lap, move a little away from her, face away from her and watch the other children, look at the teacher and nod or reply to her, accept toys or crackers from her hand or from another child's? If a trial period of attendance was offered, the decision about a clinging child would probably rest on whether, with special help from his teacher, he progressed toward separation from his mother and stayed at school alone, or whether he could make no progress and became increasingly unhappy at the thought of being left. There are other children, too, who, though not as immature, still orient around their mothers, showing everything to her if she stays and continuing to miss her and resist the separation if she leaves. Regardless of the age, such a child may need special consideration.

A child who is very aggressive toward other children, and perhaps toward materials, too, on his visit, might need to be seen more than once. Sometimes this aggressiveness has other meanings, such as fear and excitement in the presence of many unfamiliar persons. Or, since a child's mother is with him when the first visit is made, he may be trying to attack the other children because he sees them as rivals for her attention (especially if there is a new baby at home), and when she is not there he may be less aggressive. He may also be socially naive, and this apparently hostile behavior may actually be an attempt at overtures toward children. The most important question such initial behavior raises, however, is that of the child's control over his impulses. In a new setting, where a child is not yet sure of his welcome, he will ordinarily restrain aggressive impulses; he can, so to speak, be on his good behavior. Probably, as soon as he is more confident, some aggressive feelings will burst forth. But he will have shown in this initial visit that if he thinks it to his advantage to control his actions, he can do so; thus one knows that his behavior is subject to external influences. If this were not so, he, too, might need a one-to-one therapeutic relationship either instead of school or along with it. A second visit often helps clarify the problem.

A child who runs constantly from one thing to another might also need to be seen again, since a short attention span, while a disturbing sign, is for some children a first-day phenomenon attributable to the variety of new stimuli. One would want to know whether this was the first time the child had been in a group of that size and also whether he was showing behavior unusual for him or was always the same. If it was characteristic of him not to settle down to anything for more than a few moments, there might be a need for a medical opinion, perhaps with neurological and psychological study.

If a child already in the group seems disturbed during some period, evincing this by inadequate control, by chaotic, hyperactive behavior, or by being anxious or withdrawn, the teacher tries her ways of helping, along with parent conferences, and the child's response indicates whether a referral for outside care is needed. Through working more intensively with him, she comes to a clearer evaluation of both the depth and the tenacity of his disturbance and of the available strength in him. She gathers information from his play and from his reactions to others that she can share with his parents, while, at the same time, she is learning more about him from what they tell her. She also tries to get a sense of how the parents might feel about a referral if she should think it advisable. The suggestion that a child might need special help for emotional problems can be destructively threatening; some parents need time to come to this idea by themselves, if possible, and also time to experience with the teacher what counseling is—an acceptance of themselves as people with feelings, as well as the child. Their decision about whether to seek outside help will be a difficult one that only they can make. In most cases it is impossible for a person other than those concerned to know what going for such help means to them; some may feel distrust of the profession of psychiatry, and others may fear the disruption of family relationships or the exacerbation of disturbances in themselves if old problems with which they have made a satisfactory truce are reopened for examination. Usually, consultation with the child's pediatrician is a more easily accepted first step.

During the time when the teacher is trying to help the child find ways to work out his problem in school and noting his response to her help, and while she is acquiring information about him from his parents and getting to know their needs better, she must judge whether she is coming close enough to the child so that he can communicate in words or play with her, and whether his behavior can be adequately controlled in the school setting. This means a double evaluation. Can he make use of special private opportunities to express feelings in a separate room or office, and is he able to play out aggressive or frightening themes there without too much anxiety? (If he is too anxious, he will stop playing or demand the teacher's constant presence.) Does he discharge his anxiety by impulsive and compulsive behavior that bursts through the limits that she must set and to which he must be able to adhere at school without continuous attention and outer control? (Since the child would be in the office only occasionally, staying only as long as he wished, he would be with the other children most of the time.)

A child who is to be helped with special problems in the office already feels at ease there through play along with other children using toys or drums. He may also have sat on the teacher's lap in there for a while now and then, when things were too much for him. Meanwhile the teacher has been studying him to learn what will be the best materials for him to use in working out his problem. His play in the office may at first only last a few minutes, but since he is offered these materials day after day at times when his feelings run high, his time span increases, and he uses them more and more vigorously. After being in the office, when he rejoins the other children he is less apt to act out feelings on them, since the private play materials have already received the brunt of the acting out. Even though tension may rise again, he emerges more relaxed. Gradually he can begin to accept the teacher's help in the midst of play where there are other children, rather than hitting, screaming, and falling apart. He will need special play less and less, because his trust in his teacher's understanding of what is in his mind has deepened during their times alone together in the office.

For a child who progresses in the above ways, no referral will be necessary, in all probability. The child has stabilized and is ready to learn what nursery school has to teach him. Usually contacts with the parents have helped, too. Almost always, when a teacher indicates by her manner at arrival or dismissal time that she would be interested in whatever the parents of such a child have to say and is ready to consult with them about him, they will make an appointment to talk more, since they too have probably been concerned. If, in the process of playing out feelings with toys in the office, there has been a good deal of tension and bursting through of limits, probably the parents will already have been told that the child seems to have some things on his mind that he is playing out at school, so they will understand if there should be a carry-over at home. Soon, however, most children learn to channel feelings that might lead to acting out on others into the office play, thus leaving both home and school undisturbed by spilling over. This learning is facilitated by the fact that the teacher continues to expect the child to maintain adequate controls in the playroom and playground, consistently setting the same limits for him there that she sets for everyone else. In the office, too, there are reasonable limits, though the child can do what he likes with the durable play-alone toys. With most children who are receiving this kind of help, reduced tension and increased controls are noticed fairly soon both at home and school. When a teacher feels she has gained some understanding of what a child's problems are, she passes this on to the parents, usually in the same informal way she shares other news regarding the child's development. "His play seems to suggest that he has the baby on his mind these days," she may say, and the parents may want to go further into this, either at once or later, in an arranged conference. Such exchanges can help both parents and teachers to understand and help the child better, and many times the result of these direct communications is that concerned parents will then give a child direct help and reassurance in his life outside the school.

II

What is the difference between this kind of help and the psychotherapy that is practiced by psychiatrists, psychologists, and social workers? The situation is different, first of all, in that a child is not brought to school by his parents for treatment but for education. When parents take the step of seeking professional help for emotional problems, they are indicating their readiness to look at these and to work on them. Parents who bring a child to enroll in a nursery school are not in that position; where there is a problem of that kind, they may not even be aware of it. The nursery school offers them what they do feel the need for: education that is appropriate to the age level of the child. And education is the teacher's orientation, too. She is responsible for keeping the environment a stable and secure one in which learning can take place, and to that end she must sometimes work with an individual child who is unable to make use of it or disrupts it. But her work with that child is educational, too. She sees the situation as indicating the child's need to learn more about himself or more about how to establish good relations.

Through her experiences in the education of the child as a whole, the teacher knows that emotions are always involved in learning; they are therefore part of her concerns as an educator. A child cannot learn either about himself or other people or the world, in many cases, unless the deadwood of old problems is cleared away or current emotional dilemmas that keep him bound are resolved. There would not be much education if one simply stopped children's behavior without trying to understand why they were behaving in that particular way. Until a teacher knows where a child is going—what he is after—she cannot show him a better way of dealing with his problem. If a child seemed to be wrenching futilely at a wagon caught in a crack, the teacher would help him examine the situation, instead of just telling him what to do; similarly, when emotions are creating problems for him, she helps him explore those feelings, either directly in words or through the use of toys. For reasons such as these, the teacher sees the help she gives children with emotional problems as no different, essentially, from that she gives the other children, who also receive her concentrated attention at times. She sees it as education, too.

There are other differences between the education-oriented work of the teacher with a child who has problems and the treatment-oriented work of the therapist in a separate office or clinic. One difference is the degree of disturbance in the child. When a child is chronically so upset that he needs almost constant attention from someone, referral is indicated. Other children, too, who make no demands but cannot form relationships, also require an especially deep tie with an adult such as therapy provides. A child can probably be helped at school, if his disturbance lies within the range of common developmental difficulties or is a temporary reaction to current trauma or turmoil in his life.

Another difference is the involvement of parents. When parents seek treatment for a child, that commitment also involves them in a relationship, either with the child's therapist or with someone else who works closely with him or her, that encourages work on their own problems as they consider the child's. If they are ready to use it, this relationship can be more intense and intimate than the more casual and less frequent contacts of parent counseling. In the school setting, parents may be only minimally involved. They know in a general way how their children are developing, any indications for concern (and signs of growth, too) are shared with them, and they are left free on the whole to make appointments for conferences only when they themselves feel the need or desire.

An important difference between work in a school and work in a therapist's office is that when he is at school a child may have help at the moment he feels the need and in the milieu in which he feels it. The child runs into difficulties with children or teachers, for example, and is helped on the spot. At other times, if the problem is caused by feelings related to fantasies, immediate help while the fantasies are most vivid leads to their expression in play. The same person who helps in one situation helps him in the other, so it is possible to meet the child on both levels. The teacher is also in a position to provide many other means of self-affirmation; these outlets are ready and waiting for the child, to be used as soon as his emotions no longer block him.

Sometimes, at school, there will be a fairly long period when a child with problems will not use the office for his special play at all. But that there is a difference between the play he does there and his play elsewhere, and that he understands the difference, is seen in his saying now and again, "I think I'd better go in the office," or "I need the play-alone toys." The difference is only partly in the toys, selected for their propensity for releasing feelings. It is primarily that his relationship with the teacher, while not qualitatively different, is intensified in the office situation; even though she comes and goes, when she is there she gives him her full attention and watches and listens with the utmost concentration, so as to understand and respond appropriately. As a child experiences the relief of sharing troublesome feelings, he learns what the office play is—that it is something more than play in a different room with a different set of toys. After a period of playing out problems is well behind him, a child may occasionally say, "I have something I need to talk about," and go straight into the office and sit down, bypassing all toys and play. This independent seeking of help when one needs it, stopping for periods, and ending a session to engage in other kinds of self-expressive activities at will would all be unlikely to occur in the therapy situation, because appointments must be kept.

A last difference between help with emotions given in the nursery school and that given elsewhere is that both teacher and child feel less urgency. The intimacy of psychotherapy is a powerful force to bring feelings out into the open, but the teacher and the child have other concerns at school related to his total development. She puts her attention on supplying materials and on his activities and interests, as well as on his feelings; there is plenty of time to work things out, and she can follow his lead. He can thus move ahead, stop, withdraw, then move again, all with less intensity.

III

Can any nursery school teacher give help to children with emotional problems that arise in the course of normal development? The answer to that probably depends more on the kind of teacher she is than on special training for such work. The same gifts that make a responsive teacher equip her to work in the area of emotional development. This aspect of her work only requires, at certain times, an individual approach that follows the same basic philosophy expressed in the rest of her teaching. When children use art and music materials, for example, she tries to create an atmosphere of acceptance and support so they can say anything they like in these media and she creates the same atmosphere in the more intimate setting of the office, where a child, with words or through small-scale dramatic play, finds ways to externalize what is inside him. The information she gives in the school is related to a child's own purposes; she might say, for example, "Here is a tool that will hold that wood while you work on it; it's called a vise." In just the same way, when a child is tempted to take out feelings about his baby sister by putting sand on children, she might say, "Here's a rubber baby; you can use it for those cross feelings." All through the day, the teacher needs to watch and listen without making judgments so that she can understand a child's interests and learning problems, and she uses the same kind of awareness when she is concerned with nuances of feelings and direct or symbolic expressions of them. In other words, techniques for working with feelings are not learned for special use only, like skills in storytelling or piano playing, because a teacher cannot behave one way in the playroom, then close the office door and behave differently. The kind of help she gives in the office must grow right out of her deeply felt attitudes that are expressed in everything she does with children.

A teacher who works in this way can help many children, but she will need to learn to let go, too—to admit failures sometimes and turn her attention to those children whom she can help. There will be times when a child's family circumstances, his physical or psychological difficulties, or other changed situations must largely negate her influence.

● Angela began to withdraw alarmingly after the death of her baby sister; sitting alone, she looked into space, making ritualistic gestures. It made no difference where she was, or with whom, and school had no meaning for her. Clare, too, could make no progress. She was only three years old, yet she was in her fourth foster home. She just ran about slapping, screaming, and throwing toys, finding peace only momentarily, crooning in her teacher's arms while being rocked. On her medical form, the word "Encephalitis" appeared. And Petra, whose home was a scene of violent quarrels, grew more pale and tense every day. She stood by the gate awaiting dismissal time and clutched her doll in its knit cap made by the teacher, her worried face like that of a little old woman. School was postponed for all these children, and they were referred to either child guidance clinics or psychotherapists in private practice.

There are other children, like Quincy. He was improving. After four months he was just beginning to accept other children's presence, no longer sitting by the record player all day with his back turned to them. But nothing could be done about the fact that the family was moving and that, at the age of four, he would have to start all over again in a new school.

Most disturbing of all a teacher's failures will be the children she never understood. Some will have been withdrawn before she had a chance to learn to really know them, but others, although she had them in her school for a year, or even, perhaps, for two years, will remain a mystery. The variety of human beings is never-ending, and we have only made a beginning in studying their complexities. If one adds to these facts the small child's limited ability to communicate with a teacher in words, so that she must learn to read his thoughts by observing his play, gestures, and facial expressions, such failures are not surprising. Often a teacher is unable to learn enough about the child to understand him because his parents either are unaware of home situations that are affecting him or are unwilling to discuss them. Some of the information about the child that would be essential to her understanding of him never reaches her, or reaches her too late.

But there will be another child whose parents work willingly with the teacher, and information from a psychologist who sees him is available to her. Yet she still cannot find the key to his inner self, and his behavior remains troublesome. And if she has no clue to why he behaves as he does, she can only deal with him by trial and error, give him all the love she can, and hope she will stumble onto the right way of working with him, or that he will, by himself, grow past the need she cannot meet. And she must comfort herself, when she sees the child leave the school with the same problems he brought to it, that each child like this leaves a little of himself behind in her memory that will help her recognize another like him who may appear in the future. Then the patient watching and listening, the efforts that failed, the discouragement and frustration, will not all have to be repeated; she can take up where she left off, and perhaps this time she will be ready to understand that kind of child. With each failure, more experience is gained. As the years of teaching accumulate, she will have more times when, remembering a certain small face, she can say to herself, a little wistfully but with a good feeling, too, "I'd know what to do about him, now."

Along with the other gains from experience, a teacher learns humility. She is not the sole reason for a child's improving or for his failure to do so. It is comforting to know that there are other sources of support in her work; everything does not rest on her shoulders alone. Besides the occasional help of a referral, as described earlier, sometimes there is good fortune; a child in deep trouble suddenly and spontaneously gets better. She may learn later that an extramarital situation, or other problem that the parents were unwilling to discuss, was resolved. Or she may never know what change occurred in the child's life outside school. She can take no credit for that kind of improvement, but nevertheless the load is off her mind. He or she is all right.

Perhaps the most important sources of help for a teacher, which she often forgets about but that can be relied upon to solve many problems, are the other children. Chip found David, Hal entered Babette's life, and suddenly there was Anthony for Zeb. Present so often in a nursery school group is a child quietly offering friendship and getting through to the troubled one when neither the teacher nor any other adult can. This strength, available to a teacher, and right at hand, is immeasurable.

IV

How does a nursery school teacher work with a child at those times when he is unable to manage himself in the playroom or on the playground? While there will be much use of dramatic-play materials in both those places, when a child is too upset to have the necessary regard for children or equipment or is too anxious or preoccupied with worries, a "play-alone place" is required. This can be any room with a door that can be closed, preferably adjoining the common space, and provided with specially selected, indestructible toys. They would represent the objects of many children's fears and hostilities, such as family members, a fireman, policeman, cowboy, soldier, doctor, nurse, teacher, ghost, or witch. Animals might be a tiger, bear, alligator, whale, snake, spider, dog, or wolf. Some benevolent figures would be there, too, such as a rabbit, a kitten, a clown, or a family of mice. Included would be rubber cars and rubber blocks for crashing, Ping-Pong balls for throwing, and some things to use for weapons. None of the figures would be actually frightening in appearance; a child's fears are displaced onto the toys, and it is not at all unusual for him to say, after a few play sessions, "See? He's not mean any more." Weapons, too, would be ones that could change their character as the child changed, such as a rubber pocket knife, hatchet, hammer, saw, screw driver, and small bat. Sometimes a search through several stores is needed to find the right toy for a child. Rolf had a fear of "ogres," but apparently his ogre was not human. Finally the teacher brought a rubber tiger that stood on its hind legs, and he smiled in recognition as he looked into its face. "That's him!" he said; then, after a vigorous fight, he threw it into a corner, saying, "There's going to be some peace and quiet around here, now." Shown the tiger later, his mother remarked that its face looked like that of a tiger peering through trees on a hanging on Rolf's bedroom.

Most children welcome an on-the-spot suggestion, such as "It would be better to fight a rubber alligator, instead of using John for one; let's go look." Play-alone toys are not out and available for general use; saved for special play only when indicated, they are new and inviting, as well as free from previous associations. Watching a child's play helps the teacher know what is needed, and when he is overloaded with feelings that want expression, he can scarcely let the chance go by. The teacher gives him her undivided attention to help him get started and then sees that he is not interrupted, looking in and commenting frequently on what he is doing. At first she might need to stay with him to keep the play going and to make him feel safe enough to play out scary or violent themes. He also might have some trouble staying within limits; if he lets himself pound on the baby doll or fireman, this releasing of his inhibitions may make him unable to resist opening the door of the room and throwing something out. The teacher will stop him from doing that, reassuring him in this way that he can afford to let go and that she will stand by to control him where needed.

Sometimes, when a teacher is new to this way of working, she wants to go too fast. She is inclined to push herself to understand everything that is behind the child's behavior. But to think about a child, while at the same time listening to him and observing him with concentrated attention, is not possible. What is required is an intensive empathy which impresses the child with the idea that he is not alone; the thinking can come later. As he reveals his feelings, the understanding and acceptance they receive motivates him to continue; then things will begin to fall into place for both child and teacher. She may find herself wanting to urge him on, feeling that not enough has been accomplished in an interview composed of three or four verbal exchanges and a little play. But time for growth must elapse. The chance to go farther will come again if there is more to work on, as long as the child has learned to use his relationship with the teacher to safely experience emotions too strong for comfort. The teacher will need to stop when the child is ready to stop, ponder all she knows and feels about him afterward, and be ready to move forward with him again at his own pace and wherever he leads if another chance comes.

Another temptation of the helping teacher may be to explain or interpret a child's feelings or behavior to him. She may want to say, "Look, here's what is bothering you," and spell it all out for him. But there are reasons why this is not wise or helpful. Some things a child only knows half-consciously. He is keeping part of the truth hidden from himself until he is ready to see it. Only so much can be handled at each stage of development. A child has to grow into insights, bit by bit, along with his day-to-day experiences. Such growth cannot be hurried without risk of confusing a child or giving him things to worry about that he may not be mature enough to deal with. Commonly, too, what seems like a simple problem really tenuously masks a deeper, more serious one, and to break through this fragile defense might increase the child's resistance to facing uncomfortable thoughts, frighten him into retreating to an earlier, easier level of development, or worse. Thus, when a child shows anger, the teacher stays with his own symbols. "That lion is feeling very mad at that puppy." By responding only to what a child actually says or does, without interpreting it, the teacher avoids putting pressure on him. This is a safeguard. A child will not approach a problem he is not yet ready to look at, or understand the meaning of what he is doing until he can accept it comfortably. If the teacher lets him go only at his own pace, he will not be threatened, upset, or harmed in any way by expressing his feelings in play, always provided the teacher sets necessary limits on his actions while continuing to accept his feelings.

Another reason to avoid explaining a child to himself is that one may be wrong. Perhaps a teacher has been prematurely diagnosing without enough listening and watching, and an important piece of evidence that would have changed her theory has been overlooked. Sometimes, too, there is a curious obliviousness to feelings that a child is expressing, because they remind the teacher of threatening bogies from her own past. When this happens, she may blank out momentarily without being aware she is doing so. Another way of blanking out is to judge a certain bit of behavior as unimportant or unrelated to the problem. But perhaps the most common reason for missing something is a teacher's concern about facts, which leads her to question and probe, rather than being comfortable with just knowing what a child feels, without knowing why he feels it, for the present.

Still another reason to avoid giving the child interpretations is that focusing a child's thoughts on a problem interferes with his working through the emotions involved. One cannot feel intensely and think logically at the same time. When a feeling has been thoroughly experienced, however, a child can leave it behind, and often the meaning of an old feeling comes later, after distance and perspective have been gained. But insight is not necessary, though it may be helpful; essentially, it is not the point. A change in behavior comes about from a change in feelings. And a change in feelings can happen from and through a relationship. Time cannot measure the meaning of a relationship, and thus a very few moments can have a powerful and lasting effect on a child. It is the emotional climate in which these stress-provoked interviews take place that really matters—the flow of love and trust both ways, the desire for communication no matter what comes out, and the recognition and acceptance of all the feelings that emerge. More important than a teacher's intellectual understanding and diagnostic ability is her steady confidence in the process and in a child's capacity for growth. Through this kind of relationship change comes about, much as a healthful climate brings about the growth of plants.

V

Some children with problems will be described next. Several of them were helped in the playroom or playground, sometimes with other children contributing to the working out of their difficulties. Some had individual help while using special toys in the office or waiting room.

In almost every group, at one time or another, there is a child who begins to run and run as though the devil were after him. The old way of looking at this behavior was to assume that the child needed more physical activity. But it is not so simple. Small children, like cats, frequently stretch, turn, roll, sit, crawl, bend, and twist, moving in a relaxed fashion almost continuously. When they run, it is lightly and freely. It is the tense ones who must race about, sometimes with high-pitched shouting and screaming. The answer is not to be found in increased activity for such a runner. One needs to discover what the devil is that chases this child about.

- Dominic, one day, showed an extreme degree of tension, flying around the room, unable to settle down to anything. He was usually a cheerful little boy, engaged in creative, rewarding experiences—lively, but not like this. His teacher felt that something had happened. She took him on her lap when he came near on one of his flights, and said, "Something is making you feel jumpy and scared, today? Maybe so scary you don't even want to think about it? I think maybe if you can let that thought come, and tell me about it, you won't have to run so hard." This very intelligent little four-year-old lay quietly in her arms for a few moments. Then he got down, took a paper and pencil, and began to draw on a nearby table. The drawing was of a huge eye, but before it was finished, he frantically crumpled the paper. "That was pretty scary," the teacher told him. "But you let some of it come on the paper, and then made it all gone again." For quite a while he went on drawing eyes, scratching and stabbing at them with a pencil, then running to the teacher, throwing himself on her lap and burying his face in her shoulder, then trying again. Finally the eye was completely drawn, and that time Dominic didn't destroy it, but brought it to the teacher. "You take care of it," he said, "And now you make me an eye patch." Not knowing what this meant yet, the teacher did as he asked, making a patch from black paper, and he wore it until dismissal time.

  Some days later Dominic said casually, "My father's eye is better, now." "What happened to it?" the teacher asked him, matching his casual tone with difficulty. "My sister jabbed her fingernail in it by mistake," he said. "Me and her thought he'd be blind. He had to wear an eye patch." "Well," said the teacher, "Children do get mad at their dads, and might *feel* like doing something like that, sometimes." "Yes," he nodded. "I hate him. And I love him very much. I *always* want him if I get hurt, instead of my mom." "You hate him, and you love him, and you need him—all of those things," the teacher said. "Yes, that's right," said Dominic. "But most of the time I love him." And he ran off to play.

- Sometimes a teacher's support of a child's efforts to play out something can lead to the uncovering of a very old trauma, rather than a current one. Things came to a crisis with tiny, very active Mickey one busy day when the teacher's duties had piled up to almost comic proportions. Rain was pelting down, and almost all of the children were inside. They had many toys out, and the floor and tables were littered. Someone had dropped a box of raisins, and they were sticking to everyone's shoes. Two of the children needed a change of underpants. And Mickey was becoming more and more frantic in his behavior. Always a toy-thrower, on this day he threw everything about again as soon as one area had been picked up. Finally he began sweeping everything off the tables to the floor, and beads from a dumped box rolled everywhere, a hazard underfoot. The teacher suggested he go out in the covered patio where there were fewer children, but he reacted to that idea by becoming even wilder. There appeared to be only one solution. The teacher picked him up and carried him on one hip as she moved about the room. Soon he seemed to be lying back and looking at the ceiling. A strange look came over his face; he gazed vacantly, like a baby. After things returned to normal in the playroom, the teacher carried him into the office and gave him a basket of Ping-Pong balls. She wanted him to have a chance to continue his throwing.

The balls rattled over the floor, walls, and ceiling. While they bounced about, Mickey rapidly switched the light on and off, hopping in excitement. In a few minutes he peered through the door and asked for some paper, and was handed some sheets from the easel. He tore and crumpled these, then threw them around the room, too. At last he lay down on the floor, drew up his knees, and pulled the papers over himself, head and all. *"Baby, baby,"* he said, whimpering. "You're a baby?" *"Yah, yah, baby, baby."* "What's happening?" *"Water all over—lights—big noise—"* The teacher responded, "The baby is very scared of the water, and the lights off and on, and the loud noise. And he's all covered up with the papers." Mickey stood up then and leaned against the teacher. "Yes," he said. "The *baby* is *very* scared. But *Mickey* isn't." *"You're* not," she said. "You made all those things happen just now, and you made them stop, too." "Yes," he said, "I make them when I want to. Now I don't want to." "You're all done, now?" Then he gathered all the balls together and handed the basket to the teacher, telling her, "Put it away, but keep it." Children often ask the teacher to keep such materials safe; it is as though they are saying, "I'm entrusting my memory to you."

When this day was described to Mickey's mother, she remembered that once, when he was a baby, she had left him asleep in his stroller outside the supermarket where she was shopping, and a quick storm had come up, with lightning and thunder. Running out, she had found him covered with blowing newspaper sheets, soaking wet, and screaming with terror. It had taken a long time to quiet him. Probably this trauma had been behind his long-standing habit of throwing things about. The stormy day had brought the memory closer to awareness. Then, while the teacher was carrying him around, lying back in the same position as when he had been sleeping in the stroller had helped to recreate the original situation, and the sound of the rattling Ping-Pong balls on walls and ceiling and the flashing light had started the playing out of the trauma. This was a turning point for Mickey. His throwing now became purposeful rather than involuntary, and for a while he often went into the office to make "rain," finally bringing in the big drum to make "thunder." Then he was finished.

A single traumatic incident can be played out by a child fairly easily once the memory becomes accessible. Those that make more trouble are traumas that are superimposed on others. When this is the case, there may be a precipitating incident that causes what appears to be a serious upset, but when the teacher has helped the child work this out, she often finds that more lies behind it, and further exploration is needed.

● Simon arrived at school pale and weeping one day. He was reluctant to have his mother leave him, although he had for some time been making a good adjustment to school. Something that had happened on the previous day had shaken him. While riding on the back of his father's motorcycle, he had been tipped off when it turned a corner too sharply and skidded. Although he hadn't been hurt much, he was badly frightened. But, as always, this wasn't enough to explain his anxious face. In a traumatic incident, one needs also to look for wounds to the child's closest relationships. Simon knew his father had been responsible for the accident, however unintentionally it was caused; did he feel betrayed, or perhaps punished for hostile feelings he might have been having toward his dad? As he stood in the doorway with his mother, the teacher said, "You really don't want mother to leave you." "I don't want to come to school without Jeffrey," he said. This was a surprise; Jeffrey, who had recently dropped out of school, had been Simon's ride partner for a short time previously, but before that Simon had come happily without him. "You feel you need Jeffrey?" But he couldn't go on, and collapsed into sobbing. "I want to go *home*." "I see; it's something about home. What about home, Simon?" "Dad's there." Now there was a loaded association, one that pointed to family relationships.

There was a toy cash register on the table near where Simon was standing with his mother. When a child's mind is full of something, any toy or object handy may be pressed into service by him. Simon picked up the three colored discs used for money. "These are the children," he said. "Where is the father?" The teacher cut out a larger colored circle from cardboard and handed it to him. Ignoring the father, he put the smaller discs into a toy car lying on the floor and showed the teacher how the children could "drive it all by themselves." Suddenly, then, he picked up a nearby airplane and ran the entire length of the room as fast as he could, holding it high. "I can go fast!" he said. This he did several times, as though coming to terms with speed and danger by being in control himself. "You can go, now," he said to his mother. "But you stay in your chair," he told the teacher, "till I get finished." Each time, after an airplane flight, he returned to the chair. The helping teacher is the safety spot, and a child can only work out such scary things in relation to her, not by himself.

In a situation like this, special attention needs to be given to the first remarks of a child. Without trying to make sense of them at that point, the teacher salted away Simon's for future reference: "school," "Jeffrey," "home," and "Dad." They might be needed, because, even though he had probably worked out the accident through his assertion of independence and power in his play of the children's driving the car and of himself flying a fast airplane, the teacher suspected that there was another problem behind that one, probably concerned with those four words. Simon, in his associations, had been saying as clearly as possible, "When I think of *school* and *Jeffrey*, I think of *home* and *Dad*." Somehow his basic security feelings had been shaken. He would have felt fear appropriately after such an accident, but it would have been fear of a similar situation—the next ride on a motorcycle, fast car, or plane, perhaps—but not of coming back to a familiar school that he liked. What he now felt was anxiety. When anxiety threatens to overwhelm a child and he is receiving responsive listening from a trusted adult who he believes can help, he is deeply stirred, and all the material he brings up is meaningful. For this reason the teacher considered all that Simon said to be important, whether or not it made sense.

On that first day, Simon had become relaxed enough to work out the accident. Ordinarily, the most recent trauma—the covering one—is handled by a child first. Simon had taken no steps yet toward resolving, or even recognizing, the more basic concern that lay underneath. But he was no longer so anxious as to be immobilized, because on that day he had found someone who stayed close to his feelings, giving him her absorbed attention and showing a calm confidence that Simon would be able to stay at school and cope with whatever was bothering him. The exchange of words and play were brief, but because of them he had become more and more cheerful, finally running clear across the room in his usual free, light way. However—and this was important—he had told the teacher, "Stay in your chair," running back and forth to her several times before he was ready to be on his own. Through his relationship with her, he was able to surmount the trauma of the motorcycle accident and leave his deeper problem in her hands for the time being. The rest of the day was as usual.

The next morning Simon again crept in, hanging on to his mother's skirt with both hands. He was wide-eyed. *School—Jeffrey—home—Dad* swept through him in chain reaction. But he knew what to do. The toys that had helped before were ready on the floor near the door. When he saw them there, he told his mother, "You can go now." The first thing he did was to ask for a "mother," and the teacher cut out another large circle in a different color. "Oh, yes," he said, when he saw it. All the family were put into the drawer of the cash register together. "He stays *home*," he said, firmly pressing the father in. "He doesn't go anywhere, just to work; that's *all*." "He stays right there," the teacher reflected, not knowing where this was leading. Simon sat back on his heels on the floor. "Jeffrey's daddy doesn't live in his house any more," he said. "He's gone away. And Jeffrey can't come to school any more; his mom doesn't have enough money."

There was little left to be done. Simon had separated the two fathers; Jeffrey's had left their home, and there was no money for Jeffrey to come to school, but Simon's father was not going anyplace but to work; he would keep on making money and Simon would keep on coming to school. And he reminded himself that, in any case, a family also includes a mother. Simon had other feelings, of course, that lay even deeper. Among them was probably anger at his father, his rival for his mother as well as the cause of the accident, and perhaps some fear of his possible retaliation (or desertion, like Jeffrey's father) because of that anger. But those feelings were the same ones other four-year-old boys have, and he would gradually leave them behind as he grew older. It had been the coinciding of the two experiences—the accident and the news about Jeffrey—that had thrown him.

● The teacher tried for weeks to make Ann feel safe enough to play out her anger toward her mother, who had been through a period of rejective feelings toward Ann because of problems of her own. The teacher had to do this by letting Ann discover that although she would always stop her chasing and pretending to shoot the other children, she would nevertheless always accept her angry feelings. At first Ann responded to any limits set by the teacher by abruptly falling down "dead." Finally, however, she felt secure enough to go on further. She was helped at this point by Ernie, another child in the group with strong aggressive fantasies and shaky controls. For days they chased and were chased by the ghost that was on Ann's mind, which might have been a symbol for the mysterious element she sensed in her mother's attitude toward her. They both were quite frightened, but the teacher stayed right with them. She helped them work on their sand "walls" to keep the ghost under the big bush. But they wanted more experiences of being scared and yet being safe, so they said the ghost had jumped over their walls. Finally, after much shooting, running, hiding, and screaming, Ann said the ghost had been killed and had turned into a witch—her first overt recognition of the mysterious ghost as female. She then began to call Ernie "Daddy," running to him for protection from the witch, and Ernie responded beautifully to these appeals in the play. (Meanwhile he had had his own ideas of who the enemy was, as shown by his calling the ghost "the father," but neither child was in the least bothered by the confusion in the ghost's identity, since the feeling they had in common about it was so much more important to them.)

Finally one day, after a vigorous all-out session, Ernie said, "We're resting now; the fight's all over," and they lay close together in the sand for some time, at peace, with less tension and restlessness than had ever been seen before in these angry children. The result of the long series of play dramas then began to be seen as the two ceased their constant spilling over of hostile words and gestures toward the other children. When angry feelings arose later, from time to time, both Ernie and Ann knew what to do about them, and they required less and less supervision by the teacher when they played them out. In a sense, they had been trained what to do with uncomfortable fantasies; now, when one of them showed hostility toward another child, the teacher could say, "Is this really about Bobby? If it is, you can tell him." And if it was not, and Bobby was just a handy victim for the expression of some hostile feelings, this could be recognized by Ernie or Ann, who would then talk or play out what was on his or her mind. Thus this help, given when needed, was of benefit to the entire group. Just to have stopped the shooting at the other children would not have been enough. Hostility would have continued, finding other forms, and the resentment this aroused would have added to the problems of the pair.

● Tall, thin Zeb was a four-year-old redhead with a drooping posture and a way of not looking anyone in the eye. His behavior was hard to live with from the start. He taunted and teased the other children in most ingenious ways, then would run away grinning. To a teacher's efforts to find out what had made him feel like tormenting a certain child, he turned a completely deaf ear and ran away from her, too, darting round and round the big bush or climbing to the top of the jungle gym, laughing and saying, "Ha, ha, you can't catch me!" When brought face to face with a child who had a grievance to express, he would squirm, look away, and make meaningless noises so no words could reach him, grinning again. He was not selective about whom he teased; it was anyone who passed near or was in reach, anyone who caught his attention. Whatever children were doing he sabotaged, looking as though he got great satisfaction from it. He teased teachers, too, by scattering and throwing toys around, for example. He was quick to anger and often struck out at another child. And he was slow to forgive, pushing or tackling someone long after an incident in which he had felt abused or rejected.

Behavior like this in the early phases of an adjustment to school is sometimes for the purpose of testing the limits and making sure one has enough attention. It usually passes when a child feels convinced that he is liked and accepted. But Zeb's behavior seemed firmly entrenched. While informal contacts at the gate with Zeb's mother gave the teacher a chance to gain her confidence so that more could be learned about his home life, it was necessary to do something about Zeb himself. He was becoming "that bad boy" to the other children. This could only upset him further and make his behavior worse.

Firm outer controls were established first. When Zeb went out of bounds either with children or materials, then ran to hide or climbed the jungle gym to escape her, the teacher waited until he rejoined the group, then either led or carried him to another area, away from the trouble spot. If he immediately caused trouble there, too, or tried to run out again, she held him on her lap awhile, assuring him that as soon as he could manage by himself he could of course go back to play. At first he said at once that he could manage, and it was tried; but if there was more trouble, no second trial was made until he was relaxed and quiet, the explanation being "We did try that, remember? But you weren't quite ready." (It is almost impossible for a child to feign relaxation.) Sometimes, when he protested against being held, she offered, instead, to hold his hand, and they went about the school together hand in hand. His hand told clearly of his progress toward relaxation. First he held it continuously rigid and tried to squirm it out of hers, saying, "You're hurting my hand." She replied, "I'll hold it as carefully as I can. But I understand you feel cross about it." Meanwhile she kept trying to make his hand comfortable in hers, and he could tell this; he had known all along about the lack of tension in her through their body contact when she held him. Eventually a word or two—"Do you think you need to go in?" or "Do you need my help, or can you stop yourself?"—was enough to control Zeb without holding him or taking his hand. The teacher continued to make efforts toward a breakthrough in communication, sitting by him often, talking to him about things that interested her (unrelated to his behavior) that she thought might interest him, too, and listening to anything he wanted to tell her. But the impulse to torment children was still there.

One day, after many struggles with his impulses during which he continually complained that others were "mean" to him, the teacher reflected his feelings by saying, "You just feel as though *nobody* likes you." He looked directly at her then and said, "That's right. Everybody hates me. I've got no friends." However, often just when one makes such a statement, the feeling is about to change because it has been fully experienced. A few days later, after a long series of efforts to torment every child then in the playroom, followed by his complaints that they were all "mean kids," the teacher said to him, "I guess you just don't like *anybody*. Is that right?" After a moment he replied, "Yes, I do like somebody, but I won't tell you who." "You want to keep it a secret," she said. Then, to her amazement, he dropped his head and said shyly, "It's you." (Thus do teachers, in thinking about the progress of a child in socialization, sometimes leave themselves out of the reckoning.)

After this, it seemed time for some new learning for Zeb, built on the tie with the teacher that she hadn't known he felt. Since Zeb was no longer alone, he could begin to tolerate some rejection from the other children and accept help and support from her toward understanding the part he was playing to bring these rejections on himself. So the teacher began to let him experience some of the immediate results of his teasing. For example, when he insisted, against their protests, on climbing through the "window" of the playhouse that three boys were using and then laughingly made chalk marks on their clothes, she let things take their course, though staying near so Zeb should not become frightened. The boys pushed and pulled him out; then, when he went off with their "front door," they took it back again by force of greater numbers. Afterward she said to him that it looked as though he found it exciting to make people angry. He agreed, grinning and shivering, saying, "It's *ooh!*" Then she said that since he had also told her nobody liked him, that must be a problem for him; he liked to make them angry, and yet he was upset that they didn't like him. It was exciting to make them mad, and yet he wanted them to be friendly; it was a hard choice, she said, and he agreed. Thereafter, whenever Zeb bothered someone and the child reacted negatively, the teacher pointed out that he must have wanted it that way—to have the child angry at him had been his choice that time. She showed her sympathy for his dilemma, which was a real one, and now, after each painful experience, Zeb was able to use their relationship for comfort and for increased understanding.

At length something happened that could only occur in a social setting and testifies to the value of nursery school for children like Zeb. One boy, Anthony, began to be attracted to Zeb, at first, perhaps, by his dramatic antisocial behavior. "Take his bear, Zeb," he would say, enjoying the resulting confusion while safely out of it himself. But soon they began to really play together, and real play was something Zeb had not yet been able to enjoy at school. They followed each other about, indoors and out. Zeb would sometimes grab one of Anthony's toys, but when Anthony said, "Then I won't play with you," he would hastily say, "*O.K.! O.K.!*" He tried hard to be interesting and charming. "Oh, look! Come on! I see something *good* to play with!" "That's just *beautiful*, Anthony!" The teasing impulse had not quite left him, however. One day he snatched Anthony's favorite toy duck away from him and waved it in his face, holding it just out of reach and calling in his old taunting fashion, "Here, Ducky, Ducky!" Anthony began to chase him about the room and finally cornered him. When Zeb started kicking at him, Anthony nevertheless persisted in trying to get his duck, but when Zeb panicked and tried to bite him, Anthony turned on his heel and went outdoors. Zeb looked desolated, and the teacher put her arm around him. While he leaned against her, she said, "You chose making him angry, and now you haven't got him to play with you, and I guess maybe you wish you hadn't chosen that. You're feeling *very* sad and lonesome." But the next day Anthony was friendly again, and that was their last serious quarrel.

Once a child has a friend, his feelings about himself change. Others looked at Zeb differently too, now. Anthony liked him; he must be likable. Children began to be drawn by their interesting play, and watching his friendly ways with Anthony made them feel Zeb could be friendly toward them, too. Slowly the teasing dropped out, then stopped; Zeb seemed at last to have made his decision. As he accepted the responsibility for his own choices, less and less outer control was needed, and more and more inner control was achieved.

Zeb showed the kind of problem that is very difficult to solve. It is resistant to the usual approaches of a teacher, and it takes a very long time and much patience and persistence to achieve change. Like Zeb, his mother was distrustful. She never opened up to the teacher, so this was a job for the teacher alone, working in the dark. It was nearly a year before Zeb was really one of the group, even with his steady improvement. A child like this needs a more active approach from one teacher who will undertake most of his care. He will cut adults off, and, if one settles for that, one can never break through. The teacher had to batter at Zeb's gates out of her own wish for communication. She had to notice and talk to him whether he seemed to pay attention or not, and she had to be open with him about her needs in setting limits, her wish to understand him, and so on. All of this differs somewhat from a teacher's role with most young children, who need less, not more, adult intrusion; with them she is ready to give any help required, but respects their desire to explore and learn on their own without adult pressures or interruptions. As for Zeb, he too wished for communication, but he was afraid of it. He had lost hope that he would be met with acceptance. So he settled for negative attention and put all his energies into eliciting that. Otherwise, he avoided adults and closed them off from his inner life. The teacher had to seek him out actively, and by this means say, "Here I am. I care." Only in that way could she become somebody to him—the "somebody" he finally liked.

Sometimes the aggressive or fearful play themes of a child persist, day after day, leaving him with little energy or time for any other experiences in school, yet bringing no relief. Like the Red Queen in *Alice in Wonderland,* the child seems to be running as hard as he can to stay in the same place.

- Val's play faithfully reflected the television viewing that took up most of his time at home. He was admirably indefatigable in his efforts to play out the many ideas he was receiving, in order to bring them into some form he could digest. News programs suggested natural disasters, wrecks, wars, and riots. Documentaries suggested man's inhumanity to the world's starving populations and to animals becoming extinct. One program about primitive tribes was relived repeatedly with the help of his friends. Using the school's big teddy bear, he would lead his followers in a complex ritual involving dress-up materials and tom-toms; at the high moment, they leapt on the bear with their improvised spears, while Val shouted, "Kill it! Skin it! Eat it!"

The pressure under which Val labored also put pressure on the group. Always he shouted, he yelled, he roared. He talked continuously and was hoarse at the end of the day. One could see the cords in his neck stand out as he spoke, even to someone right by him. And he was constantly in action. Even more important, he always had a compelling need to control his group of friends so his play could continue as it must to relieve him. By persuasion, intriguing ideas, and rich imaginative detail, he kept them all with him, but he did make everyone do things his way and never stopped to listen to anyone else's ideas. Fortunately Val's parents accepted the teacher's suggestion that Val's television watching be monitored and gradually he calmed down. With less compulsion to play out vivid scenes he saw on television, he became able to let others contribute dramatic-play themes. Especially noticeable was the change in his voice and constant activity; he could finally have some quiet moments.

People who have led hard lives or who are fearful of the future hope for a kind of invulnerability for their children. Val's parents thought that a paced exposure to the dark side of life was over-protection, and that if their children were aware of violence, cruelty, pain, and fear in the real world from the beginning they would toughen up and not be hurt later by the prevalence of such problems. But even if it worked like that, one wouldn't want children to grow into adults who were indifferent to the pain of others through having become insensitized. As with men in battle, a child might react less and less to stimuli along those lines, requiring ever stronger ones to elicit the deadened response of empathy. But many a child would stop reacting outwardly long before that; he would acquire the ability to hide his feelings, not only from others but from himself as well. Inside, people are not so tough after all. But because the tender, caring part of him has caused him grief, he must prove over and over again that things don't bother him. And when, as an adult, he feels tender toward his own child, he hastily converts such "softness" into roughhousing, so the message doesn't come through. Thus, though wanting tenderness himself, he receives none; he is as effectively insulated against love as against hate. Real strength in adulthood comes from feelings of trust and self-confidence acquired in childhood, and no one becomes fearless and secure through being made to feel fearful and insecure then.

VI

Children can share many problems with a teacher, and she becomes sensitive to moods and feelings expressed in many ways. Her knowledge of child development helps, and since a number of her children stay in the nursery school for two years, she is able to put a child's problems into the context of the long span of growth and change in him she has seen. She knows where he is right now, where he has been, and the stages that lie ahead of him. And she knows something of his outside life; she sees his parents and may know his siblings. Perhaps she is aware that his experiences include too barren or too stimulating a neighborhood, too busy a schedule, too much television, too much baby-sitting, family disruptions, illness, problems with siblings, or a serious fright. His parents contribute by sharing important influences at home and by letting her know of any changes or disturbing incidents in his life. And the teacher learns much from her own relationship with the child. Thus, armed by understanding gained in all these ways, she tries to meet each child where he is and help him leave problems behind so he can move ahead in self-affirmation.

12 Meetings

Wes is my friend.
I would play with you, Jeff,
And I would say, "Go away, Wes,"
But then I might get thirsty for Wes.
So I want two friends—
You by my rib here,
And Wes by my rib on the other side.
                                        —Dean

I

Relationships and self-affirmation both reach a high point when people are able to talk together about problems and reach decisions that are acceptable to each person concerned. When this happens in the nursery school, a teacher sees it as a kind of culmination of her work, and, beyond that, as a hopeful augury for the future. Nothing could conceivably be better for mankind than our becoming more and more able to meet in this way.

The meetings described in this chapter were all small, involving from two to five members, and thereby permitting full and free participation of everyone on an equal basis. Examples include children's meetings, staff meetings, and conferences with parents.

● A meeting of three children, with the teacher as helper, took place following a lot of bickering in the sand area one day. "I can't understand what the problem is," the teacher told them. "How about a meeting to figure it out?" And they all trooped into the waiting room. In short order, their complaints came out. "Bobby's putting sand in our hole," Daniel said. Andy agreed, adding, "And he's scraping sand on our mountain." "Andy's putting his truck too near our hole," Bobby complained, and Daniel agreed that the truck used there was a problem for him, too. Last of all, Bobby brought out, in a burst, "They won't let me play there; that's the trouble." The teacher wrote down and reviewed each person's grievance, and they all agreed to the necessary adjustments: no sand in the hole, no scraping on the mountain, no truck near the hole, and Bobby could play there, too.

● A meeting of four children took place on another day. Benny, seconded by Bix, was fighting with Chuck, pushing him out of the playhouse and hitting him. Dennis ran over and joined in to protect Chuck, and a free-for-all developed. "What's up?" said the teacher. "Do you need a meeting?" They all came inside, enthusiastic about the idea, and brought four chairs into the waiting room. Then they looked at each other. "Who wants to talk first?" the teacher asked. Several shouted, "Me! Me!" and they giggled and continued to shout, "Me!" The teacher waited a moment, and then said, "It sounds like you're all having fun shouting together. Is the problem over?" Benny then said, "No, I have something to say. Bix and me were using the playhouse, and I went out to get something, and Chuck came right in, and he wouldn't get out when I ran back and told him, 'We're playing there.'" Chuck said, "Well, you went away and left it, so I came in." Benny protested, "But *Bix* didn't go away. Didn't you see him by the counter?" "No," Chuck answered. "I was on the floor when you came in, back of the counter," Bix told him. There was a silence. "Does anyone have something else to say?" the teacher asked. "No? What shall we do now?" "Chuck should stay out," said Bix. "Chuck and me will go to the digging place. O.K. Chuck?" Dennis said. "O.K.," Chuck agreed. "All done?" asked the teacher, and they agreed they were finished. The teacher was not much needed in this meeting, and as the year went on, occasionally this group of four-year-olds would come dashing inside on their own, saying importantly, "We have to have a meeting," closing the door to the waiting room and settling something entirely by themselves. Only the sound of their voices would be heard behind the door, and then they would burst forth, returning to play as a group.

● Meetings are often held on the spot. There were five involved in a meeting at the clay table one day. Edward, red-faced, slapped at Joe and started crying. The teacher said, "There's a problem here?" "Joe takes our clay," Edward said. "Yes," agreed Barnaby, "He pulls off pieces, like this," and he demonstrated. "Is there something you want to say, Joe?" the teacher asked. Joe shook his head. "What can we do about this?" the teacher asked. Edward said, "He can be our *friend*." "I can?" came from Joe. "And not be so mean," put in Dorothy. "Is that plan O.K. with you, Joe?" the teacher asked him. "Yes, but I need candles for my cake." "I'll give you some—here," said Tammy.

II

Teachers' meetings, of the intimate kind that seem to help most, can be very useful in gaining understanding of both themselves and the children. In these meetings, the same goals as those for the children are emphasized: building relationships with each other and with the children, and self-affirmation through sensitive, creative, and confident teaching.

● Three-year-old Frederic was the subject of a meeting requested by the teacher who was responsible for the inside areas. "Frederic is on my mind," she began. "He seems so frail and sensitive. He has that very fair skin and those long, slender fingers I associate with people like that. And right now he likes the trains so much that he just sits and cries heartbrokenly when they are all in use." The outdoor teacher nodded: "He's that way with me, too. He gets upset when he has to wait to ride in a box train. But he gets so charmingly delighted when he does have a train; he'll clap his hands and exchange all kinds of humorous remarks and twinkles of the eye. He's so small; maybe having a train makes him feel bigger." "Yes," said the inside teacher, "But I think more is involved. It seems to me he's getting worse instead of better. He cries and cries; he just can't stand it when the trains are busy, and nothing seems to help." "I know," the outside teacher agreed. "I saved the sand train for him this morning, and at least he got off to a good start, until he left it and somebody else got it." "Did you find something to use for a smokestack so you could make a box train for him?" asked the director. "I could bring something; a big can might do." "That would be good," said the outside teacher. "And it also helps to give him the engineer's hat while he's waiting; could we keep that outside?"

There was a short pause, and the teachers looked at one another. "Why should Frederic get over his fussiness about trains?" asked the inside teacher. "He's got it made." Ideas came thick and fast. "We keep saying, 'He can't stand it.' That's downgrading him." "You're right." "It's easy to get more and more protective of a child who's in tears so much." "Especially one who's so tiny and appealing." "So, pretty soon the child's problem gets so useful to him he can't give it up." "A train is a symbol of power, and he probably wants power over us." "Well, he's got it!" "He's decided he needs a train all the time. But *we* don't think he does. So why do we act as if we thought that?" "Yes—we're supporting his notion by taking too active a part." The outside teacher then summed up this rapid exchange by saying, "Hmm—we've been sucked in. It's time we got uninvolved."

As a result of this meeting, the teachers began to help Frederic as they would any other child with a special interest. He soon began to show anger at being frustrated, instead of collapsing into baby tears and sobs. They accepted his anger and helped him talk about it, but assumed he could wait for a turn with a train. Slowly he began to drop his tendency to try to control by emotion. To tide him over, he was given a small "locker train," and he would start a furious tantrum, then solve his own problems by going to get it. ("I wonder why I ever thought Frederic was fragile," said the inside teacher.) But before long, Frederic had adjusted himself.

Teaching is not easy, and perhaps a teacher may find she is often irritated. A meeting may help her learn why she has been feeling that way. She may discover that she is too tired, too hurried, or under too much pressure elsewhere in her life. Her time may need to be organized better. If she is ambitious and energetic, she may be overextending herself and then be unable to easily handle what she has undertaken. Details of her job may build up so she becomes overly tense or too tied down by them. Some thought might also eliminate unnecessary demands on her patience— things out of place or out of reach when she needs them might be one example. It is well worth the time spent to go through the day carefully, thinking of ways to ease the pressures caused by things, rather than people.

A teacher may feel irritated, or even angry, at children, too; perhaps this might happen to her when they start to get out of control. Sometimes a teacher finds this situation very frustrating because she feels inadequate to deal with it; her anger may be a reaction to her own frustration, rather than to the behavior of the children. Another teacher might even feel quite threatened when children get out of hand. She might fear being dominated by them, and find that upsetting. But if a teacher reacts with anger, children are aware of her feelings, and the steps that she takes to reestablish necessary control may succeed only because of the fear engendered. When children change their behavior because they are coerced, rather than because they are convinced, there has been no teaching. In dilemmas like these, a teacher needs to analyze the problem situation and make a plan for next time that better expresses her educational aims. If she is clear about what she wants to do and believes the steps she wants to take are the right ones, she will be prepared to respond appropriately and act less from emotion than from conviction. Then she will be able to assert control without the anger which does not belong in the situation, but, instead, arises from her need to defend her threatened control. The preschool child is not mature or independent enough to receive a teacher's discharge of anger without becoming disturbed; if such feelings need expression, she is wiser to talk them out in a meeting, or with an understanding adult friend.

Anger may also be felt by a teacher who has a troubled relationship with a certain child. Again, talking about the problem with someone who can listen acceptingly is often helpful. Of whom does this child remind her? What particular things about him are annoying? What does he do that arouses the feeling of anger? And finally, how much is his problem and how much is hers? When she regains her balance, she can keep her focus on the child's feelings without complicating them by her own. In this way, if he himself has anger to express, he does not experience, in addition, guilt over hurting her feelings, fear of her retaliation, frightening feelings of having too much power over an adult's emotions, or a sense of being unlovable and unacceptable. Then the teacher can respond in an easy, relaxed way, "I know you're angry, and you can tell me about it—it's all right." She can say something like that effectively only when it really is all right with her.

A teacher who has an unsatisfactory relationship with a child can also try to get to know him better. Once a teacher has a clear picture of a child, she can work toward understanding what has made him that way. Sometimes a home visit will help. Often she can find her way into his mind by making a continuous journal record of everything he does during a day at school. It is impossible to focus completely on a child, while making the record, without feeling empathy. One sees his face and body express his emotions in the various episodes in which he meets frustration, is bewildered, intrigued, alarmed, pleased, or angered. It helps, too, if the teacher has a chance to touch or hold the child occasionally. If she has been finding him very challenging and disruptive, his power to create difficulties for her may rob her temporarily of perspective. But when she takes him on her lap, she experiences him as the small child he really is, wanting love and care, and she thinks of him more realistically as a person, rather than a problem. And somehow, even though her mind has not figured him out, her body seems to understand him.

● In a staff meeting she had requested, a teacher got in touch with her own feelings, and these then helped her to better understand Adrienne, a child whose mother was going through a depressed period and stayed secluded in her room a good deal of the day. Adrienne had revealed an intuitive understanding of her mother's plight by talking of a witch who was lost in a dark wood. The teacher had been holding Adrienne often, and giving her special attention.

"I'm having a hard time giving Adrienne what she needs," she confessed. "I've been feeling irritated by her, and sometimes lately I really get angry with her. I can't get anything else done, because she follows me around all the time and she interferes if I pay attention to anyone else. Yet I know she needs extra affection just now because of her home situation, and I feel I ought to try to fill the gap. I know she's so clinging because she needs me, and yet I want to push her away. And that makes me feel terribly guilty. And then I guess I resent her for making me feel that way. Sometimes I really almost dislike her, poor little thing."

As she went on examining her feelings, the teacher began to see Adrienne in another light. "She clutches my hand so tight it hurts. And she plops down on my lap and gleefully holds me down that way. I feel controlled. I feel she won't let me do what I want to do. It's *hostility* I feel coming from her." The other teacher said she felt that could well be what Adrienne was expressing; she must be very angry at her mother, the "witch," for withdrawing from her, and probably displaced this feeling onto other women around her. The director contributed the thought that Adrienne was probably angry with her mother anyway because the mother had Adrienne's father's attention in a way that she herself did not have, and perhaps that attention was intensified now because of her mother's depression. Like the witch in *The Wizard of Oz*, which she had seen on television, Adrienne herself probably wanted to "kill" at times these days.

Supported by these comments in the insight which her own feelings had given her, the teacher then said she realized now that Adrienne needed help with expressing her hostile feelings. "First of all," she said, "I have to see that she doesn't express them on me, and then she'll be ready for me to help her find other ways."

In the next meeting, the teacher described what she had been doing, and the others offered ideas and prepared to work along similar lines in their own contacts with Adrienne. "Now I listen to my own feelings more," the teacher told them. "I say things like, 'I don't want you to hold my hand now; I need to use it.' Or I say, 'I want to help Susan now,' or 'I'll hold you on my lap a little later; right now I'd rather move around.' And I give her a hug and just go ahead. But the most important point is that I like Adrienne again, now that I'm not letting her do things that irritate me. And it's a good thing I do, because that hostility is really coming out, now, and I can accept it. She'll say things like, "I'll *squeeze your hand*, you witch, you.'" The teacher said she had been offering Adrienne books of blank pages and an interested ear for stories about her witches. At first, Adrienne, her hostility now clearly showing, had only grinned and torn up the books. The teacher had accepted that and offered her sheets of paper to tear up or scribble over. The director then offered to supply a witch puppet, saying, "If I can't find one, I can easily make one with some of that black cloth and a rubber ball."

As time went on, Adrienne was increasingly able to work out her angry feelings through play. The witch puppet was again and again thrown out of her locker, thus being rejected as Adrienne felt her mother was rejecting her, but she always searched her locker again for it when she arrived each morning. She also punished her witch by burying it in sand, although she always dug it up again. When she played in this way, and drew and colored in the books she now used to dictate witch stories, other children were brought into her orbit, and she depended on the teacher less. As the strength of her resentment waned, she returned little by little to her cheerful, sociable self while awaiting the recovery of her mother. "I don't give her nearly as much attention as before," the teacher said, "but it wasn't any good giving her attention when I was resenting her." "She was getting a mixed message?" "She certainly was." The director offered, "I think there is no more convincing way to show children we care than by accepting their angry feelings." "But what I learned mostly from it," the teacher went on, "was that if you accept your own hostility toward a child, and stop trying to be all things to all men—children, I mean—you can understand what their behavior is telling you."

III

A teacher makes herself available for individual parent conferences, and usually they take the initiative in making the appointments, either on special days set aside for such meetings or at other times when they feel the need. Some parents feel no need for such consultations; they judge by the child's response to the school and his or her general development that none is required. Others are interested in one or two conferences as progress reports or as a part of planning ahead for kindergarten. Still other parents may request a number of appointments, perhaps during a period of stress or crisis, or perhaps from a wish to understand their children better or to improve the quality of their dealings with them. When regular conferences seem desirable over a long period, the teacher may help the parents to find someone to see on the outside, since her own time is necessarily limited.

If a teacher herself feels the need to confer with a parent, she tries the informal contacts first, such as are made available to her at arrival and dismissal time, at times when the parent is staying at school with the child, in telephone calls, or perhaps when she makes a home visit. The response from the parent helps her to see whether the concern is a mutual one or hers alone, so that she neither pushes the parent into a meeting that would be a one-sided one or disturbs the parent by suggesting problems he or she is unready or unwilling to see or to discuss with her at that time. It is possible, too, that what the staff sees as a problem is not one that involves the child at home at all. It may belong only to the school situation, or only to the teacher's personal relationship with him.

The most frequent parent-teacher contacts occur at the school's door or gate. This can become a time to share brief school observations and anec-dotes that help a parent feel part of what is happening, and a time for parents to communicate information about a child, as well. As time per-mits, there are parents' questions about child development in general or other factual matters. "How's he [or she] doing?" is often heard from a parent, and if there is an aura of concern about the question, the teacher will need to know more about what is in the parent's mind before she can answer helpfully. "You're wondering about him?" can open the door to more; then the teacher may perhaps say something like "Children of this age can be pretty puzzling, sometimes. Maybe you'd like an appointment to talk over some of the things you've been thinking about." To other expressed concerns, information that is general, rather than personal, can be helpful and nonthreatening when there is insufficient time to talk at greater length. Examples are: "Group play usually comes later"; "He's at the stage when children like to brag"; "Children in families with new babies often revert to clinging to their mothers for a while."

Descriptions of some meetings with parents follow. They represent three kinds: conferences in the school's office by appointment, talks that occurred in the school while a parent was visiting or observing, and some that took place on the telephone or over a cup of coffee.

● Some conferences arise when parents and teachers come to the same conclusions, almost uncannily, at the same time.

The teacher watched Donavan as he sat at a table leaning his head on his hand, and a word not often descriptive of young children came to her mind. "He looks *sad*," she thought. She sat down beside him and said softly, "Something's the matter?" His eyes filled with tears. "Something happened?" He shook his head. "About school?" "No." "About home?" "No." "You're unhappy about—?" "About my mother," he said, but could go no further. At the gate that day, Donavan's mother, glancing at him as he sat on the side of the sandbox, said, "There it is again. He looks *sad*." And both the teacher and the mother spoke almost at the same time. "Let's have—" "How about a conference?"

When Mrs. Duncan came in for her appointment, she began right away. "It's about me; I'm sure of it. Donavan has been more and more irritating to me lately. And the more irritated I get, the more demanding and whiny he becomes. He and I are having some rough times. His sister is much nicer to have around these days. I think it's the age. He was a gentle, beautiful little child, and now that he's getting to be a tough little male, I don't understand him as well, and I don't know how to deal with him. I'd like to come a few times and talk about Donavan and me. Poor little guy. It's natural he should feel sad; what could be more natural? His relationship with me was his most important one, his first one, and now it's running into trouble." And her eyes filled, too.

Conferences with Mrs. Duncan helped her work out the trouble spots in her relationship with Donavan. Meanwhile, at school, the teacher helped Donavan verbalize his feelings when he seemed downcast. "Trouble again?" "My mommy got mad at me." "And that makes you feel very sad, I guess." "I want her to be always friendly, *never* cross." In this kind of talk, there is no pressure to answer, and sometimes the child just nods in recognition of his feelings and knows he is understood. Other children were helpful, too. "*My* mommy gets mad lots and lots of times," Liz said, adding matter-of-factly, "They all do." "But they don't *stay* mad," Martin put in. "No," said Norah stoutly, "That's because we're their children." "Mine gets awful mad when I talk about do-dos," Gordon said. And Donavan was able to add, "Mine gets mad when I mess up my room." Jewel often came and sat beside him. So Donavan felt less alone with his troubles while things were being worked out between him and his mother.

● Sometimes a teacher's own need for information may initiate a conference. With Mrs. Gonzales, one was enough. Her three-year-old, Pedro,
had been a cheerful, happy little boy who played at school with concentration and pleasure and was free and imaginative in his use of
materials. But he suddenly began to have violent temper tantrums. He
seemed to expect, whenever anyone entered the area where he was
playing, approached to ask him to play or share a toy, or even just
passed by, that all his toys would be snatched, his buildings toppled, or
his pictures torn up. His eyes would dilate, and he would scream
piercingly, "No-o-o!" like a siren going off. Children usually backed off
in some alarm, but the same thing happened over and over again if
anyone interfered, however innocently, with Pedro's play; and if the
child didn't go away immediately, Pedro would throw himself down
and bang his head and heels on the floor. And the behavior did not seem
to improve. The teacher always went to Pedro at once when he was in
difficulties, alerted by the shrill screams. She offered him words to
replace the screams, such as "I'm using it now," and assured him that
the others would listen and understand, and Pedro would make abortive efforts to try to talk. But he seemed very tense, and could not relax
when picked up and held on the teacher's lap. Most disturbing of all,
when he was lying on the floor in a tantrum, he closed his eyes, rocked
himself from side to side, and clutched his penis with one hand while
frantically sucking all the fingers of the other one, almost as though
trying to ram them down his throat. It was as though Pedro felt completely deserted and could find no source of comfort except in his own
body.

Signs of such serious upset in a normally stable child indicate a need
for the teacher to talk to the parent. So she met Mrs. Gonzales at the
gate and asked her, "How have things been at home, lately?" Mrs.
Gonzales replied that things had been difficult, and asked how Pedro
had been at school. The teacher said she had been wondering about his
"short fuse." Fits of temper were not characteristic of him, and she had
thought perhaps his mother could throw some light on what could be
bothering Pedro. Was anything different going on at home? "What do
you mean?" Mrs. Gonzales asked. "I can't think of anything. Different
in what way?" The teacher replied, "I can't really say; what seems to
upset him most is other children coming near him when he's playing. I
can't see why that should be, because they rarely actually interfere with
him. He seems to be losing his trust, somehow—even in the adults. I'd
be grateful for any ideas you might have; do you think we might get
together to try to figure out what's happening?" Mrs. Gonzales did not

set a time for an appointment just then, but that evening she phoned and said she had been thinking and would like to come in the next day.

"I believe I know what's the matter with Pedro," she began. "There are some older boys in our neighborhood who have been coming by the house when Pedro is playing out in front or riding his tricycle up and down, and they tease him. I expect they like to hear him scream." "You think that might be what's getting him upset." "Yes, I'm almost sure. It's like what you see at school. He screams his head off. But I don't see how I can keep him in all the time." "I see what you mean." "And we don't have any place else for him to ride his tricycle, and he loves that." "Yes, he likes ours, too." Mrs. Gonzales went on, "I try to have things for him inside, but that's no answer. I don't want trouble with my neighbors. I could send the boys home if they were in our yard, but I don't see how I can forbid them to stop and talk to Pedro on the sidewalk." "You don't feel there's anything you can do to help Pedro in his problems with the boys." There was a pause. Then she said, "It's a pretty big price to pay for peace in the neighborhood, isn't it?" "Peace in the neighborhood at the cost of Pedro's peace of mind?" "Yes. And what I said isn't true; I *can* do something about it. I can talk to those boys. And I will. How is Pedro going to trust people if even his mother doesn't take his side?" And she went off, her mouth set in determination. The teacher never knew just what Mrs. Gonzales did, but at the gate the next day, she nodded her head at the teacher and said, "It's been taken care of." From then on Pedro had tantrums at longer and longer intervals, and then they ceased altogether, and he was his old self again. Like many mothers with a sturdy sense of self, once she understood the importance of the problem to Pedro, Mrs. Gonzales could take hold and manage without further help. But she needed to find her own solution.

- Another kind of conference is a three-way meeting involving parent, child, and teacher. William had been weeping on arrival for several days, although prior to this he had come without distress. He was invited to join his mother, Mrs. Lee, and the teacher in the office. The teacher said that she and his mother could see he wasn't very happy about coming to school these days, and thought they could all three talk together to see if there might be a way to help him. At that meeting, asked if he had any ideas, he offered a few suggestions about things he would like to bring with him to school from home. He thought he would like to pack a suitcase with some of his toys and something to eat, and Mrs. Lee agreed to his plan.

After this, for a while, William and his teacher had a short meeting every day, just the two of them, soon after his arrival at school. They would go into the office, where William would sit at the desk and the teacher would sit in the chair beside it. He had almost indistinguishable speech, very hesitant and poorly enunciated, uttered in a frequently inaudible voice, with his head often turned away. However, the more the teacher listened to him, the clearer his speech became, and after several sessions he began to talk about the car-pool group in which he had been coming to school. On some days Mrs. Lee would drive him and Ralph to school, and on other days Ralph's mother was to drive the children. But he couldn't remember which days Ralph's mother was to bring them, and he was afraid that she wouldn't remember either, so that no one would take him home. Then he poured out all his doubts. His mother would forget to tell Ralph's mother that it was her turn. Ralph's mother would forget to come for him. Ralph's father might need the car that day. Ralph's mother would pick him up, but would forget where he lived. Or, when she got him home past all those hazards, his mother might have forgotten that it was Ralph's mother's day, and she might be coming to get him, so nobody would be at his house. Or she might be out in the car and have a flat tire. After he had thoroughly explored his worries, the teacher went over the facts he lacked: that Ralph's mother could reach the teacher by phone to get William's address ("Don't take my card out of your box; you might lose it," he said in his faint voice) or look up his address in the telephone book, that his mother could phone a neighbor to watch for him if she had a flat tire, and so on. When all these possibilities had been discussed, there remained the fear that his mother would forget, or somehow inefficiently be late or upset arrangements. Here he said, his voice breaking, "Would *you* take me home? Would *you*?"

It is always a great temptation to momentarily reassure such a child by saying "Yes, of course I would." But this would be like agreeing that his mother might be unreliable. So instead, the teacher said that William's mother or someone she sent for him would always come, and that the teacher would stay with him until then. William's problem seemed to be his lack of communication with his mother. He saw her as someone with a confusing and unpredictable schedule, whose comings and goings he could never understand, so that at times when he himself was involved in a similarly confusing schedule, he felt panic. The teacher, together with William, then invited his mother to meet with them again on the problem of why he wept at the door, and this time he said the car-pooling worried him. Mrs. Lee responded promptly that if the new plan bothered him they would go back to the old one for a while until he felt better about it. She would bring him and come for him every day herself. This she did, but for quite a while his anxiety during story time at the end of the day brought him running out to the dismissing teacher to ask "Who's coming? Who's coming today?" Finally he could hold in mind the "always mother" plan. Because his mother did have a complicated schedule, she was sometimes late, but he learned to wait trustfully for her.

The three-way meetings were followed by a conference that William's mother requested for herself. Mrs. Lee discussed her thoughts since the last meeting, saying that she had decided she should always explain any plan she made for William simply and clearly, and that if she had practical problems in arranging for his care, she should not discuss all the alternatives with him or in front of him; "They're my responsibility," she said. And she commented on the improvement in his speech, saying it would be easier, now, to answer his questions; there was no need for him to be a "little Worry Willie" all by himself. Her last words were: "When you asked *him* to tell what was bothering him, I thought he wouldn't know, or if he did know he wouldn't be able to say what it was, or that, even if he *did* say it, I certainly wouldn't be able to understand him. I'd never really tried to find out things like that or talk them over with him. I always thought he was too young." A few weeks later, after William had regained his sense of security, the ride-group plan was successfully resumed. One of the most important functions of three-way meetings is to help in communication problems between parents and children.

● Not all meetings take place in conferences by appointment. Short, informal ones occurred at school with Mrs. Minnick, caught in the midst of a stressful relationship with her son Jasper. Jasper controlled his mother by emotional outbursts that she resented but felt powerless to resist. He was an only child, a sturdily built four-year-old, just starting nursery school. He demanded not only his mother's presence at school, but also her services, insisting that she bring him toys he wanted, push him on the swing, pull him in the wagon, put his pictures in his locker, and so on. He refused to allow her to stay and read or sew in the waiting room, constantly calling her out, though he was free to go in and out and stay there with her if he liked. When Mrs. Minnick tried to get out of this dilemma by having a friend bring him to school, he refused to get into the car and threatened to "throw up" on the seats if she insisted. From the start, it had looked like a contest between mother and son, and it appeared that the boy was winning.

Whenever Jasper was out of earshot, Mrs. Minnick used the chance to talk to the teacher about her feelings. Her patience was wearing thin. She felt that she was helpless and, understandably, protested against her bondage. She described Jasper's tantrums at home and said she had always done a good deal to avoid causing them. She felt her position in the family to be that of a peacemaker, as far as Jasper was concerned. After talking in this way for several days, she tried to get another private moment with the teacher by suggesting that Jasper make a painting for his daddy. But he wasn't interested in doing that. The teacher reflected what her restlessness seemed to mean by saying, "You'd like us to have a little time alone?" "Yes," she said, and then added, surprisingly, "Will you say it for me?" The teacher told Jasper, "We'd like you to go back into the big room now. We're going to have a little talk here." After he left, Mrs. Minnick said, "That just shows how hard it is for me to stick up for myself. If you hadn't been there, I don't know what he would have done; I could never have gotten away with telling him something like that. And I'm getting so tired of jumping at his commands. But what can I do? If I don't do what he says, he gets furious." "It's a pretty tough spot to be in—I can certainly understand that." "Yes—he's so strong.—What should I do?" "You're very anxious to find an answer, I'm sure. You're thinking maybe I could advise you?" "I guess I want even you to tell me what to do! What's the matter with me, anyway? No! I want to be my own boss. I'm going to write some letters in the waiting room today, and not do anything for Jasper. But it's the first time I've really opposed him, and his dad isn't here to help by spanking him. I don't know what to expect." "Kind of like stepping off into space—I can see that." "I did see a contest like that here, though. One child wore another down by sheer persistence. It took a long time, but he won, and he was smaller, too." "Strength didn't seem as important?" "No, it was who could hold out longest. And I know Jasper. He's no good for the long haul. He has to have everything right away."

With the teacher standing by, Mrs. Minnick went to Jasper and told him she was going to stay in the waiting room until going-home time. He said, "No! You can't!" and he wrapped his arms and legs around her. She loosened his grasp again and again, staying fairly calm. Once she looked at the teacher, her eyes saying, "Stay with me." Finally Jasper threw himself on the floor, red-faced and screaming with rage, and his mother left him there. The teacher told him, "Yes, I can see you're very angry. You didn't want her to do that, but she did it anyway. It's all right to be angry about it, and it's all right to scream." After a while, he climbed onto the teacher's lap, fitting his long body into her arms. This day was the turning point for both Jasper and his mother, and a few days later she started leaving him at school for gradually lengthening periods.

For a while, Mrs. Minnick came for an occasional observation at the school, staying in the background. Jasper, as is natural, was in competition with his father for his mother's love. He had identified with the powerful, dominating side of his father, and he was also carrying old feelings of omnipotence that dated from his baby days, when cries and screams worked magic. His mother had supported him in these tendencies by submitting to him, as she did to her husband, whose protective role had played its part in making it unnecessary for her to assert herself with Jasper. At school his mother watched him try to dominate the teachers as he did her, and she noticed their responses. At first he felt himself to be as strong as, or stronger than, the teachers. In many ways, they treated him as an equal, as, together, they discussed problems, found solutions, and enjoyed each other. But when issues arose that made it necessary, the teachers never hesitated to act as adults. When he was resisting limits, he tried to intimidate them with glaring eyes and threats like "I'll break your glasses." They encouraged him to talk about how he felt but stopped him from acting out his anger, saying, "I can see you really want to do that, but of course I couldn't let you." "But I really will," he would say, and for a while he kept his belief that the teachers, too, were unable to stop him and were afraid of his anger.

The only way to modify this firm conviction of his power over them was to let him experience its limits, which he did many times at school. Though he continued to be difficult for quite a while, he gradually began to change. He often called the teachers names, or yelled or hit at them, but none of this aroused any counter-furor or changed anything; they only responded by verbal reflections of his anger that helped him talk it out. What Jasper needed to experience was quiet steadfastness. On the jungle gym one day, after many encounters like these, he was unwilling to stop pretending to shoot the other children climbing there, and they were becoming upset and overexcited. The teacher told him, "I guess you'll need to come down, then," and he said, "I won't come down! You can't make me!" But even as he said this he doubted it and began to come down, not even waiting for her foot on the ladder. Earlier he would have had to test this out to the finish.

Mrs. Minnick's conferences by appointment dealt with her feelings about herself as growing up and changing from an obedient little girl to a responsible adult. She said she was realizing there were times when she knew what was best for Jasper, and, like it or not, he was under her care. She said she thought that since she was unsure of herself she had put the burden on Jasper for many decisions he was not yet old enough to make, "Like deciding what toys I should buy him, what I should cook for him, what TV shows he should watch—all that. I know I may make mistakes sometimes, but that doesn't mean I should just give up." From being disgusted at her immaturity Mrs. Minnick moved to more acceptance of that part of herself, saying, "But I did have some good ideas; I wanted to respect his individuality and his right to make his own choices. I had dreams of a democratic family, and there wasn't anything wrong with that. But that also fit in with my feeling reluctant to be grown-up. I was very young and scared, and wanted to depend on my husband, and then on Jasper, to tell me what to do." She began to see Jasper in a different light, too. "I always thought of him as power-ful—much too strong and self-assured for me to oppose. But I'm begin-ning to see that all the things he's had to decide about his life have made him feel inadequate—just like I do if I have to make decisions I don't feel qualified to make. I think that might be why he does so much shooting play; it makes him feel big, like those TV characters, and covers up his feelings of littleness. And incidentally, now that I'm convincing him I can take care of him, he's not so interested in having me buy him guns."

One day Jasper's roars and screams were heard on the front steps of the school at dismissal time. The teacher looked out the window. Jasper was yelling that he wanted to cross the street without his mother's holding his hand, and she was sitting on the steps, keeping him on her lap to prevent him from going on ahead of her. She sat there very quietly, not responding to his storming, and soon they got up and went off, Jasper holding her hand. Mrs. Minnick discussed the effect of this incident on her later. "I think I've really grown up," she said. "The other day I told him he couldn't play with something of mine, and he went into his usual threats. He told me if I didn't let him, he'd wait until I wasn't looking and then break it. I suddenly realized I wasn't reacting to that, and without thinking I said to him, 'You know something, Jasper? I'm not afraid of you any more.' He looked astonished and he said, 'You *used* to be.' I told him, 'I know, but not any more.' And it's true. I found it out when I held him on the steps the other day. But it started the day he put up that big battle about my doing my own thing in the waiting room. It was awful!" She laughed a little. "I kept telling myself, 'Time is on my side. Time is on my side. He's just a child. He can't hold out, but *I* can.' And I'd look at you. My mother was a doormat, like me. But you're a woman, too, and you're not one. And

I'm so glad I'm not one either, anymore. Jasper's going to be better off this way; just imagine him grown up! He'd have married another doormat; I just know it!"

● Lark's mother, Mrs. Jerrold, was receiving psychiatric help on the outside when she enrolled her daughter. Her contacts came in the form of visits and observations at the school, telephone calls, and an occasional talk over a cup of coffee.

When a mother is in intensive therapy, her moods often vary widely, and a little girl who identifies strongly with her is apt to be much affected by these swings. Sometimes Lark had no problems about separating from her mother at the gate, but on other days she came to the door clinging, asking to be carried into the room, and refusing to let her mother go. Mrs. Jerrold seemed to be clinging to Lark, too, on those days, and she was invited to stay at school as long as she wished. Since she was examining her problems with her psychiatrist, help at school was focused on situations that arose there, and whatever feelings these aroused were worked out in her therapy sessions.

While she was observing Lark at school, Mrs. Jerrold noticed that Lark asked to go to the bathroom, go outside, sit at a table, use a toy, or even touch things, prefacing her questions with the phrase "Would it bother you if I . . . ?" The mother saw the teacher, in response, pick Lark up and say, "I'll always tell you how I feel. If something bothers me, I'll say, 'Lark, that bothers me,' and you'll always know." Later the mother said, wistfully, "Lark has never known how I felt about anything. I've been afraid to tell her—or anybody else, I guess." After she had observed more interactions at school in which all kinds of feelings were being openly expressed by children in the group, she said, over after-school coffee, "When I was a child, I never showed my feeling until I got so angry I couldn't help it. And I'm still that way. When I blow up, Lark gets scared. I know that's one reason she's so unsure of herself. I don't know how to be a good mother; I'm just no good at it." The teacher smiled at her and said, "Lark's not the only one who's unsure of herself?" and she smiled back, ruefully, and said, "No, I always have been."

A few days after these observations and talks, Mrs. Jerrold telephoned the teacher to say that she really didn't want to stay at school with Lark when she was feeling depressed or upset. She said, "I just feel at those times that I have to get away from her for a while. Can I do that?" She was encouraged to follow her feelings, and when she was clear and definite, Lark seemed relieved and turned to play. This then helped Mrs. Jerrold take new steps in being direct with Lark. When a mother's deeper motivations are being explored through psychiatric treatment, observations in the nursery school and the friendly support of teachers can help her to change old patterns.

The series of discussions with the parents of Julian that ends this book represents the kind of conferences most often seen in the nursery school setting, though initiated in this case by an unusually severe upset. In these conferences, a teacher and a child's parents work together over an extended period to help him through a stage in which he is experiencing developmental stresses, and the teacher's role is primarily educational and supportive.

● Julian, a three-year-old with a baby brother, appeared on entrance to be a bright, verbal child who was fond of stories, sang songs, used puzzles and construction materials, climbed well and rode a tricycle, and liked exploring art. There were no transition problems for him; he entered the stream of play, saying goodbye cheerfully to his father, who was to bring him and pick him up. He adopted social customs readily, too, and was independent and creative in his choice of activities. He was friendly and talkative with the teachers and enjoyed the children, learning all their names very soon.

After about two months there was a disturbing change. Julian began to come into the schoolroom door hanging on to his father's hand and whining and whimpering. His speech regressed dramatically, and he became very hard to understand. If a child approached or anything startled him, he ran and hid behind the teacher, clutching her, or lifted his arms, saying, "Up! Up!" He began to be wet every day and put things into his mouth constantly. His long attention span vanished, and if a block fell off his building or a piece of puzzle wouldn't go in at once, he cried or threw it. Often he asked, anxiously, "What shall I play?" unable to get started without much teacher help. He would repeat requests to the teacher unintelligibly, over and over, and become increasingly upset when not understood. A crisis came with an all-out temper tantrum over his block building. He was taken into the office, where the teacher held him, telling him that she knew how angry he felt and that he could scream there as loudly as he liked. When he tried to hit her, she said, "I can't let you do that," and when, then, he got off her lap and fell a little way to the floor, looking at her questioningly, she said, "And I won't let you hurt yourself, either." This seemed to reassure him, at least temporarily.

While Julian, during this period, looked extremely disturbed, the staff decided to try to help him in school rather than to make an immediate referral. There were many positive aspects. The family was a stable one, and the parents were sensitive and loving. Julian had had a very good developmental history up to that point. And the parents were ready and willing to work with the problem at home and keep in close touch with the school. Understandably very concerned, they had frequent conferences and telephone talks with the teacher. They described his home behavior as "impossible," and were particularly distressed by his crying and getting out of bed at night. When taken back to his room, he screamed hysterically, waking the baby and robbing his parents of needed rest. They felt he was frightened and anxious and had been sitting by his bed in turn to try to comfort him. But nothing seemed to help.

Julian's baby brother now walked and ran about, and when he was held up by his father to wave over the school gate, he looked like a miniature copy of Julian, rather than the baby he had been. Julian had never seemed jealous of the baby, and the teacher suggested that sometimes this came later, when the sibling began to seem more like a rival. Much of Julian's frighteningly bizarre behavior, she suggested, might seem more comprehensible when seen as appropriate to the playing of a baby role. His use of the school bathroom was a case in point. He would stand at the toilet and say, in his new odd speech, "It won't come—it won't come—," only to flood the floor moments later, exactly as babies do in the training period and as his own brother was doing at that time. A similar episode occurred one day when he began to moan and wail after climbing into the big office chair. He was apparently convinced that he couldn't get down, and finally managed to say, in a high, tiny voice, "Me want *little* chair." To be lifted down and put into a chair his own size was a sensible wish for a baby. Appropriate, too, for the role, was Julian's butter-fingered use of the blocks and puzzles, which made the three-year-old part of him so angry and frustrated. He would try to mash and pound a piece of puzzle the wrong way around, exactly as a toddler would.

The teacher suggested to Julian's parents, Laura and Tom, that his playing the baby role was involuntary at these times and that consequently it was as bewildering and upsetting for him as for them. For example, perhaps at night he would feel an urge to wet the bed, as the baby was doing, and the part of him that had begun to master this old habit would feel anxious. Seeing the baby with his bottle would also make him miss his own, now given up, when he was in bed, and perhaps a small one filled with water would help him over that hump; if he could be a bottle baby, he might not have to be the more worrisome (to him) bed-wetting one. This suggestion was tried, and helped to relieve the immediate sleeping problem.

At this point, it was necessary for all who dealt with Julian to look at him as two people, the baby he had been—and wondered if he should continue being in order to get the same attention as his baby brother— and the well-adjusted, competent three-year-old now seen more and more rarely. To aid him in achieving control over his changes from one to the other, rather than being swept helplessly into regression, the teacher suggested that his parents help him play the baby role at home. He would be given props such as bottles, pacifiers, rattles, and blankets and be encouraged with words like "Of course we know you're not *really* a baby, but sometimes children like to pretend they are. So here are some things to do it with." Then one or the other parent would play out a part in the drama as a caretaker of a baby, picking him up lovingly, rocking him, carrying him about, talking baby talk to him, and so on, "hamming it up" just enough so he would be aware throughout that it was a game they were playing with him. As soon as he changed back into his three-year-old self, they would at once assume an ordinary tone, saying, "That's enough for now?" and then talk about his three-year-old interests with him. At times when Julian's change into a baby was unexpected, as when he suddenly fell down and his speech couldn't be understood, they would say, "You're a baby, now?" and join in with something appropriate like "Here, baby, *I'll* pick you up." They would need to be firm, too, sometimes—for instance, when the baby Julian spilled or threw things—saying, "Oh no, baby, you can't do that," but in the loving, smiling way one would talk to a baby. As he was helped, by means of this play, to understand what he was doing, Julian's anxiety would diminish, and he would gain voluntary control over the role-playing.

Frequent conferences, either face to face or by phone, were very important at this time. The parents needed explanations of the strange behavior of their child. Regression is very alarming to parents, and their anxiety can be quickly picked up by the child. In his primitive state, while identifying with his baby brother and his earlier self, Julian had very few defenses against anxiety. He might become more and more confused and frightened and have an additional reason for regressing to what seemed an easier time of life. Understanding what was going on with Julian also helped his parents not to feel annoyance because of their disappointment in the child of whose good development they had been so proud. This would have been destructive, too, confirming Julian's fear that it was the baby brother who now possessed their love. And the parents were reassured when the teacher told them that in her experience, even though young children sometimes looked very disturbed when passing through such common crises as jealousy of a sibling, they could usually be expected to return to their former level of development afterward.

Meanwhile the parents, supported by the teacher, were working out their own solutions to various situations that arose at home. The father decided to put the baby's potty chair in the bathroom so that Julian could take his choice between that and the regular toilet, and when he didn't have to give up his baby role completely, Julian stopped having toilet accidents. His mother had bought some baby toys in thrift shops for Julian's use alone.

Some time later, Julian came to the school door crawling between his father's legs, and the teacher, knowing that his brother no longer crawled and that identifying with an animal is another way to be something small, needing care, said to him, "You're on all fours, today; are you pretending to be some kind of animal?" "Yes," he replied at once, "I'm a baby guinea pig." The meaning of his wild, frightened look and his strange sounds on coming in recently became clear now. The teacher said, "Oh! I'll make you a cage, baby guinea pig," and she put chairs around a table, facing outward, so as to make a barred enclosure. For several days afterward he crawled under the table on arrival and accepted food and pats from the children before emerging as himself. Periods of being his three-year-old self were becoming longer, but he still had trouble at dismissal time. Apparently the idea of returning to the seat of the trouble swept away all his shaky control of the wish to be a baby. At this time he would have a tantrum over almost anything. One day he screamed and threw himself about because his father wouldn't lift him over the railing of the steps, which was impossible to do from outside the gate where his father waited with other parents. The teacher said, "Perhaps now you'd like to be little again. Shall I carry you to your daddy, little one?" and he lifted his arms with a sigh of relief.

After several weeks, Julian began to show the first signs of the integration of his two sides. He made his own guinea pig cage, an arrangement of chairs, table, and blocks, with a place on the roof to "sit in the sun," windows, and front and back doors. He had stopped bringing a bottle and blanket to school, and he began to take over the responsibility of attending to his toilet needs. "Oh-oh, my wee-wee's coming!" he would say, and run to the bathroom, managing from there on by himself. Most of his school day now began to go fairly smoothly, and he looked relaxed and happy much of the time. He was able to go from child play to baby play and back again quite comfortably for the most part. Real recovery, however, was not so fast as relief from anxiety. Social play was at a standstill, with Julian either playing alone or in parallel fashion. All "power play," so typical of the older three-year-old and four-year-old, had stopped; he didn't use trucks or trains, ride a tricycle, swing, climb the jungle gym, or use the slide. He engaged mostly in manipulative activities like those of two-year-olds, such as fitting pegs into holes, stacking rings on sticks, and nesting boxes. Puzzles still bothered him, as did matching pictures and similar intellectual tasks. Though formerly capable of a high level of achievement with such materials, now perhaps he found it worrying to face such clear evidence that he was really not a baby. He was not ready, either, to commit himself to being adequate with such symbols of grown-upness as books, pencils, paintbrushes, or hammers. And some kinds of play clearly showed his sensitivity in the area of size. For example, one day he was using a set of pink plastic sticks, each of which could be inserted into the next, so a long chain of them was easily achieved. At first he talked of making his chain "as big as the room," but he had to stop abruptly when the chain was baby-sized, about two feet long.

Nevertheless, bits of maturity began to come through more and more. When he sat on the teacher's lap as a baby and she sang to him, he tried to join in; then he wanted to sing the whole song himself, saying, "Let *me!*" eagerly. He had formerly been very concerned about being hungry and had nibbled much of the day. Now he prepared the crackers at snack time for the other children, though he played this parental role while holding firmly to a small basket for himself in the other hand. The school's stuffed-rabbit family next began to replace Julian's playing the role of a baby or small animal. Each day he would seek out the father, mother, and baby rabbit, putting the "boy rabbit" away in a corner. That he identified with the baby rabbit seemed clear; for example, he would say, "The baby rabbit is hungry," and then feed it and himself alternate bites of cracker. Like Julian himself, the little rabbit didn't seek out friends or assume a "big" role, like that of a train engineer or truck driver. It had a little bottle and a blanket, and Julian made it a bed in a trailer which he pulled around on the floor. Thus he gave himself some vicarious babying. His play was more independent, too, at this point. He would close the office door so he could play alone with the rabbits, although frequently emerging to tell what was happening.

At home Julian had begun to be difficult again, but in a different way. He pushed limits to the hilt and was again demanding attention at bedtime, though in a dominating way rather than an anxious one. In another conference, Julian's parents, together with the teacher, worked out a new bedtime routine geared toward self-sufficiency. Either Laura or Tom, on putting him to bed, would plan with him what he might do if he was not ready to sleep or if he woke up in the night. He could put on his own light by means of a long attached string; he could look at a few books he would have by his bed; he could help himself to a snack or pour drinks from a small pitcher on his bedside table; and he could play his music box. Firmness during the day was also discussed, because, as Julian was able to act more and more mature and powerful, if not under control he might become frightened at what he could do and perhaps regress again.

At school, too, Julian was starting to push the limits. When it was time to go home, he had heretofore been asked to choose whether he wanted to walk or be carried to the gate and had always answered, "Carry." But one day he refused to do either and had a tantrum at the top of the steps. The limit set by the teacher was that he cry inside the door, rather than at the top of the steps. After finding the limit a firm one, he allowed the teacher to pick him up as usual and carry him to his father.

Laura and Tom were reassured again by the teacher at this stage that in a normal child the urge to grow and learn can be relied upon to revive, once conflicts about it are resolved. Julian's present tendencies to explore limits and try out his strength against that of the adults could be seen as part of this reviving urge. If both parents and teacher could take a neutral position, allowing him to make his own choices by clearly saying in many ways, "Sometimes you feel little and sometimes you feel big, and it's all right with us either way," Julian would feel free to swing back and forth between baby helplessness and power voluntarily, until he came to rest at a midpoint that reflected his real level of development.

After the tantrum at dismissal time and the setting of limits by the teacher, Julian could feel reassured that she would control him and that it was probably safe to feel powerful again. Now followed another day of consolidating and moving ahead. Arriving cheerfully, he began to make a chain of the pink plastic sticks on the playroom floor, saying it was to go "clear to the rabbits' house," thus linking baby play with big-boy play. (Progress is most safely made by linking, not by a splitting off of past from present.) As he worked, Julian said, "It's getting bigger. It's growing. Like me. I'm growing, too. See? See?" (It was very necessary to him that the teacher notice, and that in this way he could know she was neither alarmed by, nor disapproving of, his growing up, so he said, "See? See?" at each step all day.) Later, as he reached the halfway mark in his chain-building, he said, "It's about big enough." The teacher said, "You can make it any way you decide— little, middle-sized, or big." "Middle-sized" was a new word that he needed now, and he picked it up at once. "Like me," he said. "My daddy is big, and my baby is little, and I'm middle-sized." He left the chain then, and went to work with a box of assorted mosaic tiles, practicing his new awareness and acceptance of size differences there, too. "I'm going to make a big building, and a middle-sized building, and a little building with these," he said.

Next Julian moved to watch another child playing on the floor with a train. This was the first time since his disturbance that he had displayed the typical three-year-old's interest in others' play. After a few minutes, he suddenly ran to the teacher, smiling, and gave her a hug. Later the teacher told Laura and Tom, "Perhaps I was projecting a meaning into this, but it felt as though he were saying, 'I could play like that, too, if I wanted, but it's all right with you no matter what I do.'" Then he asked the teacher for "another game." With the pegboard and pegs she handed him, he went straight into his baby role. All the pegs were spilled in a pile on the table, and instead of fitting them into their holes he stirred them and smeared them about with his hand, fingers unseparated from thumb like a baby's, and put some of them into his mouth, all the while uttering what was now recognizable as his baby murmurings, frettings, and whimperings, along with a mishmash of unintelligible words like his mishmash of pegs. The teacher smiled at him and said, "It's a baby doing that," and he smiled back. In a moment some pegs spilled on the floor, and, jumping up, he said clearly, "I'll pick them up," making another of his fast switches of role, uncolored by anxiety as they once had been.

A day or two later, Julian went into the doll corner for the first time since his trouble. Initially he seemed a little bothered by its many possibilities. Baby dolls, boy and girl dolls, a big bed and smaller ones, chairs his size and a doll's high chair, presented him with a host of choices. He seemed to need the teacher there. "What shall I do? What shall I do?" he asked. He picked up a baby doll and made it stand up. "It can stand up," he said, "but it can't walk very well. It falls down." And he dropped it on the floor. "He fell down," he said, a little worriedly. "He went ker-plunk," the teacher said, smiling, and he smiled too and kept dropping the doll on the floor, saying "ker-plunk!" each time, as though it were a great joke between them. Banging the doll harder and harder, he then made crying noises for it, saying, "He's calling his Dad. He's too little to say 'Dad!' He cries instead." Here was his first overt display of the antagonism children usually feel, at least to some degree, toward their siblings. Julian was beginning to have feelings about his baby brother as a separate person, rather than identifying with him. And later, leaving the doll corner, he showed again how he was coming to terms with his problem. Looking at the pictures hanging on the screens there, his comment was: "Some are little and some are big."

At the very end of the day, he went overboard a little at the growing-up end. Typically, boys of his age want to think themselves bigger than anyone (particularly their fathers) and make outlandish claims as to size, strength, and superiority. The teacher wanted Julian to keep in touch with reality at this stage of his recovery and not to swing into a denial of his baby feelings too fast, lest they again overwhelm him at unconscious levels. It would be important for him to keep both aspects of himself in awareness. When it was nearly time for him to go home, he swelled his chest and said, "I'm big! I'm bigger than my Dad!" Here he foretold the Oedipal stage, suggesting that the baby identification was losing its hold on him. Glad to see this happening, the teacher gave him a warm smile, but she also said, "He's really bigger, but I expect you'd *like* to be bigger than he is." Julian looked a little downcast and then said, "But I *am* bigger than my baby brother." "Is this a carry or a walk day?" the teacher asked as usual, when Tom arrived at the gate for him. "It's a walk day," he answered. "Dad! Dad!" he called from the door, "It's a walk day!" As he reached the top of the short flight of steps, he stopped, and there was a pause while the watchers held their breath. Then down he went, and out. In that pause, he had made his final choice.

Letter to a New Teacher

Dear Teacher,

As you start your work, I know you'll also be starting a long process of meeting new problems and seeking new answers, and that this will continue, as it has with me, as long as you are a teacher. You'll have puzzling days, discouraging days, and days when you felt you did nothing but pick up toys and run hard to keep ahead of chaos. Teachers of older children may tell you that yours is an easy job; you'll know it isn't. (Few parents will tell you that, though.)

Yet many of us continue. Our overtime is never-ending: at home we sew on a rabbit's ear, scrounge out art supplies, make to-do lists for maintenance people or for ourselves to stem the inexorable wear and tear children inflict on their surroundings; and in our beds at night we try to find our way into Nancy's or Peter's mind, or replay something we said or did that left us feeling uncomfortable, so as to be ready for the next time. We are under an enchantment.

On the night before school opened I was there for a long time. I was arranging toys, putting bouquets of flowers around, labeling lockers with new names, and double-checking everything. There are so many details to make right in a playroom. All the pieces must be in the puzzles. Any dress that won't go on easily must be taken out of the dolls' bureau. And where is the small father doll?

At last I've done all I can. The school looks wonderful to me. And now begins that feeling of excitement about the children who are coming. Never, even after so many times, do I anticipate meeting a new child without this feeling. What will he or she be like? Soon I'll find out. And one thing I know: This child will not be like any I've ever met before.

The next morning I'm there early. The first arrival is Giles, who is three years old. His mother and his two older brothers have brought him. From the inside I see them open the gate. He is small, blond, and square, wearing a minute pair of white gloves. He walks through the gate purposefully, ahead of them. He is leaning a little forward, and his whole look is of expectation. His mother stays back, and I see her gesture to the big boys to be still. And I am still, too. Giles is coming up the center steps, one foot at a time, carried steadily on by his inner momentum, and never looking back. He opens the door. I have made myself lower by sitting on a small chair by the long table, not too close to the door, and I smile at him and say, quietly, "Hi, Giles." He looks at me, gives a little duck of his head, then goes straight across the room to the shelf of toys.

Giles's mother is now at the half-open door, just outside it. Our eyes meet, and hers look a little teary, but she is smiling. The big boys peering from behind her smile, too. She says, "O.K., Giles?" quietly, and he nods, looking only momentarily at her, then back to the fire engine he's chosen. A child who is ready, and a sensitive mother who can let him leave her and go forward to the new experience—I feel touched by this little scene and impressed by the family. But I know I need to be available to Giles on his first day if he should waver later. (And he did. When the room activity was in full swing, something made me go and kneel down close to him, and he buried his face in my shoulder, staying that way for just a few moments with my arms around him. Then he turned back to play, and he never faltered again.)

That long-ago day had the indescribable charm of any day in nursery school, given a special color and luminosity by its being the opening day of a new school. And I remember parts of it. Two children, friends from the same neighborhood, came together in a car pool. Alan, a tall, slim four-year-old, introduced me. "That's Samantha," he said, "The one with the tail." A long strip of cloth was pinned to the back of silent Samantha's dress. "Oh," I said, "Does she always wear it?" "I'll ask her," he told me. "No," he reported back, "She says she didn't have it when she was a baby."

I remember Alan brought a fat, stuffed ladybug, about six inches across, which, when he marched with a drum, he carried on his head under his hat. Samantha called him tenderly "Old Stupid Hat," and he replied, equally lovingly, "Old Tomato Face." Later in the day Alan told me, "I was sitting in Samantha's locker because we're going to get married when we grow up, but now I'm sitting in my own locker because I really belong to myself."

Stuart, who called himself Mrs. Lobodowsky, stands out too. He was chubby, sun-bronzed, and beautiful, and discovering a puddle of water in a corner of the playground, sat down in it joyfully.

And there was Tully, a four-year-old, who made a series of objects at the carpentry bench. I remember his saying, "I made a helicopter, and a bridge, and a bindy." "What's a bindy?" I asked him. He answered, "It's when you hammer the nail in and it goes all crooked, but you go ahead and paint it anyway." (Told about this, an artist friend said, "I have a studio full of bindies.") Later I offered Tully some spools, saying, "I'm afraid those nails won't hold them on, though. The heads are so small they go right through." "You use two nails," he told me kindly.

I remember two little girls sitting quietly on the floor in front of a mother who held a baby on her lap, each holding a soft, bare foot in her hand.

I remember "Salad Soup" being made out of sand.

I remember an upturned face and earnest eyes: "Mrs. Griffin, when you were not born yet, was your name Mrs. Houston?"

And more memories come, as I read those old notes.

"I'm here!" calls Manuel from the door. "*Now* you won't miss me!"

On the steps to the playground, I ask a child, "Is this belt too tight for your waist if I buckle it here?" "What's 'waist'?" "Do you know?" I say to a watching boy. "Sure. A waist is for leaning over railings," and he shows us.

A boisterous group tumbles in a pile of sand the workmen have left in a wheelbarrow. Royce issues a friendly invitation. "Mrs. Griffin, do you want to jump up and down in the wheelbarrow, too?"

And Elsa—she looks like a Christmas-card angel as she fills a pail in the sandbox, the sun shining on her blonde curls. She glances up with clear blue eyes, and smiles radiantly as she says, "I'm making poison."

As always, I'm caught by their language. "It's time o'clock." "My sock is leaking down." "Will you higher this swing for me?" "I'm going to *frop* this nail right in."

I overhear a conversation in the doll corner. Rick, ready with the doctor's kit, rings the bell and says, "Can I come in? I'm the doctor." But he is not like the doctors of the real world; in this one, he has no authority. The mother of the house says, "I guess so, if you hurry." "She'll have to have medicine," he says, looking over one of the dolls. The busy mother, a little impatiently, tells him, "There's medicine in the cupboard." The doctor says, tentatively, "Well, I have some medicine here in my bag—" "No," the mother tells him firmly, "we have our own medicine."

A friend of mine returned to nursery school teaching after a long, enforced absence. At the end of her first day back I met her—hair mussed, makeup long gone, skirt askew, but eyes shining. "Back to cloud-cuckoo-land," she said. "I've just been fishing for a pair of panties through a fence with a Simple Simon fishing rod."

Who can describe this charm? Nursery school is more, much more, but its enchantment is always part of whatever we try to tell about it.

I am deeply committed to giving all I can for these children to whom the future belongs, but, in the end, they give me as much. I have sometimes gone into this island of childhood when in trouble, in bodily pain, even in grief, yet once there it is always the same. All else fades away, and I am again at the heart of life.

With my best wishes,

Elinor Griffin

Suggested Reading

For Teachers

Ashton-Warner, Sylvia. 1963. *Teacher.* New York: Simon & Schuster.

Axline, Virginia. 1947. *Play Therapy.* New York: Houghton Mifflin.

Beck, Helen L. 1973. *Don't Push Me, I'm No Computer: How Pressures to Achieve Harm Preschool Children.* New York: McGraw-Hill.

Cohen, Dorothy. 1972. *The Learning Child.* New York: Random House.

Davidson, Margaret. 1978. *Children's Minds.* New York: Norton.

Dennison, George. 1969. *The Lives of Children.* New York: Random House.

Dewey, John. 1938–72. *Experience and Education.* New York: Macmillan.

Fane, Julian. 1957. *Morning.* New York: Reynal.

Fraiberg, Selma H. 1959. *The Magic Years.* New York: Charles Scribner's Sons.

———. 1977. *Every Child's Birthright: In Defense of Mothering.* New York: Basic Books.

Ginott, Haim. 1972. *Teacher and Child.* New York: Macmillan.

Goodell, Carol, ed. 1973. *The Changing Classroom.* New York: Random House.

Holt, John. 1967. *How Children Learn.* New York: Pitman.

Kohl, Herbert R. 1976. *On Teaching.* New York: Schocken.

LeShan, Eda. 1968. *The Conspiracy Against Childhood.* New York: Atheneum.

Montagu, Ashley. 1958. *Education and Human Relations.* New York: Grove Press.

Pratt, Carolyn. 1970. *I Learn from Children.* New York: Cornerstone Library.

Read, Katherine H. 1960. *The Nursery School, A Human Relationships Laboratory.* Philadelphia: W. B. Saunders.

Redl, Fritz. 1966. *When We Deal with Children.* New York: Collier Macmillan.

Rogers, Carl. 1969. *Freedom to Learn.* Columbus, Ohio: Merrill.

Rudolph, Margarita. 1954. *Living and Learning in the Nursery School.* New York: Harper & Brothers.

Spock, Benjamin. 1974. *Raising Children in a Difficult Time.* New York: Simon & Schuster.

For Children

Green, Mary McBurney. 1948. *Is It Hard? Is It Easy?* New York: W. R. Scott.

Krauss, Ruth. 1950. *The Backward Day.* New York: Harper & Brothers.

Lenski, Lois. 1942. *The Little Auto.* New York: Walck.

Minarek, Elsa. 1957. *Little Bear.* New York: Harper & Brothers.

Index